VISION 2020
CHALLENGES
FOR THE NEXT DECADE

OTHER LOTUS TITLES:

Hindustan Times Leadership Summit	*The Peace Dividend: Progress for India and South Asia*
Hindustan Times Leadership Summit	*India and the World: a Blueprint for Partnership and Growth*
Hindustan Times Leadership Summit	*Building a Better Future*
Hindustan Times Leadership Summit	*India the Next Global Superpower*
Hindustan Times Leadership Summit	*Imagine the India that Can Be*
Hindustan Times Leadership Summit	*Ambitions for the New Century*
Ajit Bhattarcharjea	*Sheikh Mohammad Abdullah: Tragic Hero of Kashmir*
Amarinder Singh	*The Last Sunset: The Rise & Fall of the Lahore Durbar*
Anil Dharker	*Icons: Men & Women Who Shaped Today's India*
Aitzaz Ahsan	*The Indus Saga: The Making of Pakistan*
Alam Srinivas & TR Vivek	*IPL: The Inside Story*
Amir Mir	*The True Face of Jehadis: Inside Pakistan's Terror Networks*
Ashok Mitra	*The Starkness of It*
H.L.O. Garrett	*The Trial of Bahadur Shah Zafar*
M.J. Akbar	*India: The Siege Within*
M.J. Akbar	*Kashmir: Behind the Vale*
M.J. Akbar	*The Shade of Swords*
M.J. Akbar	*Byline*
M.J. Akbar	*Blood Brothers: A Family Saga*
Maj. Gen. Ian Cardozo	*Param Vir: Our Heroes in Battle*
Maj. Gen. Ian Cardozo	*The Sinking of INS Khukri: What Happened in 1971*
Madhu Trehan	*Tehelka as Metaphor*
M.B. Naqvi	*Pakistan at Knife's Edge*
Mushirul Hasan	*India Partitioned. 2 Vols*
Mushirul Hasan	*Knowledge, Power and Politics*
Nayantara Sahgal (ed.)	*Before Freedom: Nehru's Letters to His Sister*
Nilima Lambah	*A Life Across Three Continents*
Robert Hutchison	*The Raja of Harsil*
Shashi Tharoor & Shaharyar Khan	*Shadows Across the Playing Field: 60 Years of India-Pakistan Cricket*
Shrabani Basu	*Spy Princess: The Life of Noor Inayat Khan*
Shyam Bhatia	*Goodbye Shahzadi: A Political Biography*
Sunil Gupta	*Living on the 'Adge' in Jhandewalan Thompson*

FORTHCOMING LOTUS TITLES:

Michel de Grece	*The Rajah of Bourbon*
M.J. Akbar	*Have Pen, Will Travel*

VISION 2020 CHALLENGES
FOR THE NEXT DECADE

EDITED BY

NAMITA BHANDARE

Lotus Collection

First published in 2010
The Lotus Collection
An imprint of
Roli Books Pvt Ltd
M-75, G.K. II Market
New Delhi 110 048
Phone: ++91 (011) 4068 2000
Fax: ++91 (011) 2921 7185
E-mail: info@rolibooks.com; Website: rolibooks.com

Also at
Bangalore, Chennai, Jaipur, Kolkata, Mumbai & Varanasi

Cover: Naresh Mondal
Layout Design: Jyoti Dey
Photo Credit: HT Media Ltd

ISBN: 978-81-7436-803-4

Typeset in Photina MT by Roli Books Pvt Ltd
and printed at Polykam Offset, Delhi.

VISION 2020
CHALLENGES FOR THE NEXT DECADE

Hindustan Times
Leadership Summit

Dr Manmohan Singh
Prime Minister of India

Pranab Mukherjee
Finance Minister of India

Efraim Halevy
Head, The Shasha Center for Strategic Studies, Hebrew University of Jerusalem

Shaun Gregory
Founder-Director, Pakistan Security Research Unit and Associate Dean, School of Social & International Studies, University of Bradford

Brajesh Mishra
Former National Security Advisor, India

Dr Naresh Trehan
Chairman and Managing Director,
Medanta –The Medicity

Dr Salim J. Habayeb
WHO Representative to India

Dr George W. Weightman
MD, Associate Director and COO, Professor,
Wake Forest Institute for Regenerative Medicine

Nikesh Arora
President, Global Sales Operations and
Business Development, Google

Sunil Gavaskar
Former India Captain

Ravi Shastri
Former India Captain

Sir Richard Hadlee
Former New Zealand All-rounder

George W. Bush
43rd President of the United States of America

Anshu Jain
Head of Global Markets, Member of the Management Board, Deutsche Bank

Chanda Kochhar
Managing Director and Chief Executive Officer, ICICI Bank

Kareena Kapoor
Indian Actor

Saif Ali Khan
Indian Actor

Sukhbir Singh Badal
Deputy Chief Minister of Punjab

Sitaram Yechury
Member, Rajya Sabha and Leader, CPI (M)

Sushma Swaraj
Deputy Leader of the Opposition, Lok Sabha

Richard Olivier
Artistic Director & Founder,
Olivier Mythodrama

Rajiv Bajaj
Managing Director, Bajaj Auto Limited

Malvinder Singh
Group Chairman, Religare Enterprises
and Fortis Healthcare

Preetha Reddy
Managing Director, Apollo Hospitals

Atul Kumar Rai
CEO and Managing Director, IFCI

Shobhana Bhartia
Chairperson & Editorial Director,
HT Media Ltd

Contents

Hindustan Times
Leadership Summit

In the eight years since it began, the Hindustan Times Leadership Summit has become a platform for thought, debate and the voicing of concerns that affect our times. Each year an invited panel of distinguished speakers – heads of state, cultural icons, sporting heroes and CEOs and entrepreneurs from all over the world – gather together in New Delhi to discuss contemporary issues and set the agenda for the future.

In a rapidly changing world where political equations are being constantly rewritten, terrorism has become the number one threat for all humanity, global warming is imperilling the future of our planet and the world's economic stage shifts from west to east, it has become all the more imperative for visionary leaders to be able to step back from daily responsibilities and pressing concerns to consider longer-term issues.

The 2009 summit was held in the backdrop of renewal and also, destruction. Even as the world was returning to normalcy in the aftermath of the financial crisis, the city of Mumbai faced a horrific terror strike that struck at the core of its nerve centres. The fallout of that attack had reverberations not just in the neighbourhood but all the way up to Washington.

There were other changes to be considered. Technology was breaching new frontiers in medicine and in communication, changing the way we as human beings interact with each other. The rules of engagement were changing not only in security concerns but also in the subcontinent's most beloved game, cricket. Globally, America's re-engagement with the world was impacting geopolitical equations and closer home, what role could a constructive opposition play in a coalition government? These were questions, and answers, that were deliberated.

Welcome Address

▪

Shobhana Bhartia
Chairperson & Editorial Director
HT Media Ltd

▪

WHEN WE FIRST PLANNED THE HINDUSTAN TIMES LEADERSHIP SUMMIT EIGHT YEARS AGO WE WANTED IT TO BECOME THE SINGLE-MOST important gathering of its kind in India. This we knew was an ambitious goal and one we could only achieve if we maintained a high level of discussion and made it a destination for the world's leaders.

Eight years later, I am pleased to say that we are well on our way to achieving this goal. Prime Minister Dr Manmohan Singh has been kind enough to attend our summit every single year since his government was sworn in. I know there have been years when the pressure of work should have kept him away but he has always found the time to come and inaugurate the summit.

One of the many advantages of having an intellectual as prime minister is that his speech is usually one of the most anticipated events of the summit. Over the years, he has addressed the need for social justice, for equality in our society and, most recently, on how India would cope with the global economic crisis.

Last year, in 2008, our summit was dominated by apprehensions about the state of the economy. Those of you who were here will recall the prime minister's words of encouragement, tempered with caution. Times were difficult, he said, but India would manage. Today as the Indian economy bounces back we have Dr Manmohan Singh to thank for the intelligent and strong leadership that ensured the India story was not destroyed by the global economic downturn.

Over the next two days you will hear speakers discuss the near meltdown in the global economy and about the search for new solutions and a new paradigm. We will also discuss the other global crisis of the twenty-first century – the rise and spread of terror. We are a few weeks short of the first anniversary of the Mumbai terror attacks. Those attacks showed us how vulnerable all great cities are to the designs of cowardly but ruthless terrorists who cross borders with impunity and care nothing for the traditional rules of war.

Terror is just one of the challenges that India and the world face in the twenty-first century. There is also the challenge of coping with change and, as the events of the last few years have demonstrated, the changes are coming faster than anyone could have predicted. In the past, India was heard only by itself when it wanted the rest of the world to pay more attention to the upheavals in its neighbourhood. Today, there are few countries in the world that do not see South Asia as the epicentre of concern. Last month, in September, at the G-20 Summit a new world order seemed to be emerging. Who would have thought it possible even five years ago that emerging and developed nations would be able to work together so harmoniously?

We at the *Hindustan Times* believe in a future of hope and promise. We have hopes when it comes to cricket and we have faith in the promise of technology; we have panels on both these topics. We will discuss the future of the Internet now that we are well into the age of social media. We will consider the challenges and changes that we have seen in the way India's most beloved game, cricket is played and whether the game as we knew it is now dead.

Business always forms an integral part of the summit and this year too we have the finance minister of India to tell us how the economy will be revitalized. We will try and find lessons from the crash and ask if the apparent global recovery is for real. The world may seem hopelessly divided at times. It may seem fettered by past prejudices and present biases but the old does fall apart and the new does arise. And it is leadership that gives birth to, and accelerates, both. Future historians will ascribe to President George W. Bush and Dr Manmohan Singh's leadership what was long considered an impossibility in diplomatic circle, ending sixty years of estrangement between the world's two largest democracies.

The changes will keep coming and with them will come the challenges. The task before all of you as decision makers and thought leaders is to cope with the unexpected and to respond with speed and clarity. I do not pretend that you will find all the answers in the next two days but I do know that if this summit follows the precedent, we will all leave tomorrow evening better informed and much more thoughtful about the challenges that confront India and the world.

Those who do not remember history are condemned to repeat it and those who do not anticipate the future will forever live in the past. This summit is about the future and about what we will do when we get there.

'Real change in India will come when we get the right kind of state level and local leadership – a forward-looking, modern and compassionate leadership that strengthens the foundation of our great Republic. The focus of the debate on leadership for building a new India should, therefore, shift to the states.'

Building the India Decade

▪
Dr Manmohan Singh
▪

Moderator
Amit Mitra
Secretary General, FICCI

Dr Manmohan Singh

Prime Minister of India

The seventy-seven-year-old Oxford-educated economist is on course to becoming the third longest serving prime minister of India after Jawaharlal Nehru and Indira Gandhi.

Dr Manmohan Singh is the first Congress leader outside the Nehru-Gandhi family to have led the party to victory after he was declared prime ministerial candidate for the 2009 general elections.

Known for the economic reforms during his tenure as Finance Minister in 1991-96 and for clinching the Indo-US civilian nuclear deal in his first stint as Prime Minister in 2004-09, Singh has kept political pundits and analysts busy trying to fathom what his big-ticket step would be this term.

Singh has been a member of the Rajya Sabha since 1991, where he was Leader of the Opposition between 1998 and 2004.

Before he became Finance Minister he had been Governor of the Reserve Bank of India and Deputy Chairman of the Planning Commission of India.

A soft-spoken person who initially appeared to be a reluctant politician, he is proving to be one of the ablest leaders of our times.

Dr Manmohan Singh is the first prime minister in more than three decades to have won a second term, after a challenging first term.

I AM TRULY DELIGHTED TO BE BACK AT THE HINDUSTAN TIMES LEADERSHIP SUMMIT. I COMPLIMENT SMT SHOBHANA BHARTIA FOR THE DEDICATION AND COMMITMENT WITH which she has been organizing this event every year.

This year we will have an opportunity to hear the former president of the United States, President George W. Bush who is a great friend of our country. We, in India, recognize the very important role that he played in the fruition of the civil nuclear cooperation initiative. We are working now with our international partners to give a boost to our nuclear power programme. This will be an important contribution to our efforts to use cleaner fuels and thus combat climate change.

I mention this today because this day happens to be the birth anniversary of the great Indian scientist, visionary and nation-builder, Dr Homi Bhabha. In concluding the civil nuclear agreement we sought to realize Dr Bhabha's dream of tapping the atom for the welfare of our people. It is only fitting that we pay tribute to Homi Bhabha's genius at this Leadership Summit.

In reflecting on what I should say today, I was recollecting in my mind what my key messages have been to you over the past five years that I have been regularly attending this summit. I believe I had placed before you three related thoughts.

First that our challenges in nation-building are primarily at home. And that these are best addressed by ensuring sustained and inclusive economic growth and development. We do face external and global challenges. The global slowdown is a reality. Rise of terrorism is also a reality and we have to face these challenges. But I sincerely believe that they are nowhere as daunting as the ones we face at home. If we get our house in order, if we can liberate each and every citizen of this free nation from the tyranny of poverty, ignorance and disease, there is no external challenge that we cannot overcome.

Secondly, I have said here before that our composite culture is based on our rejection of the notion of an inevitable clash of civilizations. Our philosophy of *vasudhaiva kutumbakam* has encouraged us to accept pluralism as the natural order of all civilized existence. Freedom, democracy, pluralism and secularism go together. You cannot have one without the other.

My third submission to you has been that we seek to live in peace with our own neighbourhood and with the world at large. We have always been and wish to remain good neighbours and good global citizens. I do believe our destiny is intrinsically linked with that of all our neighbours. We seek good relations with each one of them. I have repeatedly said that we see our security and prosperity in their progress and stability. We sincerely wish to resolve all outstanding issues with our neighbours through dialogue and in the spirit of partnership and friendship that should rightly characterize our relations.

As responsible global citizens, we wish to be partners of all nations in humanity's struggle for the preservation and protection of the environment and in giving meaning and substance to the notion of sustainable development. We will approach the international negotiations on global warming, climate change, and carbon emissions as responsible global citizens. We will fulfill our obligations to nature and to humanity consistent with our commitment to the welfare and well-being of our people, and the poor of the world. Equally, we expect the developed nations and those who have so far drawn unduly on nature's bounty to bear their due share of the burdens as well. Ours is not an unreasonable stance. It is based on our worldview that the 'whole world is one family', and on our commitment to the principles of inclusive growth and development.

These three messages are relevant to the theme of this year's summit as well. They will remain the three pillars on which the India of 2020 is built. 2020 is not far away. Our primary challenge in the next decade will be to sustain high rates of economic growth, to ensure that the growth process remains equitable, to invest in the education and health of every child and adult, to generate gainful employment, to build modern, efficient and environment-friendly infrastructure and to ensure that government and public services are efficient and responsive to our people's needs and function transparently. We should aim to sustain annual growth rates of 9 to 10 per cent per annum. We have to increase investments in physical and social infrastructure, paying particular attention to the needs of our agriculture and the transformation of our rural economy. The fact that our savings rate is as high as 35 per cent of our GDP suggests that what I am saying is eminently a realizable goal. The challenge for political leadership at the national, at the state, and at local levels will lie in ensuring the realization of this outcome.

I submit to you that India cannot be built from Delhi alone. No doubt the Union government has an important developmental role, apart from its central role in providing national security. But with the growth of the market economy and with individual talent and enterprise being unleashed, no agenda for building a new India can any longer be imposed from Delhi. India lives in the states. The future of our country depends, therefore, a great deal on the quality of political leadership and of government at the state and at local levels. In this context, great importance is attached to the revitalization of the institution of the Panchayati Raj which was a dream of late Shri Rajiv Gandhi, former Prime Minister.

One of our biggest challenges remains the challenge of reducing regional disparities. Equally important is the challenge of ensuring the economic and social uplift of our scheduled castes, scheduled tribes, other backward classes, less privileged sections of society and religious and linguistic minorities. These challenges have to be addressed at every level of the policy pyramid.

Our government has launched a series of development initiatives since 2004. These initiatives are aimed at investing in rural and urban infrastructure, at guaranteeing minimum employment and generating maximum employment. These initiatives are aimed at improving access to and the availability of education and health care to all our citizens. These initiatives need to be carried for they seek to improve the productivity of our farm economy and the income of our farmers where 65 per cent of our population still depends on agriculture.

But for each of these initiatives to be successfully implemented, we need proactive and creative leadership at the state and district level. We need a more active civil society and media focus on the quality of governance at the state and district levels. Urban governance has to vastly improve to make our cities and towns meet the needs of a burgeoning urban population. We need a creative entrepreneurial class that can compete both at home and abroad without artificial props. A visionary national leadership alone cannot do much when the challenge of development is in the realm of policy implementation and where states must be active partners.

For us this challenge is compounded by the fact that our less developed regions are also the more populated ones. This has contributed to the persistence of poverty and to the problem of internal migration and it has also given rise sometimes to law and order problems. In these states we need a forward-looking, development-oriented political leadership. We need a committed and proactive civil service. We need an active civil society. We need a professional middle class. We need a combination of all these participants to transform our less developed regions and take them forward on the road to sustained development.

Sitting here in Delhi, we can endlessly debate the qualities of national leadership. But real change in India will come when we get the right kind of state level and local leadership – a forward-looking, modern and compassionate leadership that strengthens the foundation of our great Republic. The focus of the debate on leadership for building a new India should, therefore, shift to the states.

While such domestic, regional, and local leadership will build the new India we aspire for, we also need in our region, in South Asia, an equally forward-looking leadership. Each of our neighbours faces similar developmental challenges. Some of them face bigger existential challenges.

India seeks a neighbourhood of peace and progress. We wish our neighbours well. We would like to see them develop and wipe out poverty and overcome the burden of history and we would like to work with them to achieve these goals. India is always happy to extend a helpful and supportive hand to all our neighbours. We wish to see democracy take deep roots in all these countries so that the people of South Asia are fully empowered to take their destiny into their own hands.

We need a leadership in our region that can take a long-term view and which has the courage to take bold decisions. We must not allow our past to limit our future. To paraphrase Gurudev Rabindranath Tagore, we must not allow 'narrow domestic walls' to confine us to 'the dreary desert sand of dead habit'. Instead, we should dip into the 'clear stream of reason' and walk forward into 'ever-widening thought and action' so that we can build not just a new India by 2020 but a new South Asia.

Moderator | **Amit Mitra**

Secretary General, FICCI

Q: The tenth anniversary of the annual India economic conference at Stanford recognized our resilience, and that economic recovery has begun. There is a preponderance of evidence that poverty and employment coefficient of our growth is significantly lower than in some emerging markets, particularly China in the absence of structured reforms. But there were concerns whether in the near future this purposive and stable government would accord priority to many stalled economic legislations, particularly on labour, on insurance, on manufacturing, and the reform of the financial sector, which can impart a great impetus to the ongoing economic recovery process.

Dr Manmohan Singh: You are right. We need to push forward the reform process in areas that you have mentioned, and we will do so. But the reform process has many dimensions and in the situation in which India is placed, increased investment in rural infrastructure, increased emphasis on education and health in our rural areas is probably of the greatest importance. We have to create an environment conducive to the growth of entrepreneurship in our urban economy. At the same time, we must ensure our government's greater involvement in rural development, in rural infrastructure and in rural social development. So there has to be a mix of both types of reform commitments. That is our challenge.

Q: The growth of the knowledge economy requires the creation of original content and in a sustainable future of not jobless growth. All the resources gathered here today could not match up to the potential of India's traditional knowledge sector, not only in terms of a unique and contemporary content but in terms of ecological livelihood right across the country. Do you position this sector as an important subset in your economic policy?

Dr Manmohan Singh: It goes without saying that the type of transformation you have referred to is something which must go hand in hand with the normal processes of economic and social development which I have been talking about.

Q: You spoke about entrepreneurs and democracy. I think two facets which definitely need your attention are reforms in the police and reforms in the judiciary, because if there is no rule of law, then you cannot expect democracy or entrepreneurship to flourish.

Dr Manmohan Singh: The enforcement of law and order is the first and foremost responsibility of every civilized state. The area of reform that you have hinted at, police reforms is something which has not received the attention it deserves. We have the report of the Administrative Reforms Commission. In the months ahead, we would tackle this aspect of reform as well.

Q: The UPA government seems divided as far as its approach to tackling naxalism is concerned. You are willing to undertake joint operations with the ruling Left in West Bengal and other governments in the states. Yet your own cabinet colleague and railway minister, Mamata Banerjee seems to be giving a clean chit to the Maoists. Does her stand complicate your approach to the issue?

Dr Manmohan Singh: We are a functioning democracy. There are occasions when there are differences of opinion among various leaders of our coalition but let there be no doubt that law and order is the primary responsibility of every civilized state. Whatever comes in the way of maintenance and enforcement of law and order will be dealt with as it ought to be dealt with. The India of tomorrow cannot be built from New Delhi alone. We need the active cooperation of state governments that applies not only to developmental processes but also the enforcement of law and order. We will work with all the state governments regardless of their political complexion to strengthen the processes of enforcement of law and order.

Q: Could we know something about your perspective on healthcare reforms?

Dr Manmohan Singh: Our primary concern is to ensure that our rural areas also get the benefit of health and education that we are emphasizing in all our developmental processes. Our basic concern is to strengthen primary healthcare in our rural areas and simultaneously move towards a system where, over a period of time, health insurance becomes a viable instrument to provide effective healthcare to all our citizens, particularly the poorer sections of our society.

Q: For the third consecutive day you are talking about peace with Pakistan. You spoke about this at a speech in Srinagar and, again, at your press conference and now here at the summit without actually mentioning Pakistan. How encouraged are you by the internal situation in Pakistan to pursue your agenda of peace and dialogue with them?

Dr Manmohan Singh: I think Pakistan is tackling many internal problems. The rise of terrorism is one of them and I wish them success in dealing with it. Without going into greater details, I would like to say that the destinies of our two countries, and indeed the destinies of all countries in South Asia, are closely interlinked. There are difficulties of expanding areas of cooperation but they have to be overcome. I believe tough, visionary leadership in all our countries can make the future happen.

Q: What do you think about the need and desirability of the inter-linkage of rivers to solve the problem of drought and floods?

Dr Manmohan Singh: The interlinking of the river systems is something which can help in expanding areas under irrigation but there are also problems and environmental concerns. There is a difference of opinion among experts about how far we can go to use the interlinking of the river systems to provide water security to our people. Two or three projects are under preparation and project designs are now available.

I believe we have to move with caution in expanding the scope of linking our rivers because environmental concerns and related issues are something which have to be carefully attended to otherwise there is every danger that we might do irreparable damage to the ecology and environment.

Q: We are surrounded by hostile countries and there are a lot of internal security problems we face. I think we should be more concerned about the strategy China is developing around India. China is building the entire neighbourhood, extending from Tibet and Nepal and into Pakistan. Taking this into consideration, I hope you are preparing your defence and armour system equally robustly to face this situation.

Dr Manmohan Singh: Security concerns are the primary responsibility of every civilized country. Hence, you have my assurance that we have been paying adequate attention to protect and preserve the security of our country. As far as India-China relations are concerned, I have said on more than one occasion that both India and China have immense opportunities to work together in cooperation because there is ample space in the world to accommodate the growth ambitions of both the countries. We have problems on the border but we have also agreed that pending the resolution of the boundary question, peace and tranquility should prevail.

'We require institutional changes in the reform process which began in 1991. Reform is not a stop-and-go process. It is a continuing process. Therefore, the process which began in the early '90s will have to be taken to its logical conclusion. For that to happen, a convergence of views across the political spectrum is called for.'

Reviving India's Economy

Critical Factors

■

Pranab Mukherjee

■

Moderator

Rajdeep Sardesai

Editor-in-Chief, IBN18 Network

Pranab Mukerjee

Finance Minister of India

The most experienced minister of the UPA government, Pranab Mukherjee, seventy-four, is the ace trouble-shooter for Congress President Sonia Gandhi and Prime Minister Manmohan Singh.

He is that rare senior political leader to have handled the key ministries of defence, external affairs and finance, along with a host of other ministries in his nearly four-decade-long parliamentary career.

Known for his sharp negotiating skills and vast knowledge of governmental functioning, Mukherjee was the points man for dealing with the Left parties in the UPA government's first tenure.

He headed more than fifty Group of Ministers on various subjects between 2004-09, other than handling key assignments for the party.

He also held the position of Deputy Chairman, Planning Commission from 1991 to 1996.

Pranabda, as he is fondly called by cabinet colleagues, party leaders and journalists, is quite accessible for a leader of his stature and has a rare quality of meeting people even at odd hours.

First elected to the Rajya Sabha in 1969, Mukherjee was a five-term MP in the Upper House, until he won his first Lok Sabha election in 2004. He was re-elected this year.

A post-graduate in Political Science and History, Mukherjee is a trained lawyer and has authored five books on politics.

I AM INDEED HAPPY TO BE PRESENT AT THE HINDUSTAN TIMES LEADERSHIP SUMMIT WHERE PEOPLE FROM DIFFERENT WALKS OF LIFE – POLICY MAKERS, CAPTAINS OF INDUSTRIES and those who represent views from different sectors – articulate their views.

Like most countries, India could not escape the adverse impact of the international financial crisis. In one stroke, our growth trajectory came down to 6.7 per cent. Prior to this year, it was 9 per cent for three consecutive years. Our exports have been badly hit. Another important component, our IT sector has also been affected and this has had cascading effects. With the slowdown of growth, the revenue buoyancy which the country had been enjoying for quite some time has also got adversely impacted.

Today any finance minister of India must confront three major problems. First, how do we return to the higher growth trajectory of 8 to 9 per cent? Second, how do we come back to fiscal consolidation? We deliberately overshot the fiscal limitation imposed on us in terms of fiscal deficit by the FRBM (Fiscal Responsibility and Budgetary Management) because we thought that we would have to inject resources to generate demand, particularly in the rural sector, internally.

In one go, our developmental expenditure was stepped up from Rs 2,85,000 crore to Rs 3,25,000 crore. There was a substantial step-up of gross budgetary support, higher allocation in important social sectors like the Employment Guarantee Scheme for jobless rural youth and higher allocations for education and health. In this atmosphere of security concerns, the expenditure overshot. We did not have the resources for it and had to borrow substantially. As a result, the fiscal deficit was coming to 6.8 per cent. This could not have been sustained for long. So, in the same budget, I mentioned that by 2011-12, I would like to return to 5.5 per cent and, later, to 4 per cent. That is the second task for any finance minister to have to implement – fiscal consolidation and to bring the fiscal deficit down to prudent limits.

The third is to ensure inclusive growth. For that we have to have both institutional arrangements, sometimes backed by legal rights and entitlements and sometimes through normal executive orders.

What are the major hindrances in achieving these three major objectives of higher growth trajectory, inclusive fiscal consolidation and inclusive growth? First, it is important to have world recovery. I will give you just one example. Merely by generating demand in the internal sector or even by exploring the possibilities of the external market for our exports, it would not be easy for us to have any recovery within two to three years unless there is robust economic recovery in the industrialized world. Europe, Japan, and USA together account for nearly 62 per cent of our exports.

One of our key strengths is our IT industry which has been hit because outsourcing has been affected substantially. We had started having substantial inflow of FDI and in 2007-08 in particular, there was a robust inflow of external resources. But there has been a slowdown and although there is some recovery, particularly with institutional finances, FDI is still to achieve the same momentum.

The second hindrance is the security environment. The security environment must improve in order to have faster growth. I am not talking merely as a finance minister to allocate more resources for security. The budget of our home ministry has increased by almost 25 per cent in just one year because no finance minister can compromise on the country's external or internal security. Constitutionally, it is the responsibility of the Union government to protect the country from external aggression as well as from internal disturbances. If the law and order situation assumes a magnitude which may be described as an internal disturbance, then the Union government has to step in. It is a constitutional requirement. Therefore, in collaboration with state governments, we have to maintain the security environment so that smooth transportation and industrial activities can take place.

The third area of concern is that we require institutional changes in the reform process which began in 1991. I have always believed that reform is not a stop-and-go process. It is a continuing process. Therefore, the process which began in the early '90s will have to be taken to its logical conclusion. For that to happen, a

convergence of views across the political spectrum is called for.
Sometimes we find that this is not very easy, particularly in our system where we have to take certain legislative steps to have reforms in the insurance or pension sector. Bills have been pending for quite some time. The ruling coalition does not have a majority in both Houses to get them translated into legislation. Therefore, a broad political consensus is needed, and we are working towards that.

Now, what are our achievements? We have yet to arrive at the ultimate figures but currently we have two important studies: an assessment by the RBI and an assessment by the Prime Minister's Economic Council. There are similarities in both. Growth projection is around 6-6.5 per cent.

In the first half of the last year there was a phenomenal rise in commodity prices all over the world. In August 2008, oil prices were as high as $147 per barrel. In the earlier part of the year, the price of food grains and other essential commodities went up. There were mixed reactions and a mixed picture, but it had its impact.

At some point of time our WPI (Wholesale Price Index), registered negative figures. But that is no consolation to us because that was a statistical advantage on a year-on-year or from the base year. The real market price is reflected in four sets of Consumer Price Index. It is reasonably high. We are expecting WPI to be around 6-6.5 per cent.

I would say there is recovery. But this recovery is halting and slow. Numbers for the second quarter are not yet available and I cannot say whether they will be steady or not. But I am optimistic that from the third and final quarters we will be able to achieve the targets which we projected as the short-term strategy for the year concerned.

We still have a long way to go. And in that long way our journey will not be easy. We shall have to overcome so many hindrances. But there is one point on which I am confident. I have tremendous faith and confidence in the young entrepreneurs of India. Today, whenever there is a challenge, they do not remorse or lament. They understand and appreciate it; take courage in both hands. Sometimes those of us who belong to the older generation do not understand them, but we appreciate and admire them. They take courage in both hands, face challenges and ultimately succeed.

Moderator | **Rajdeep Sardesai**

Editor-in-Chief, IBN18 Network

Q&A

Rajdeep Sardesai: Dr Mukherjee, you have been saying that you are looking at 9 per cent growth rate possibly after two years. Are you still sticking to 9 per cent, given what's happening in agriculture and to farm outputs?

Pranab Mukherjee: When I talked of 6 to 6.5 per cent GDP growth, I had in my mind the possibility that agricultural growth this year could be negative, around minus 2 per cent. This is an extraordinary year where we are bearing the adverse impact of drought as a consequence of which our *kharif* crop production may be down by almost 15 to 16 million tonnes. We have also had floods. If you look at the micro level, some crops which were protected in Andhra Pradesh, for instance, were able to sustain the adverse impact of drought but ultimately were affected by floods. Therefore, we lost out both ways. Keeping that in view, with this negative growth, we are still expecting to have 6 to 6.5 per cent. In order to achieve 9 per cent GDP growth, agricultural growth should not be less than 3.5 to 4 per cent.

Q: We in business need a firm visibility of when and how GST (goods and services tax) will take shape. We need to prepare ourselves so that there is no disruption in the marketplace. You have been consistent in your position that GST will go live by 1 April 2010. Can I have some further inputs from you?

Pranab Mukherjee: The empowered Finance Minister's Committee is meeting in Delhi. We are seriously trying to have a convergence of views. In large areas we have been able to arrive at a convergence. Divergence of views is limited but at the same time it will take some legislative measures, including a constitutional amendment.

I am trying to stick to the time schedule but I will not be surprised if there will be a delay of a few months. There will be two major tax reforms which you are going to have, on the indirect tax side as GST, and on the direct tax side as direct tax code.

Q: You said that some of your reform legislations are held up because the ruling coalition doesn't have a majority in both Houses of Parliament. You also said that you are now working to build a consensus. The BJP has stated that they are willing to support several of these bills, particularly on insurance and pension. Will you be willing to go ahead and pass these bills now? What is building consensus if not persuading the major Opposition party to your point of view?

Pranab Mukherjee: Consensus means consensus should be within the coalition. I cannot run a government if I have to take support from somebody outside as happened last time there were serious differences among the ruling coalition. We are running a multi-party coalition government. There are difficulties from the floor management point of view. Therefore, we have to converge views within the coalition and also outside the coalition.

Rajdeep Sardesai: Isn't it easier this time around now that you don't have the Left parties? Surely your friend in Bengal, Mamata Banerjee cannot be a hurdle towards major reform in sectors like insurance. I know land acquisition has been a problem for you. But to take the point further, isn't it easier now in UPA-2 than it was in UPA-1?

Pranab Mukherjee: We did not have the experience of running a coalition before 2004 at the Centre because numbers were never a question and the Congress itself was a coalition. Since its inception, the Congress has accommodated various viewpoints. Divergent views have converged within the platform of the Congress. But, I would not like to sit on value judgement. My job is very plain: whenever legislation comes for adoption and discussion before the floor, I have to see that my coalition partners support it and I can get as much support from those who are outside the coalition. That is my simple task.

Rajdeep Sardesai: Would it be fair to say that you are more confident now than you were in the first term?

Pranab Mukherjee: I will be able to get these legislations through. But I cannot say exactly when and during which session this will happen. I will try to get them passed as fast as I can.

Q: This whole austerity business has been seen in large parts of the country as tokenism; a form of appeasement. You still haven't been able to curb government expenditure. We still have a very bloated government. Ministers fly economy class but then stay in presidential suites of hotels like the Four Seasons in New York. Do you as a long-serving politician genuinely believe there is a change in the value system of politicians today? And can you expect them to be Gandhian in today's new order?

Pranab Mukherjee: It is not merely a question of being Gandhian. The question is that certain actions are to be taken, and should appear to be taken. Whatever I have done in the name of austerity – the circular was issued by the finance minister before I assumed office – has been reiterated by me. That is the practicable and practical point of view

For instance, I have requested officers of both Houses to ensure that Parliamentary Committee meetings – with the exception of the committee on public undertakings where members must interact with public undertakings outside Delhi – take place in the Capital itself. Apart from any tokenism, my experiences both as a minister and chairman of the important standing committee on Home for five years have shown that committees can do a much better job when they sit in Delhi and cut expenditure by almost one-third. This is the practicability which I wanted. To what extent I will be able to succeed depends on the cooperation of the entire system.

Rajdeep Sardesai: The Prime Minister spoke about the need for better leadership, but what about corruption? In all his interviews, Telecom Minister A. Raja asks why we are targeting him. Decisions on spectrum were taken by the CCEA (Cabinet Committee on Economic Affairs) the FDI proposals were cleared by the FIPB (Foreign Investment Proposal Board)_headed by the Finance Minister. So why are you singling him out? Isn't corruption the real issue that you should be looking at seriously? Do you agree that there is a serious crisis of corruption at the highest levels in government and that this should be the focus, not austerity?

Pranab Mukherjee: First of all I would like to point that allegations of corruption do not mean that this is the proof of corruption. I would refer to just one case without mentioning any names. A gentleman was arrested by the CBI (Central Bureau of Investigation). He was known to be a competent technocrat and managed many public sector undertakings. Then he was arrested and refused bail. Ultimately, nothing was found against him. But the damage to his reputation was done. Therefore, we should be careful.

Rajdeep Sardesai: Are you giving a clean chit to the Telecom Minister or are you saying that in a coalition government you have to wink at corruption?

Pranab Mukherjee: I am not saying that. There is no coalition with corruption. What I am talking of is the system. The Election Commission requires candidates to file a list of their assets at the time of filing their nomination papers. If elected, they have to give a list of their assets again to the Chair of the House. If you are a minister, you must give it to the prime minister or chief minister. Anybody filing an RTI (Right to Information) can get this information. It is an entitlement we have given to the people of this country.

I do not say that corruption is not there or that there should be no action against corruption. For instance, with regard to tax evasion and tax avoidance, we are taking up the amendment of avoidance of double taxation agreement with 77 countries. But this will take time. It has been clearly indicated that the CBI will directly act under CVC (Central Vigilance Commission). The administrative minister has no control over it.

Rajdeep Sardesai: You are talking of double taxation. Is your government serious about bringing back black money, which is stashed in Swiss banks by Indians? Do you even have an estimate of how much black money there is?

Pranab Mukherjee: We are very serious and we are pursuing it. The government has not made any estimate on how much money there is. There was one estimation done in 1985. Thereafter there has been no effort. But there have been studies by experts and professors and these figures are available.

Q: India has traditionally been a nation of savers. Now we are hearing

that we want to be a nation of investors. In many parts of the world, there has been a very conscious effort towards the establishment of regulations, investor protection as well as regulation of financial planning. What step is the Indian government taking to regulate financial advisers towards consumer protection? Secondly, how do you see pension reforms?

Pranab Mukherjee: We have various regulatory authorities. But in a developing economy like ours, the role of the government is not merely to be a regulator or to create institutions of independent regulators but also to be the facilitator. That is a much more important role.

Q: Why cannot political parties select their candidates on a pattern similar to that of Union Public Service Commission and State Public Service Commission?

Pranab Mukherjee: I would have loved to appear before any service commission to enrol myself as a political activist. But if you look at the growth of the political system not only in India but all over the world, the system is completely different. Nowhere in the Constitution is it written that you shall have to engage yourself in political activity. It is a voluntary action.

Rajdeep Sardesai: Are you happy that so many sons and daughters of politicians are entering politics? Are you happy with the fact that in today's politics you need only two things to fight elections: money power and family connections?

Pranab Mukherjee: It's not a question of being happy or unhappy.

Rajdeep Sardesai: Do you think that is good that India should be run by 200 families?

Pranab Mukherjee: I do not find anything wrong in it. I can give you a number of examples. Out of 56 prime ministers in UK, as many as 21 were related to each other. I may be wrong by one or two. As many as 6 US presidents were related to each other. It is quite natural in a business atmosphere for children to join business. The same holds true for any profession like medicine or law. Therefore, what is wrong if the children in a political leader's family decide to join politics? In democracy there is no nomination. There has to be an election.

Q: My question relates to the proposed Direct Tax Code and its potential implication on the high savings rate we have as a country. I am referring to the removal of a distinction between Capital Gains and Marginal Rate of tax. I don't think this distinction has been removed in any part of the world. Why are we trying to fix what is not broken? We have a high savings rate, so why are we proposing such radical changes?

Pranab Mukherjee: Even earlier when I was Finance Minister, one of my basic objectives was to discourage expenditure and encourage savings. If somebody takes the trouble of going through the budget proposals of the early '80s, they will find one running theme in my various fiscal proposals. Apart from that, what has been stated in the Direct Tax Code is a proposal for discussion. We have not reached a decision but have raised many issues – Capital Gains tax, different aspects on savings, housing and so on.

Rajdeep Sardesai: Isn't that the problem? The BJP has put together a list of over 300 issues with the Direct Tax Code. It is great to have open debate and discussion. But in a democracy like India, a billion people have a billion views. Isn't it better to end the uncertainty?

Pranab Mukherjee: There is no question of uncertainty because when I introduced the Direct Tax Code I said I would give enough time for debate and discussion to get inputs. I myself have attended three meetings. My officers are going all over the country interacting with stakeholders. Anybody can make a list of contradictions, but that is not the point.

Q: My question is related to PPP (public-private partnership) projects. We work in seven states where the state governments do not seem to be aware of their obligations in a PPP. All the pressure is put on the private party and we are treated exactly as if the government owns everything and we are the interlopers. I am talking of heritage hotels in our case.

Pranab Mukherjee: I cannot know about the details of individual cases but the basic philosophy of PPP is that everybody is an equal partner; co-sharers of the same approach and objective.

Rajdeep Sardesai: You have been finance minister, defence minister and external affairs minister. I think only Yashwant Rao Chavan completed the full circle by also being home minister. Do you have ambitions beyond these ministries? You were quoted in some Bengali newspapers saying that you have fought your last election. Does that mean you are looking at Rashtrapati Bhawan? Where do you go from here?

Pranab Mukherjee: I will go to my study where I have collected a large number of books which I have not had the time to read. When this tenure is over I will be seventy-nine. That perhaps is the time for having a little bit of rest.

Lessons from 26/11

Securing India Against Terror

■

Efraim Halevy

■

Shaun Gregory

■

Brajesh Mishra

■

Moderator

K.C. Singh

Former Secretary, Ministry of External Affairs and Co-ordinator, Joint Anti-Terror Mechanism between India and Pakistan

Efraim Halevy

Head, The Shasha Center for Strategic Studies, Hebrew University of Jerusalem

Head of the Shasha Center for Strategic Studies at the Federmann School of Public Policy and Government, Hebrew University of Jerusalem, Efraim Halevy serves as a consultant to Israeli government ministries and agencies on strategic issues. He was recently re-elected unopposed for a second term as Chairman of the Israel Intelligence Heritage and Commemoration Center (IICC). He has also been elected Chairman of the Zalman Shazar Center for Jewish History.

Halevy served as National Security Advisor to Prime Minister Ariel Sharon from 2002 to 2003. Prior to that he was the head of the Mossad from 1998-2002. He has been Israel's Ambassador to the European Union (1996-1998), deputy head of the Mossad (1990-1995) and Senior Command Echelon of the Mossad (1967-1990). He served in the Mossad for close to forty years.

Halevy studied law at the Hebrew University in Jerusalem and graduated M.Juris (cum laude). While at university, he was president of the National Union of Israeli Students.

Halevy has served as a secret envoy for five Israeli prime ministers, Yitzhak Shamir, Yitzhak Rabin, Benjamin Netanyahu, Ehud Barak and Ariel Sharon and in 2005 was awarded the President Herzog Prize for his unique contribution to the security and diplomatic concerns of Israel. Among other honours, he has received the Order of Istiqlal (Independence) first class, by King Abdullah II of Jordan for his contribution to the relations between Jordan and Israel. In 2002, he was awarded the Director's Award by the Director of the Central Intelligence Agency of USA.

Halevy's book, *Man in The Shadows: Inside the Middle East Crisis With a Man Who Led the Mossad* was published in 2006 and has been translated into eight languages. He has written articles for *The New Republic, Time, The Economist* and is a regular contributor to *Yedioth Acharonot* and *The Jerusalem Post* in Israel.

IT IS A GREAT HONOUR AND PRIVILEGE FOR ME AS AN ISRAELI, AS AN INTELLIGENCE OFFICER, AS A FORMER HEAD OF MOSSAD (ISRAEL'S SECRET INTELLIGENCE SERVICE) AND, if I may say so, as a citizen of the world to be here today. It is my intention to address the future, not to talk of the past and I would like to speak of issues which I think are common to all areas in the world that are infected by terrorism, and let me say there are very few areas in the world that are not infected by terrorism today.

The greatest human right we have to protect is the right to live. This is a basic human right; not the right to die, not to sanctify death, not to idealize death but to idealize life and to do everything possible to save every human life and every possible human life that we can save. In our tradition, he who saves one human life is equivalent to a person who has saved the world as a whole.

We are now facing a new period in the history of the world. I would like to refer to a document issued by the National Intelligence Council of the United States of America, called *Global Trends for 2025: A Transformed World* and give you two quotes from the executive summary. The first: 'The whole international system as constructed following World War II will be revolutionized. Not only will new players, Brazil, Russia, India and China have a seat at the international high table but they will bring in new stakes and new rules of the game.' I emphasize 'new rules of the game'.

The second: it says there will be growing influence of non-state actors including tribes and various organizations. I will say also terrorist organizations and criminal networks. What we have to see are the new rules of the game and what you as Indians, probably one of the upcoming and emerging great powers of the world, can do. What could you do to take us forward into this new world which we are entering in the next decade or two?

First, we have to be realistic of the fact that we are facing changed rules of combat. We are involved in what we call 'asymmetric warfare'. The two sides are not equal. Not only are they inequal in their strength, they are also not equal in their moral views and in the way they approach life. We have to be conscious of this and we have to tailor what we have to do in this situation, which is unique in the annals of the world. It is no longer possible to defend a country from within its borders. This is not practical. This is not possible. India cannot defend itself within Indian borders. Israel can't defend itself from within Israeli borders and the United States or Russia or any other country in the world cannot defend itself from within its own borders.

Second, the rules of international law and the rules of war as they were fashioned in the years gone by when there was conventional warfare between armies are to a large extent no longer applicable. We have to fashion new rules; rules concerning rendition of changing and transferring prisoners from one country to another, for instance. All the rules of extradition originally had been formed in order to deal with criminal acts. But you cannot

Non-state actors who do not conform to the rules and to the defences of the rules of law as we practice them. When human shields, for example, they should not be able to them in our own countries.

extradite a terrorist simply to interrogate him. You have to indict him and put him on trial. If you don't have any issue on which you can put him on trial, you cannot extradite him. It has become necessary now to enable extradition for interrogation which is a very key issue in the years to come.

We have to be conscious of the fact that national sovereignty is no longer a key element of international society. We have many areas around the world where we have what we call non-state actors. In this part of the world, you have a country nearby which has a government that doesn't control more than 10 per cent of its territory. The rest of its territory is controlled by others. These are new situations which need new guidelines and new methods of combat.

Non-state actors who do not conform to the rules and to morals as you and I apply them should not be entitled to the defences of the rules of law as we practice them. When they engage in certain practices, using human beings as human shields, for example, they should not be able to request or obtain the guarantees of law the way we apply them in our own countries.

We have to have rules which apply to combat as they are forced on us by them. We have to have rules of what we call hot pursuit. In other words, if you have a terrorist attack on Indian soil, you must have the legal right internationally to pursue the attackers and pursue those who have given them safe haven across your borders to apprehend and deal with them and with those who give them commands. Hot pursuit must not be simply gauged in hours or days. The right of hot pursuit should be a prolonged right in order to be able to apprehend those who have carried out terrorist acts and as deterrence because one of the key elements

morals as you and I apply them should not be entitled to they engage in certain practices, using human beings as request or obtain the guarantees of law the way we apply

in any combat, whether it's terrorist or otherwise, is deterrence. If you cannot hit those who are attacking you, you will never be able to deter them.

It is no longer possible, as the chief justice of Israel once said, 'to fight terrorism in a democracy with one hand tied behind your back'. That is a very, very noble statement. I suggest to you to go home and take a rifle in your hands. Tie one hand behind your back and try and fire the rifle. I am not sure whether you will succeed but if you do manage to fire it, look how far you are off the target. In this new world of ours, we no longer will be able to combat terrorism with one hand tied behind our backs.

We have to also change the rules of conviction when we have terrorists. It will no longer be possible to present to a court of law for the perusal of the defence all the evidence and all the information which has been gathered through secret and clandestine means in order to achieve a conviction. It must be possible in a court of law to present evidence solely to a judge or justice panel and let them weigh the evidence without making it available to the defendant. Otherwise we will have a situation where you either decide not to prosecute in order to protect resources and methods or try to put the evidence before the court and run the risk of causing grievous damage to further capabilities of collecting evidence and intelligence.

I also believe we have the perfect new means of collecting information. We are living in an age in which the terrorists are not just people who are in backward places. They are highly sophisticated, knowledgeable and, sometimes, brilliant. I would say demonically brilliant in the way they think up of all kinds of schemes, like the scheme which was perpetrated on 9/11 on the western coast of the United States of America or acts which have been committed on Indian territory or acts committed against Israel or in the Middle East. We are up against a highly sophisticated enemy and we have to put the best minds together in order to fashion a proper response.

We have been in this situation for the last ten to fifteen years. I don't think we can expect that this war will be resolved within the next ten to fifteen years. We are going to have at least another two decades of struggle. We have to be prepared for the long haul. And to prepare for the long haul, we have to take up cudgels; take up the challenge and change the rules of the game. This is an area in which international cooperation, both in combating terrorism and in setting the rules of the game is vital. It can be successful.

Shaun Gregory

Founder-Director, Pakistan Security Research Unit and Associate Dean, School of Social and International Studies, University of Bradford, UK

Professor Shaun Gregory is the founder-director of the Pakistan Security Research Unit (PSRU) and an associate dean of the School of Social and International Studies at the University of Bradford, UK. He was formerly the head of the department of Peace Studies from 2002 to 2007.

Professor Gregory has held visiting research or professorial posts including, in 2006, at the Institut de Etudes Politiques at Sciences Po in Paris. He was a visiting fellow at the Australian National University (Canberra), at the Institut de Relations International et Strategiques in Paris, at the International Strategic Studies Institute in Islamabad and at the Institute for Defense Studies and Analysis in New Delhi.

Professor Gregory's work focuses on terrorism, extremism, and nuclear weapons issues in South Asia. In recent years he has centred his research on Pakistan.

He is the author of four books and more than 120 papers on nuclear weapons, security, and terrorism issues, the most recent of which are working with Pakistani Intelligence agency, the ISI, terrorist groups in Pakistan, the stability and cohesion of the Pakistani state, and the role of the Pakistan Army in the war in Afghanistan. He contributes periodic articles to *Open Democracy* and *Oxford Analytica*.

Professor Gregory's latest book, *Pakistan: Securing the Insecure State* will be published in 2010. He is regularly consulted by various branches of the UK government and the French government, and has worked recently with NATO, the EU, the US Army, and the UNHCR (United Nations High Commissioner for Refugees) on issues related to Pakistan and the war in Afghanistan. Professor Gregory is also widely consulted by the national and international media.

I HAVE BEEN ASKED TO REFLECT ON THE ROLE OF PAKISTAN IN THE MUMBAI ATTACKS OF NOVEMBER 2008, TO THINK ABOUT LESSONS AND FUTURE TRENDS, AND TO OFFER SOME thoughts about responses to terrorism in this context.

Pakistan has a long history of supporting terrorists and insurgent groups in pursuit of its internal as well as external policy objectives. The use of these actors is intimately linked to, what I have called, a set of structural drivers shaping Pakistani polity.

The first of these drivers, of course, is that Pakistan is a revisionist state which disputes its borders, rejects original status quo and seeks to exploit the instruments at its disposal to maintain the instability that is necessary to keep these issues alive.

Second, having been through the trauma of national break-up in 1971, Pakistan is acutely sensitive to what it sees as threats to the integrity of what remains of the country.

Third, antipathy towards the non-Muslim Other, particularly though not exclusively, towards India and to Hindus is deeply woven into the fabric of the nation through the polity, through national schooling and through elite discourse.

Fourth, Pakistan and its main intelligence wing, the ISI, seeks to maintain and manipulate that antipathy both to underwrite their own claims on national resources and to maintain a degree of autonomy from civilian governments.

Fifth, in common with many Islamic nations and Muslim diasporas post 9/11, Pakistan is, to some extent, in the middle of a re-envisioning of the meaning of Islam for the state and the nation. This re-envisioning is characterized in part by the growth of Islamism and Islamic extremism, a rise in anti-Americanism and anti-Westernism, and a shift in the centre of gravity in the country in a more Islamically conservative direction.

The exact details of the attacks in Mumbai have been widely discussed and there is no need to rehearse them here. The salient points that I want to bring out are these:

- The terrorists were trained and directed by Lashkar-e-Taiba

(LeT), a Pakistan-based terrorist group with strong and current links to the ISI.

- The ISI was involved at some level in the planning and conduct of these attacks.
- No evidence has been provided that really ever could prove that case in Pakistan. For the rest of us, though, the evidential case that helps in the three-part dossier that Pakistan was given by India is persuasive though perhaps not conclusive on its own. But coupled with the circumstantial case it is overwhelming.
- Pakistan continues to support Afghan Taliban groups, not least that of Siraj Haqqani [Pashtun warlord Sirajuddin Haqqani], in relation to the Afghan theatre. It continues to support the LeT in relation to the Indian theatre.

There are no doubts about the fact of these relationships, even if there are uncertainties about the power relations within them, simply in terms of personal contacts or of instrumentality. We see jihadi anger against the so-called Crusader-Zionist-Hindu enemy mirrored within the Pakistan Army and ISI. Strategic cultural jihad and martyrdom remains pervasive even if this is played down for obvious reasons by the public face of the Pakistan Army and ISI, which appears pro-western and they are banned.

Nor should we be sidetracked by talks of 'rogue elements' within the ISI or of a 'state within a state'. As former Pakistan President Pervez Musharraf himself said to the *London Times* in 2006, the ISI is a disciplined force, doing what the army tells it to do. We should accept his word. If the ISI acts itself or through former members retained by it because of its personal contacts with, or sympathies for, Islamism and terrorists, then it does so at the behest or with the tacit assent of the army.

This relationship, we must remember, is underwritten by staff rotations between the army and the ISI that sees about 80 per cent of ISI staff turnover every two years. Almost all of them are from the army. The scale, the character, the timing, and the targets of the Mumbai attack have given rise to much analysis about actors and intentions. For me the most persuasive of these are those which link to the structural drivers that I just outlined, namely that the attacks were intended to provoke a crisis with India; a crisis which would refocus Pakistan's military attention on India and, to some extent, relieve US pressure on Pakistan in the tribal areas. It was intended to weaken and increase international pressure on the civilian government of Pakistan, to torpedo the peace process between India and Pakistan, to apply pressure to India at the time of elections, to increase tensions with India thus making a US resolution of the Afghan question more difficult for the incoming Obama administration, and, of course, to poison, or seek to poison, relations between India and Israel.

Looking forward, the implications would appear to be that organizations as long as these continue to serve its policy supporting these groups can be borne.

The question of *cui bono*, who benefits, from the Mumbai attacks seems to me answered most clearly in terms of the Pakistan Army/ISI. Looking forward, the implications would appear to be that the Pakistan Army/ISI will not abandon its links to terrorist organizations as long as these continue to serve its policy objectives and as long as the internal and external cost of supporting these groups can be borne.

The Pakistan Army/ISI clearly believes that it can maintain the separation between those terrorist groups in Pakistan which threaten the Pakistan state and those which function directly or indirectly as instruments of the Pakistan state. That may prove to be hubris. Groups like the Afghan Taliban and Lashkar-e-Taiba have grown very powerful in recent years and now hold the Pakistan Army/ISI to some extent in a kind of fallacy and standoff. Elsewhere, groups like the TTP (Tehrik-i-Taliban), Lashkar-e-Jhangvi and Jaish-e-Mohammad have joined up with Al-Qaeda both in enhancing the reach of Pakistan Taliban groups beyond the Pashtun belt and in enlarging the ideological vision of these groups in South Asia and beyond. Finding a response to terrorist threats originating in other countries, which are both antipathetic and actively support terrorism, is the most difficult challenge of all.

Understanding Pakistan's relationship with terrorist groups may offer us a possible framework for movement. It follows from what I have said that the Pakistan Army can be pressured and supported to abandon its links to these groups and to turn its security apparatus on them only when these groups no longer serve Pakistan's policy objectives or when the internal and external costs become too great. I think there is scope for movement, albeit it is very difficult along all three of these axes.

Firstly, the United States and India should increase cooperation

the Pakistan Army/ISI will not abandon its links to terrorist objectives and as long as the internal and external cost of

on regional dispensation, particularly with respect to Afghanistan and Kashmir, which responds to Pakistan's concerns. I am open, when I say this, to the charge that this is bowing to terrorist threat. But my answer to that would be that it is important to maintain a positive environment of engagement in order to draw the sting of the Pakistan Army/ISI's paranoia to help strengthen the civilian government and less hawkish forces in Pakistan and also to begin to offer over time calibrations in Pakistan around continued support for terrorist groups.

Secondly, the internal costs for Pakistan are rising and it is in no one's interest to see that country break up or descend into chaos. This is why I am a strong supporter of the Obama administration that tends to shift support in Pakistan from the military to the civilian realm and to condition and link military aid to precise counter-terror and counter-insurgency outcomes. Indian restraint in denying the Pakistan Army/ISI an excuse to reduce pressure in the tribal belt is a powerful force multiplier in that regard and is greatly to be welcomed. If I was in Washington and if there are US leaders here, I would be arguing for greater investment and support for policing in Pakistan and for the reconnection of the US and Pakistan armies.

Finally, in relation to external cost, it is evident that neither India nor anyone else can find a means to militarily punish Pakistan for its continued support to terrorist groups which do not undermine other objectives or exacerbate the problems. Therefore, perhaps the most significant external costs are being paid in terms of Pakistan's dwindling circle of friendly nations; its cost in terms of lost investment and business, economic and social opportunity, particularly in the context of India's enormous economic growth and potential and, of course, also being paid in Pakistan's drift towards pariah status.

It falls, therefore, to those outside Pakistan to continue to signal the problem which attaches to Pakistan's links to terrorists but also to bear the costs of separating Pakistan's terrorists from those within the state.

Brajesh Mishra

Former National Security Advisor, India

A former Indian Foreign Service officer, Brajesh Mishra was appointed the country's first National Security Advisor by former Prime Minister Atal Bihari Vajpayee.

In April 1991, Mishra joined the Bharatiya Janata Party, which he quit in March 1998 to become Principal Secretary to the Prime Minister. From November 1998 to May 2004, he was also the PM's National Security Advisor.

As Vajpayee's trouble-shooter he was one of the most powerful principal secretaries the PMO had ever seen.

Mishra was the key motivator of foreign policy and principal spokesman on all major issues. The opportunities for him were endless. From Pokhran-2 to Kashmir, and from Vajpayee's historic visit to Pakistan to engaging the United States in a strategic dialogue, he was behind a never-ending series of foreign policy and security manoeuvres.

Born on 29 September 1928, his father, the late D.P. Mishra, was a former chief minister of Madhya Pradesh.

Brajesh Mishra served as India's ambassador to Indonesia. He was also the country's permanent representative in Geneva. From June 1979 to April 1981, he was India's permanent representative to the United Nations. He continued with the United Nations on deputation until June 1987.

Once out of office, Mishra welcomed the Indo-US civilian nuclear agreement signed by Prime Minister Manmohan Singh after he was convinced that it was in the country's best interest.

TODAY'S DISCUSSION HAS TWO DIMENSIONS – ONE IS EXTERNAL, THE OTHER IS INTERNAL. MUCH HAS BEEN SAID ABOUT THE EXTERNAL DIMENSION BY THE TWO previous speakers. Of course, Pakistan is a big actor in this entire situation and let me state outright that as long as the Pakistan Army is in charge of Pakistan, this type of action – whether it was in the '90s or in the beginning of this century or last year – will continue. We must never fool ourselves into thinking that the Pakistan army will give up its privileged position in the near future or even perhaps in the distant future.

We talk about democracy in Pakistan but we know through our experience that it is the army which is in charge. It is the army which is in charge of relations with India. It is the army which is in charge of relations with Afghanistan. It is the army which is in charge of the country's nuclear weapons.

As far as we are concerned, and I don't want to dwell too much on Pakistan because that can take a long time, the problem we face today is the following: the Pakistani army's ambitions vis-à-vis India are known to us. China is supporting Pakistan and especially the Pakistani military for reasons which are well known. It is the support of China which is becoming more and more open in the last few weeks. You must have read about the change in their attitude towards the Kashmir question. You must have read about the claim to disintegrate India, which was published in official media some time ago. So, China's help to the Pakistani military is a very important factor in aiding and abetting its designs on India.

But we also have the United States. The United States is not our enemy. It is our friend. But the policies being pursued by the United States for the last eight years vis-à-vis Pakistan have the same adverse impact on India as China's policies towards Pakistan. We all know that President Musharraf has himself declared publicly that the financial and material aid given to Pakistan by the United States during the Bush administration was used for purposes other than for what it was intended, if not for lining one's own pockets.

That is a very clear admission from President Musharraf who

was in charge for most of that period. Although conditions have been put today on the aid to Pakistan by the US Congress, we know that those conditions will be bypassed, subverted – use whatever word you like -- and the money will still go, quite a lot of it, to the Pakistan Army to help Pakistan's designs against India.

In addition, there are voices from Washington asking us to settle Kashmir with Pakistan on the basis of the wishes of the people of Kashmir. This is a very old mantra as you all know. There are also voices from the United States asking us to reduce our presence in Afghanistan. Now, if all this doesn't serve the interest of Pakistan, then I don't know what serves its interests.

We are facing a situation, so far as the external dimension of terrorism is concerned, where we are up against an unprecedented challenge. We have to face this challenge through diplomacy plus – and this is more important than diplomacy – increasing our military strength. Without that you will not be able to overcome the problem or even face the problem as it exists.

One last word on the external aspect: we have had two fronts since 1962. Fortunately for us, these two fronts were never simultaneously active against us in the past. But I will not rule out that within the next five years, given the change in the attitude of China which we have been seeing in the last two years, the two fronts could be active simultaneously. We have to have the military strength to face the two fronts. I don't mean that we should be offensive about it. I mean that we should be able to defend ourselves both conventionally and through non-conventional strategic weapons.

Coming to the domestic aspect of this, much has been talked about 26/11. There are four points which need consideration. One is the will of the political leadership to face terrorist activity. This means one does not communalize the terrorist situation. Let me say to you that it is not one party which is responsible. All are responsible for communalizing the terrorist situation. We have to discard this and this can be done only through the political actions of political parties and through political will.

Second, politicians have to show the way to the people as to how to conduct themselves in this situation. Rules have to be accepted. We must give up the habit of some MLAs stopping a train in some station where the train is not supposed to stop because he has to get into the train and travel. What kind of example do you set to the people when you do that? Or then, some members of Parliament recently stopped an aircraft from taking off because they were delayed. As recently as two days ago, a technocrat wanting to delay a flight in order to catch it said there was a suspected bomb in the plane. What kind of example are we giving to our people? So, we need leadership in order to educate people to accept the fact that their actions have to correspond to the terror that we are facing. They have to take into account the fact that they have to give up some of their freedoms.

It is well known not only in India but almost every country that

We talk about democracy in Pakistan but we know charge. It is the army which is in charge of relations with Afghanistan. It is the army which is in charge of

Intelligence agencies never cooperate with each other. They don't want to share information. Either they are hiding their sources or they are hiding their incompetence. Having been in the seat of power for six years, I can testify to that. It is very important that Intelligence agencies cooperate with each other, share information with each other and act together, not merely at the centre but also in the states. The Intelligence Bureau has a presence in all the states of the country. It has presence perhaps in all the districts of the country. But what is the coordination between the Central Intelligence Bureau and the local intelligence bureau? That is something which has to be worked out by the government.

Political interference in the working of the police force or in matters relating to the recruitment, transfer and promotion of police must be stopped immediately. Unless you have a police force which is able to react to the situation fast enough and with competence, you are not going to be able to prevent terrorist activity. Not every terrorist activity can be prevented. But you can prevent a vast number of terrorist plans if the police force were to act in a way corresponding to the dangers that we are facing. Because of political interference in recruitment, transfers, postings and promotions, we have a nexus between politicians and the police, which is very dangerous.

The second aspect of this is that police training has to change in order to take care of the new terrorist situation we face. It is not just an ordinary law and order problem. It is a much bigger problem.

Finally, the police force has to earn the respect of the people, and the people have to respect the police force. It is not happening today. I am afraid to go to a police station to register an FIR (first information report) because I don't know what will happen after

through our experience that it is the army which is in with India. It is the army which is in charge of relations the country's nuclear weapons.

that. This fear must go. At the same time, the most important element of the police force is supposed to be the beat cop, the one in the *mohalla* (neighbourhood) where he finds out what is happening. Today, that is not the situation. Incompetent people are put in that position. They cannot find out what is happening in their territory.

Unless we do all these things, the prevention of terrorist activity is not going to be possible. While you act diplomatically and otherwise with Pakistan or any other source of terrorist activity that might come, you have to improve your internal situation. You have to change your habits here at home. You have to reform the police. You have to re-train the police. You have to see that the people respect the police and are not afraid of it. Unless you do that, we will not be able to handle the situation in the way in which we should.

K.C. Singh: We have to look at the history of Indo-Pak relations and terrorism in three phases from 1990 to 1998. The first phase begins around 1990 when Soviet withdrawal had taken place in Afghanistan. Spare capacity was available, the Mujahideen had come home and Pakistan started pushing this trained group into Kashmir and igniting the fire of terrorism there.

The second phase begins in 1993 after the destruction of the Babri Masjid, the riots that ensued and the culmination of events in the Mumbai blasts which led to the blowing up of financial institutions there. Pakistan did not succeed in what was attempted because the blasts were really done by Dawood Ibrahim's group. It was not a terrorist organization as much as a crime syndicate to which organizations in Pakistan outsourced the blowing up of the Stock Exchange and other buildings. But Pakistan could not ignite a communal holocaust in India which could have been set off after the Babri Masjid episode. This demonstrated that the Muslim community here was integrated, at peace and in harmony with social life.

In 1998, the NDA government came in and ushered in the third or nuclear phase which is from 1998 to 2001. Suddenly, the eyes of the global community were focused on India and Pakistan. There were now two countries with nuclear devices, and there was terrorism. Now this was incendiary and Pakistan reveled in it because it was getting attention at last. So, it focused on Kashmir and that is when during those three years starting from 1999 were very critical.

There was the peace journey, with Prime Minister Atal Bihari Vajpayee travelling by bus to Lahore. This was followed by Kargil with 1999 finishing on a negative phase with a bad taste in the mouth that a prime minister had been sacked in Pakistan.

The NDA began with a democratically elected leader and ended with a dictator in Pakistan. The UPA government began with a Pakistani dictator and ended up with a democratically elected government. But, twice in the case of the NDA, once in 1999 and the second time in 2001 when our Parliament was attacked, dialogue was started and dialogue was thwarted because a major terrorist attack took place.

Twice in the life of the UPA, the same thing happened. In 2006 we had the Mumbai train bombings coming after 2004 in Madrid and 2005 in London. These attacks took terrorism to another level. Then, the dialogue process began. The UPA came in saying we should not allow terrorism to interrupt the dialogue process. In fact, they were very critical of the NDA earlier. But they realized that once the threshold is raised, it becomes very difficult to continue a dialogue when public fear and public anger is aroused.

This was overcome by constructing a joint anti-terror mechanism on the sidelines of NAM (Non-Aligned Movement) in 2006, which I was asked to lead from the Indian side. But we realized even when the mechanism was set up that this could only be a temporary fix. This was not going to fix terrorism. This could restart the dialogue process but could also insulate the dialogue process for all time to come from another terrorist attack and that is precisely what happened with 26/11.

Where do we go from here? Twice, talks were restarted by the NDA with assurances given by President Pervez Musharraf from a public platform that the soil of Pakistan would not be used for any abetment of terror in a neighbouring country. Once in the case of the UPA, a mechanism was set up in the presence of President Musharraf and it was thought that perhaps this would get rid of the problem. Now we are again encountering the same problem. So, therefore, the dialogue process and terrorism are closely intertwined. How do we past get it? Sharm el-Sheikh [where India and Pakistan held meetings for the resumption of bilateral talks] was an attempt and we saw a public reaction that worked rather badly for the prime minister.

It was mentioned to the prime minister at this summit that he has been articulating the need for dialogue and peace. But is articulation enough? Is ours a voice in the wilderness? Whom do you talk to? What is happening to Pakistan? Where are the president and the prime minister? What is their relationship to the army chief? What is the battle they are fighting in the West? Is the pressure going to bear on India?

We will examine these questions but another issue of significance is that we used to treat West Asia as a problem far away. We had sympathy and empathy at a public level with Israel but public articulation was always for the Palestinians. We thought it was a problem which we could articulate in multilateral fora and leave it there.

But Al-Qaeda has a global agenda and West Asia is on the global agenda. Where does Kashmir fit in? Has the agenda got mixed up? Have the barriers gone, where even if Kashmir was settled terrorism would not go away? Hakimullah Mehsud recently said: 'I will first get Pakistan and then I am going to be at India's border.' If there is going to be a global Caliphate, then Indian Muslims can't be insulated.

Therefore, is Kashmir a core issue or is it just an ancillary issue? These are the issues we will examine.

Moderator | **K.C. Singh**

Former Secretary, Ministry of External Affairs and Co-ordinator, Joint Anti-Terror Mechanism between India and Pakistan

Q: My question is to Brajesh Mishra. Why is India numb to China's growing discomfort over the visits of the Indian prime minister and the Dalai Lama to Arunachal Pradesh?

Brajesh Mishra: I am not in the Indian government, so how can I answer that? But, let me say that in the last two years or so, Chinese claims on Arunachal have acquired a stridency which was never there before. They are doing everything possible internationally and otherwise to see that Arunachal Pradesh is not recognized as a part of India. Their opposition to the Prime Minister going there – this is not the first visit of a Prime Minister to Arunachal Pradesh – their opposition to the Dalai Lama going there – this is the fifth visit of the Dalai Lama there. Earlier there weren't so many protests from China with regard to these visits. The situation has changed in the last two years. But for a proper answer as to the government's response, you must ask the government representative about it.

Q: Mr Halevy, I think you underscored a very fundamental dilemma which confronts every democratic state in the fight against terror. To what extent should the state really internalize authoritarian impulses and what is the limit of those authoritarian impulses? India has had two very successful experiences over the last sixty-two years in the fight against terror. The first is in Mizoram, which of course was supported by the Chinese, and which was sorted out through a negotiated political settlement. The other one is in Punjab which was the first frontier the Pakistanis had opened up. In Punjab too we were able to find a solution to the problem of terror without fundamentally changing the rules of the game. The point that I am trying to make is that there is scope and there is space to fight the battle against terror without really becoming like them (the terrorists).

Efraim Halevy: I don't want to dispute your examples and I am not suggesting that there should be no checks and balances. What

I am suggesting is that in this new climate, especially after Mumbai and similar acts that have never been perpetrated before, we need new rules of the game. We are in this for a very long time. The intentions of the terrorists who attacked Mumbai were not similar to the intentions of those who carried out their acts in the cases that you mentioned. In Mumbai there were aims that are far-reaching and global in intent. So, we have to think about this differently. If we don't, we will succumb and if we do not learn now, we will have to learn later after paying a much heavier price.

Q: The Prime Minister has said on a number of occasions, if Pakistan takes action on terrorism we can resume the composite dialogue. What do you think can be such action by Pakistan, given the experience of the last ten years?

Brajesh Mishra: I don't think we can expect Pakistan to meet all our demands. There are quite a few of them, but certainly we cannot move forward on a dialogue with Pakistan unless they punish the perpetrators of this crime in Mumbai, openly and in court. Today, they are playing games: the court is adjourned, the prosecutor does not want to take the case, the judge does not want to take the case. All these things have been going on for the last so many months. They do not give us the impression that Pakistan is very sincere about what it has said it will do in this regard. Therefore, in my view, with all due respect to the Prime Minister, I don't think we can go back to a dialogue without Pakistan first taking some action to convince us that it is going to fight terrorism.

Q: Mr Mishra, can we expect Pakistan to not perpetrate another attack with or without the help of other countries?

Brajesh Mishra: I think we would be fooling ourselves if we came to that conclusion. In the last few days, you have heard how another LeT attempt was foiled by the United States. I don't think you need any further proof.

Q: Mr Halevy, does the Israel government have any technological equipment that can protect its public places against terror attacks?

Efraim Halevy: Yes, there are many technologies in Israel related to these affairs. The Israelis are operating all over the world in protecting public installations, hotels and so forth with much success.

Q: How is the Indian government taking a lead from your resources of this technological advancement?

Efraim Halevy: I have not been in government for several years but from my experience and during my previous visits to India, I have had extremely fruitful conversations and discussions with my counterparts here. We have found in successive Indian governments a very willing and very capable partner as far as we are concerned.

Q: Professor Gregory, the kind of attacks we have seen in Pakistan in the past few weeks seem to suggest that Pakistan's war on its east, west and northern fronts is coming together. There is Harkat in Kashmir, Lashkar in Punjab and Tehrik-e-Taliban on the western front. They are all working in tandem. One study seems to suggest that those who went to the general headquarters in Rawalpindi could quite easily have received the same training and the same commanders even as the men who came to Mumbai. What is your perspective?

Shaun Gregory: There is no question that some of these groups are beginning to join hands. This is beginning to pose a new kind of threat inside Pakistan. But, these groups aren't all yet connecting up. The LeT, for example, has never conducted an operation inside Pakistan. The Afghan Taliban groups like Haqqani and Omar still have the support of the Pakistani state so that in the seven years since the Afghan Taliban were pushed across the border following their overthrow in Afghanistan, we have seen nothing against those groups that matches what is taking place in tribal areas now. One of the things that I heard was that the Pakistan Army/ISI, was using Mullah Omar in order to try to control the TTP to scale down the attacks against Pakistan cities and, therefore, there is a kind of standoff. You are absolutely right in saying that the great nightmare for most Pakistanis is that the Afghan Taliban and the LeT and others will actually join up. But that hasn't happened yet. The army thinks that it can keep the two separate. I am not persuaded that they will actually be able to do this in the long run. I have been cautioning the army, to the extent that I have been able to, that the distinction between so-called good terrorists and bad-terrorists is phoney and it is eating away at Pakistan. It is in no one's interest.

Innovative Solutions for Health Challenges

▪

Dr Naresh Trehan

▪

Dr Salim J. Habayeb

▪

Dr George W. Weightman

▪

Moderator

K. Srinath Reddy

President, Public Health Foundation of India

Dr Naresh Trehan

Chairman and Managing Director, Medanta – The Medicity

A graduate of the King George Medical College Dr Naresh Trehan subsequently practiced at the New York University Medical Center, where he obtained a diplomat from the American Board of Surgery and American Board of Cardiothoracic Surgery, Dr Trehan is a renowned Indian cardiovascular and cardiothoracic surgeon.

Dr Trehan is the Chairman and Managing Director of Medanta – The Medicity, a 1,500-bedded multi-super-specialty institute that offers cutting edge technology and state of the art treatment. The institute is governed by the guiding principles of providing medical services to patients with care, compassion and commitment.

Dr Trehan founded the Escorts Heart Institute and Research Centre where he was the Executive Director. Escorts was conceptualized, created and managed by him from November 1987 to May 2007.

Among other prestigious awards, Dr Trehan has received the Padma Shri and Padma Bhushan by the President of India.

He was President of the International Society for Minimally Invasive Cardiac Surgery, Minneapolis, USA, from 2004 to 2005. He has also received honorary doctorate degrees from three prestigious universities.

YOU HEARD THE MOST EXCITING JOURNEY INTO THE FUTURE. LET ME TAKE YOU BACK TO THE BASICS. THERE ARE HUGE CHALLENGES WITH INDIAN healthcare.

The story started way back in 1978 when India became a signatory to the Alma-Ata Declaration (International Conference on Primary Healthcare) along with 134 other countries. These countries committed that by the year 2000, they would provide basic healthcare to all citizens.

It was a no-brainer that this was not going to happen, so we commissioned Mckenzie (consultants) to do a health status report with two briefs: where are we, as opposed to where we should have been by 2000, and, if we are not there, what will it take to get there in the next ten years?

The data showed that we are actually about 40-50 per cent of where we should have been. Some of the other countries who were co-signatories like Mexico, Brazil, Thailand, have made significantly more progress than we have. So we are actually now at the same level as Sub-Saharan Africa.

But as always in India there is a flipside. We have multiple centres of excellence where we can perform procedures and deliver treatments of the highest level at a fraction of what it would cost in America, albeit it's still too expensive for our Indian population to access.

We spend 5.2 per cent of our GDP on health. Only 20 per cent of this comes from the government, 80 per cent comes from private pockets. We are hoping that this GDP will grow to 7 to 8 per cent. In the United States, it is 14 per cent. In other countries it is 9 to 10 per cent. We need to reach that level to be able to attach appropriate importance to healthcare in our country.

The current size of the healthcare system is about US$ 36 billion and we hope it will grow to about US$ 45 to 50 billion by the year 2012. To double our infrastructure, because that is what our data showed, we are at about 50 per cent of where we were. We would require an incremental investment of about $25 billion.

At the current spend rate, we would spend about $10 billion, so you can call it a deficiency or an opportunity, but there is huge scope for participating in the investment of healthcare provided it is done in the right proportion.

Worldwide, the enablers of healthcare access are insurance companies. Although 10 to 15 per cent of Indians are covered by either the government or their employers or some sort of insurance, private insurance penetration was only one per cent as of 2002. It has gone up to about 3 per cent now. We are hoping that over the next five years it will reach a premium level of four billion which will make it possible for many more people to access healthcare.

India is not alone in this crisis. The United States has its own problem. At $2.2 trillion, they cannot even provide services to 300 million people; 50 million Americans are out of the scope of the healthcare delivery system. If that is the cost of healthcare as we know it, there is no hope for countries like India and countries in Asia and Africa. We need to think out of the box to see how we are going to cope with this crisis. It's the same problem with UK and France. It is predicted that most of these systems are going to collapse in the next fifteen to twenty years and go bankrupt.

To understand the Indian healthcare situation and how we could possibly find solutions to it, I have sliced the problem into four parts. The first is preventive care. We can decrease the burden of disease that by itself will not only decrease expenditure on health but also lead to a healthier India, healthier workforce and more productivity.

Similarly in primary healthcare, we need to come up with newer solutions. The old adage that you need a doctor in every village, is not happening. It is unrealistic, a fantasy. Where do you get 600,000 doctors when the total population of Indian doctors is 500,000? How do you get 600,000 doctors to live in a village where there is no school, no drinking water, no amenities for the family? It is not going to happen. We need to come up with solutions to address this problem.

The secondary care we talk about happens in district hospitals where simple operations and a little more complicated treatment can be performed at the district level. The government has a very large network of district hospitals. Unfortunately, there is an uneven standard and not all these hospitals function well. So, that is another challenge.

With tertiary care we are talking about high-end, complicated operations requiring huge investment in technology and great expertise of doctors. It presents two challenges. One is that the investment required to create tertiary facilities is huge. Second, the doctors who have specialized for many years to perform those procedures expect to earn much more than a government system can pay. So that area naturally falls in the private sector. Yet, we can do better.

To cite one example. We looked at a typical village in Daruhera, sixty kilometres from here. It is close to one of the biggest manufacturers of motor cycles in India. But when we went in, we found roads filled with slush where mosquitoes were breeding in the millions. There was no proper garbage disposal. Sewage flowed between homes and even right next to the hand pump where the people drew water from. The school was deserted; the girls had a 100 per cent dropout rate because there were no toilets in their school.

This was the state of affairs right in our backyard. We thought about what we could do to change this and came up with a programme called the Healthy and Educated Village Programme. We launched this programme with the help of some corporates. Four months later we converted that same village into one with *pucca* roads, a sewage system that runs around the village and goes into septic tanks. We made four walls for garbage disposal. The hand pump was dug deeper until we found potable water. We put toilets in the school and the children came back. All this cost a total of Rs 12 lakh. We were able to transform a village of 2,500 people with the help of corporates including the *Hindustan Times*.

Corporates adopt villages. They provide drinking water and whatever their speciality is. HCL provides computers to schools.

Bharti provides teaching to teachers. Jubilant and *Hindustan Times* adopt villages. Collectively, we have now adopted 100 villages and hopefully will complete work in this coming year.

The second thing I was talking about was primary care. As I mentioned, you cannot have a doctor in every village. I took one district of Sonepat with a population of 22 lakh people. Going by the headcount, you would require 150 doctors in this district alone. This is not going to happen. But what if you took four small towns in that district and set up base mobile systems in the hospitals there? There are schools for the families of doctors, there is security and the doctors will not mind staying there. With 16 doctors and their attendant staff of equal number, you could actually cover the entire Sonepat district with four to eight mobile vans that would visit every village every other day. In case of an emergency, there is telephony; you can always ask for an ambulance from the hospital.

The healthcare sector needs to be given infrastructure It can create a new stream of revenue generation

We have been talking about public-private partnership for five years now. We still don't have a reliable model to speak of. So I wanted to stress that we already have those district hospitals. We must leverage the already existing networks. Take help from the private sector, the NGO sector, funding, professional services, systems and staff and you can actually participate, provided the private sector agrees to do it on a no-profit-no-loss basis. We are stuck with the idea: are we going to make money by helping the people or not? But there is great room in creating a public-private partnership and accelerating it right away.

For tertiary care delivery we must come up with innovative low-cost solutions for rural areas. That means that we build small hospitals with basic facilities where you don't have to provide the most complicated tertiary care. But the network will lead to tertiary care in case somebody needs it. We have economies of scale which we can leverage to reduce the cost of tertiary care even in cities.

You can use cross-subsidies to help poor people because you must bring everybody into the loop. The cost of technology has to come down and that's where we need partners from our manufacturers who can actually bring costs down. One idea we took from all this was to create Medicity, now known as Medanta, The Medicity. What we have done here is create an institution with 1,250 beds that can be expandable to 1,800 beds. We put in all the technology in the world. This cost quite a bit but when you divide it by 1,500 or 1,800 beds, the cost becomes affordable and we were able to reduce the cost of delivery by 20 to 25 per cent.

The institution is now open. We have used cross-subsidies, we can amortize it over a larger base and accept all sorts of insurance and try to see if we can serve a whole cross-section of society.

In the end, what can the government do? First, healthcare has not been on the political agenda. Lack of healthcare does not translate into lack of votes. We are hoping that with the new awakening, it will take centre stage. That's when the government will get more serious about healthcare.

status .... There is huge employment potential for our country. by taxes.

Second, the healthcare sector needs to be given infrastructure status. This will help create the infrastructure that we need across the world. We need to double it. There is huge employment potential for our country. It can create a new stream of revenue generation by taxes. The minimum salary of a hospital employee is about Rs 5,000. Most employees are tax payers. This is a huge area.

The government should realize that the more it stimulates the health sector, the better off we will be not only in terms of healthcare but as a country. We have lost sixty years. We need to create a national task force right away and converge all the points, all the different participants in the healthcare delivery system. Whether they are in the villages, whether they are private doctors, whether they are *hakims* and *vaids*, ultimately they are all a part of India.

We should not waste any more time. We need to set a five-year time bound agenda to say that we will accomplish the standards to which we committed in 1978. There is a cartoon of President Barack Obama standing on his head, trying to solve the healthcare problem of the United States supported by Hanuman. If we don't do this, our leaders will be standing on their heads with Obama trying to support us. The time is here. And we must get serious.

Dr Salim J. Habayeb

WHO Representative to India

WHO Representative to India since January 2003, Dr Salim J. Habayeb was earlier the lead public health specialist at the World Bank headquarters in Washington, where he has worked for sixteen years in the regions of Europe, Middle East, North Africa, Latin America and the Caribbean, and South Asia.

Dr Habayeb pursued his training in France and USA. He obtained his medical degree from the University of Bordeaux. He holds a master's degree in Health Planning & Administration and a joint master's in Public Health in Epidemiology from the University of Michigan. His post-graduate training includes Internal Medicine, Preventive Medicine and Tropical Medicine. He is a Fellow of the American College of Epidemiology.

Dr Habayeb's main professional interests include outcome-oriented national health planning; health systems strengthening; sectoral reform; sustainable development, financing, resource mobilization and partnerships; poverty alleviation; essential public health functions; communicable and chronic disease control; teaching, training and coaching; public health policy; regulatory and legal aspects in public health.

THE WORLD HAS ALWAYS BEEN THREATENED BY EPIDEMICS AND PANDEMICS. A PANDEMIC IS A GLOBAL EPIDEMIC. THE WORD COMES FROM GREEK AND MEANS 'total in all'. While it has been a threat for the last several decades, the threats have increased immensely due to more interactions. This is not a linear situation, like a triangle where you stop one item and it stops.

Think of a pressure cooker where everything is mixed, constantly interacting with each other, especially the host population and other environments affecting mankind. For the agent or the host, microvisually this nature cleaves with the host in perfect harmony but sometimes there are imbalances where it is allowed to spread in a formidable way or to jump species from animals to humans, causing pandemics.

For the host, there are many characteristics. There is no need to go there but mainly there are immunity levels and some areas

There are new emerging infections globally and, whether have many more if we didn't have the technology and

with genetic factors. The most important ones are the physical environment affecting pandemics and also the socio-economic environment. The physical environment includes natural disasters that cause epidemics. Water, sanitation, deforestation, and recent studies on climate change show that India will have an expanded window of transmission for malaria by three months. This is the phenomenal impact of the environment on disease spread.

The socio-economic environment is most important and relates to lifestyle issues. For many epidemics like HIV/AIDS, it is a major contributing factor. The speed and intensity of travel and transportation has certainly impacted the way diseases behave. There are new emerging infections globally and, whether you call it an epidemic or pandemic, the point is we would have many more if we didn't have the technology and the know-how to alleviate or to prevent them.

Global health security has become an important topic for the whole world. WHO and 594 countries have got together and updated International Health Regulations and have started implementing these with benchmarks and deadlines. We have a hub in Geneva, the Global Outbreak Alert and Response. It is a network for identification and response. We have an Event Management System that is connected with state parties and governments. We have a focal point in each country that facilitates interactions.

Influenza is on everybody's mind. We also have a Global Influenza Surveillance Network. We have 128 institutions globally from 99 countries that are providing inputs to global surveillance. WHO advises twice a year on the kind of strain that should be included in the seasonal influenza vaccines.

Our vision is to have an integrated system based on the National Health Systems themselves. My colleague Dr Srinath Reddy published recently that you cannot have a rush response.

you call it an epidemic or pandemic, the point is we would the know-how to alleviate or to prevent them.

You cannot press a button and respond to the influenza pandemic or to any other pandemic. You need to be prepared and to build the response block by block. Fortunately, the world did learn from Avian Flu and from SARS and was relatively better prepared to deal with this current scare.

Our vision is to have a network of networks. Of course, part of this is already functioning but can be made much more effective. What this means is that we don't' need just technical areas in the health sector. We don't just need physicians. We need all the specialties. We need managers, IT experts, media, and lawyers to deal with rules and regulations affecting countries.

Dr George W. Weightman

MD, Associate Director and Chief Operating Officer, Professor, Wake Forest Institute for Regenerative Medicine

Formerly, commander of the United States Army Medical Research and Material Command, Major General Weightman oversees the day-to-day operations of the Wake Forest University Health Sciences Institute for Regenerative Medicine of which he is the Associate Director, Chief Operating Officer and Professor.

His awards include the Distinguished Service Medal (one Oak Leaf Cluster, Legion of Merit (three Oak Leaf Clusters), Bronze Star Medal (one Oak Leaf Cluster), Meritorious Service Medal (two Oak Leaf Clusters), Joint Service Commendation Medal, Army Commendation Medal (three Oak Leaf Clusters), Armed Forces Expeditionary Medal (with Bronze Arrowhead device), and the Army Superior Unit Award.

A native of Eden Mills, Vermont, Dr Weightman received his bachelor's degree from the United States Military Academy at West Point. He was awarded a medical degree from the University of Vermont and completed his family practice residency training at Eisenhower Medical Center, Fort Gordon, Georgia. He is board certified by the American Board of Family Practice and is a Fellow in the American Academy of Family Physicians.

Dr Weightman's military assignments have included commanding the North Atlantic Regional Medical Command and Walter Reed Army Medical Center; commanding the US Army Medical Department Center and School and Fort Sam Houston, San Antonio, Texas; serving as Commanding General, 44th Medical Command/Corps Surgeon, XVIII Airborne Corps at Fort Bragg, N.C., and serving as Assistant Surgeon General for Force Projection and Commanding General, 3rd Medical Command (Forward), and Coalition Forces Land Component Command Surgeon for Operation Iraqi Freedom.

I WANT TO TALK A LITTLE BIT ABOUT REGENERATIVE MEDICINE AND WHAT THE FUTURE MAY HOLD FOR THE PROMISE OF BETTER WORLD HEALTH. WE HAVE HAD AN explosion in the technology of medical science over the last twenty to twenty-five years. Starting with the human genome and carried on through a greater understanding of proteomics and genomics, we now understand what goes on in the human body at the genetic, molecular, cellular and even tissue and organ level. This is an understanding we didn't have even half a generation ago.

We have developed new systems in the last decade where we can grow cells outside the body. That is a tremendous advance. We also found out that for many organs and tissues, you need a scaffold, something to build these cells on to take correct shape, whether it's a heart or a kidney or a liver. We have had breakthroughs in those scaffolds that we can build on, add cells and then once they are transplanted into the body, they can disintegrate, so that there is no foreign body reaction.

What is the potential for regenerative medicine? Just looking at the United States, there are 58 million people who have cardiovascular disease and 16 million people with diabetes. The number of people waiting for transplants has doubled in the last decade. This is a tremendous problem. The average cost for one year of kidney dialysis in America is $250,000. The average length of life on dialysis in the United States is five years. This has an impact not only in economic terms but on quality of life as well.

Regenerative medicine is not just about growing tissues and organs. There are also cellular therapies. For instance, one of the clinical strategies we now have is where we inject muscle cells into the sphincter of the bladder to control urinary incontinence which is a fairly widespread problem. Injecting cells into the sphincter recruits additional healthy cells and makes the new cells correct the problem. You don't necessarily have to transplant an entire organ or part of an organ. Sometimes cellular therapy will recruit the body's own natural mechanisms.

We have also developed diagnostic platforms using standard platforms within the laboratory. Using PCR technology, we can detect if a patient is infected by up to 36 different organisms within three hours. Traditionally you have to take samples. You have to send them off to a microbiology lab and you will not get results for 24 to 48 hours. This is one of the technologies that we have developed at the institute to help our clinicians treat their patients faster.

We are also working on healing therapies. We have developed technology where we can encapsulate an oxygen-producing compound, so that it releases oxygen over a period of time. This has great application in wound-healing; certainly in infections, maybe even for cosmetic purposes. That's an additional technology that is not traditionally associated with regenerative medicine. Supporting technologies – building those scaffolds or those matrices to build new organs upon that is called bio materials – is a burgeoning

What is the potential for regenerative medicine? Just who have cardiovascular disease and 16 million people has doubled in the last decade. This is a tremendous

field that is a spin-off from what we traditionally think of as regenerative medicine.

We have grown some cell types outside of the body at the Wake Forest Institute. Some have been grown from the patient's own organ-specific tissue; kidney tissue from the kidney and so on. We cannot as yet grow organ specific tissue from the heart, the nerve, the liver and the pancreas. But we can grow those from stem cells. Right now up to about twenty-two different tissue types can be grown in the lab. Not all these projects are ready for clinical application.

I would say that the whole field of regenerative medicine is truly a global effort. Within our laboratory, we have scientists and students from twenty-three countries and we have international collaboration with over fifty different countries, including India at the present time.

In our war in Afghanistan, we partnered with our Department of Defense to look at five major areas that are specific to our wounded warriors. These include growing skin, scar-less healing, and therapies for growing digits. We are very focused on producing products. Now a question that often comes up is, how soon can you grow a new kidney or how soon can you grow a liver or how soon can you grow a new arm? Right now I predict that we will have solid organs – liver, kidney, pancreas – probably in the fifteen to twenty year timeframe. These are much more complicated than say hollow organs, such as the bladder, blood vessels and the trachea. These we will see ready for clinical application within the next five to ten years. Whole limbs are probably also about fifteen to twenty years down the road.

I want to set realistic expectations. Part of this is technological;

looking at the United States, there are 58 million people with diabetes. The number of people waiting for transplants problem.

we need to learn more. Part of it is regulatory. In all countries there are regulatory agencies that govern how quickly we can put products to human and clinical use. This is a new field for all our regulatory agencies. We are working with them to determine the right safety levels.

The near-term deliverable is rapid pathogen detection where we can put a sample in a standard PCR machine and get a read-out of not only what a patient is infected with but also the sensitivities. That technology is ready today.

Bio-reactor and bio-printing manufacturing are two new technologies that we also have right now. A bio-reactor can grow muscles cells outside the body in a dish. That doesn't mean that they are going to work like muscle cells in the body. So, we put them in a machine, a bio-reactor, and start stressing them like you would a normal muscle cell. They grow along the lines of stress and act more and more like muscle tissue, not individual cells. That is all a bio-reactor is.

Bio-printing is a new concept. We took a standard inkjet printer that you get from HP. We took the ink out of the cartridge and replaced it with cells. Then we wrote the software and programmed it and got a printout of various tissues up to 20 cells deep. It's pretty awesome when you see it. I think it has a lot of applications, especially for those areas that you are trying to recreate, say on the surface of body skin. We can now take a sample of skin, stretch it up to five times its normal surface area and then transplant it back on the donor. For many burn patients with significant 50 to 60 per cent burns, this marks a significant decrease in their morbidity and mortality.

Take drug toxicity testing. How do you know if a new drug that's come up by a pharmaceutical company will do more good than harm? Right now the protocol is to do the testing outside the body, or on animals. If we can grow new liver cells outside the body and test a new drug on those cells, then we're going to really shorten the experimental and the regulatory period until we can prove whether it is safe or not safe to get it back into humans.

I already talked about incontinence treatment and burn treatment techniques. These are some things that are I feel you will see in the marketplace within the next two to three years. These will probably be available worldwide. This is our mission. I think we share this across our international borders.

Moderator | **K. Srinath Reddy**
President, Public Health Foundation of India

Q: Dr Trehan, one notices a lot of pharmaceutical companies coming up alongside hospitals. How ethical is this in your opinion? Don't you think that on many levels healthcare has become nothing but a business because it is not at all affordable for the common man?

Dr Naresh Trehan: As far as pharmaceutical companies are concerned, you will have to ask them what their interest and ethics are. But it is true that when a pure businessman gets into the healthcare field, there is a top line and there is a bottom line and there is nothing in between. When healthcare providers like doctors and associated people get into healthcare, there is a top line and a bottom line, but there is always a patient in the middle.

I believe, and I always say this, that healthcare is a business with a soul. You need to make money. You need a return on the capital. But it does not have to be 25 to 30 per cent. It could be 7 or 8 or 10 per cent. It gives you huge gratification to do something in the healthcare field than, say, by manufacturing cars or something else.

There is an inverted view right now in some people's mind that healthcare offers huge money-making opportunities. First of all, it is the most difficult business to do and people realize this once they get into it. It will level itself out eventually. But we must remember that we need to bring to the centre stage the patient, his needs and affordability.

Q: Is there a remedy or innovative solution to send doctors to rural areas? Dr Trehan rightly said that there have to be facilities. When we

talk of sending doctors to rural areas, they say there are no teachers there. When you want to send teachers, they say there are no doctors. How do we break this deadlock?

Dr Naresh Trehan: First of all, we need to pay attention to what we actually have. Right now a lot of efforts are being made in a desperate manner that are not coming to convergence. We talk about doctors in the villages. But first we have to make villages look different. Second, we don't have that much time. Which government can be proud of not being able to provide drinking water to its people? This is a shame. It doesn't take that much to provide drinking water to people.

I spoke about an interim solution through mobile units. Bring the backend up and then expect them to go.

Q: Dr Trehan spoke about primary care but what about training nurse practitioners? Second, when we talk about economics and reducing the cost of the cardiac care, let me take an example of a stent, which in the US will cost something like $1,000. The income generated by a receptionist is $2,000, which means that any receptionist or anybody at the lowest position can afford a stent. In India, if we started encouraging Indian manufacturers to produce stents, it should not cost more than Rs 5,000. What have we done to produce stents indigenously in the country?

Dr Naresh Trehan: I couldn't agree with you more. We need 750,000 more nurses just to service the healthcare sector and it takes on an average three years to start a nursing school. I had spoken to the Prime Minister of India back in 1991 and had asked him for single window clearance. It was promised on the table that it would be done within three months. But we are still waiting.

Time has passed us by. We have done many things for many industries but healthcare has been a stepchild for a long, long time. Part of the fault lies with us. We are so busy with our own practices that we haven't bothered. We need to create a task force of all thinking people who will take it on themselves to transform the sector in the next five years.

K. Srinath Reddy: Tamil Nadu is now training nurse practitioners but some of the regulatory cobwebs that exist in terms of the Medical Council and the Nursing Council need to be cleared in order to have nationwide replication. In terms of stents, the Kalam-Raju stent produced by our former President along with Dr Soma Raju from Hyderabad is undergoing clinical trials and the Department of Biotechnology is also collaborating with Stanford to produce stents in India.

Q: I would like to point out there are a number of corporate hospitals that have been given concessional land in the heart of major Indian cities in exchange for the promise of free care to poor patients. Somehow the land shows up but the free care to the poor does not. I don't know what is the reason for this. There are arguments about what defines treatment; what is covered and what is not. Is private-public partnership in this form truly the way forward or is this a model we should abandon?

My second question: of the 750,000 cardiac surgeries done around the world, India does only about 80,000 every year though our need is for three million. How can we make cardiac care more affordable and more widespread in our country?

Dr Naresh Trehan: To answer your first question, the government is the enforcer of the law. If the government finds itself unable to enforce, then it has lost control. Why does it take twenty years to file a case and then keep going because the government is also involved in this? We need to look at making people live by their commitments. When the government gives concession to people for duty drawbacks, it makes them pay. So, why is it that the government finds itself unable to enforce policies in healthcare? Is it possible to tell a poor man to give up; to tell him that he will not get medicine?

I am acutely aware that healthcare is unaffordable for many people. We have developed in India the use of the heart-lung machine, and reduced the cost by about Rs 30,000. We have held the price since 1995, despite it going up in human costs by at least 50 to 75 per cent. We are talking about doing heart surgery through minor holes and making it cheaper by another 30 per cent. That is the model we are working on at Medanta, the Medicity.

If a surgeon needs to make Rs 5 lakh a month, does he want to spread it over 5 patients or 50 patients? That's where the economies of scale come in and where we can cross-subsidize.

Q: My question is for Dr Trehan. How can we provide quality healthcare for a common man in the current scenario of this country?

Dr Naresh Trehan: It all comes back to a collaborative effort. We need the inputs to be reduced. I see some of my colleagues from the medical industry make huge profits. If they cut their profits a bit, it will help to reduce costs. Second, doctors need to spread their income over a larger population base rather than choose just a few patients. Third, we need to look at innovative patterns in therapy. Ayurveda and herbal medicine has huge potential which has fallen by the wayside. There are hidden gems in herbal medicine which we can put to the test of modern science and bring them into our therapies today to reduce the cost by half in the next five to seven years. New era medicine can emerge from India and we are working feverishly at that. These are some of the things that we can do to reduce costs.

K. Srinath Reddy: Over the last thirty years, every year there has been a new outbreak of a virus or a pathogen, threatening a pandemic. About 60 per cent of these come from animals to humans. It has been said that commercial-scale livestock breeding with factory farms bring wildlife, veterinary populations and humans into close contact. This sets up a conveyer belt for transmission of viruses and is something that we should be cautioned against. What is your response as a public health person, Dr Habayeb?

Dr Salim J. Habayeb: You will put me into trouble with the industry. Let's say developing countries have an informal sector in the backyard poultry and backyard industry. Public health purposes related to vet medicine will be limited. But from the health side, certainly at the nutrition level, it's good to become vegetarian and to reduce risks. The biggest benefit would be environmental benefits. We know that investments in water and energy to develop livestock is very high. Certainly the shift to a more vegetarian natural food chain, would be very, very beneficial.

The British economist, Nicholas Stern cautioned us against climate change and its economic impact. Last week he called for reduced meat consumption to protect against climate change. So this is another reason.

Q: You mentioned professor that 45 per cent children who are underweight in the world live in India. I would like to get your perspective on malnutrition. Although the severe acute malnutrition rate in India is about 7 to 10 per cent, it can be as high as 20 to 25 per cent in the villages. Even our prime minister has referred to it as one of our biggest curses of our country.

K. Srinath Reddy: Clearly we need a nutrition policy which addresses all facets of malnutrition whether it is inappropriate over-nutrition or under-nutrition. We ought to be able to have nutrition delivered through the Integrated Child Development Scheme (ICDS) much more effectively in villages and for this we may require a second Anganwadi worker.

But we also require a great deal of health education. Breast feeding which is continued up to six months, and preferably beyond six months, is absolutely necessary. Unfortunately, universal breast feeding up to six months is not always practiced even in India. The introduction of complementary feeds at six months is again pretty deficient. So it requires a combination of educating people, especially mothers, activating child nutrition services through the Anganwadis, and even giving training to new mothers about child-rearing practices, even in institutionalized hospital settings.

Q: Dr Trehan, how is Medicity going to have policies that are different from the previous organizations you worked in?

Dr Naresh Trehan: Earlier also, I was in charge of defining policies and my policy has always been: never turn back anybody who reaches your door. You cannot tell a poor man to go away and that he cannot be treated. You have to find a solution. We have made a commitment for free treatment. We have made a commitment for 6,000 villages progressively to be connected 24x7 by telemedicine, for free. We are creating a foundation, outside of the business part by the same partners and families of the partners to raise more funds, to ensure that anybody who needs treatment will get it through the foundation. The hospital can always give 30 per cent concession over its rack rates because that's the EBIDTA (earning before interest, taxes, depreciation and amortization) they are looking for.

It's very easy to cross-subsidize, as I said earlier. You have to ensure that all the physicians who work with you must also play ball. They must be of the same ilk. So if you ask me how am I going to do it, there are three things. The first is economy of scale, so that we can cross-subsidize many more people. We have only chosen doctors who already have this idea in their head. They are ready to service everybody and will not cringe from providing free services. We also have the foundation which is committed to help people, especially children. So these are some of the things that we are going to develop.

Q: Regenerative medicine is a brilliant scientific percept. But for how long can you delay death? We already have a problem. We don't have resources. We are fighting for resources for the existing population. What are we going to do by delaying people's final departure?

Dr George W. Weightman: I am a family physician, so I have a primary care orientation. I personally think we should be worrying about preventive care. Why worry about stents? We should worry about preventing cardiovascular disease in the first place. We should be worried about cleaning up water in villages so that the number one killer of kids in the world is not diarrhoea. We ought to be worrying about basic issues. It doesn't always take a doctor to do that. Certainly a nurse, a physician's assistant or even a healthcare technician would help us on the front end. That way we won't have to make tough resource decisions towards the later end of life.

"People are asking where the internet is going. What is going to happen? We have barely scratched the surface ... We are going to see a world where everybody is going to be connected to the internet in some way, shape or form, whether with their PC or with their mobile phone."

The Internet is Social

Now What?

▪

Nikesh Arora

▪

Moderator

Anubha Bhonsle

Senior Editor, CNN-IBN

Nikesh Arora

President, Global Sales Operations and
Business Development, Google

Nikesh Arora oversees all revenue and customer operations, as well as marketing and partnerships. Since joining Google in 2004, he has held several positions with the company. Most recently, he led Google's global direct sales operations. He also developed and managed the company's operations in the European, Middle Eastern and African markets and was responsible for creating and expanding strategic partnerships in those regions for the benefit of Google's growing number of users and advertisers.

With a background as an analyst, Nikesh's main areas of focus have been consulting, IT, marketing and finance. Prior to joining Google, he was Chief Marketing Officer and a member of the management board at T-Mobile. While there he spearheaded all product development, terminals, brand and marketing activities of T-Mobile Europe. In 1999, he started working with Deutsche Telekom and founded T-Motion PLC, a mobile multimedia subsidiary of T-Mobile International. Prior to joining Deutsche Telekom, Nikesh held management positions at Putnam Investments and Fidelity Investments in Boston.

Nikesh holds a master's degree from Boston College and an MBA from Northeastern University, both of which were awarded with distinction. He also holds the CFA designation. In 1989, Nikesh graduated from the Institute of Technology in Varanasi, with a bachelor's degree in electrical engineering.

IT IS BOTH AN HONOUR AND PRIVILEGE TO COME BACK TO INDIA TO SPEAK. BEFORE I COME TO THE INTERNET, IT IS IMPORTANT TO UNDERSTAND THAT WE ARE IN THE midst of one of the biggest revolutions of our time. Most of the other revolutions that have happened in the past have been very easy to spot because they have happened around the world.

But this is a disruptive force that we are dealing with. It is actually happening around the world at the same time. You wonder why; what is happening at this point in time that is causing this technological revolution to happen. It is very hard to spot a revolution when you are in the midst of it. If you think about what is happening around the world, there are technological forces that are conspiring to make this revolution happen.

The first and foremost thing we are beginning to see is ubiquity in terms of Internet access. I know India does not see that just yet. But there are 1.8 billion people around the world connected to the Internet. There are about 4 billion people connected via mobile phones. If you consider this, 1.8 billion people are still only about 25 per cent of the world's population. Seventy-five per cent of the world's population is yet to connect. If you look at it differently, today over 90 per cent of the world's GDP is connected to the Internet. If it was a country by itself, it would be the largest GDP country in the world where people would share similar beliefs, similar behaviours and perhaps similar preferences over time.

The other interesting trend that is going on is a trend around storage. If you look, most people today have iPods. An iPod today can store 80 gigabytes worth of information. If you follow Moore's law, an iPod in ten years from now can possibly store the entire content created in the last hundred years. This is a very interesting trend in storage. Going forward, it makes it very, very cheap for us to store data.

The third interesting trend in technology that is going on is that all of us are actually carrying the tools of production of content in our hands. In the past if you worked in the newspaper or television business, you had to have cameras and fancy equipment.

Today, I was noticing in the morning, people in this audience were taking pictures and twitting and writing updates on Facebook. They were actually creating content on the fly. You have the tools of production.

The challenge we have at Google is that Google is often held synonymous with the Internet. People believe that Google is responsible for the Internet, which is good most of the time when people say, 'I love Google and I use your product.' But it is also hard because very often we are held responsible for some of the sweeping changes that are going on around the world, in the world of business, in the world of social media and in the world of advertising.

If you look at where we are, from our perspective, the Internet is the world's largest information communication and distribution network. Ten years ago when you went on the Internet or when you wanted to find information, you were happy if you found an old brochure or a piece of marketing from a company. You were so excited that you had found it.

Today people's expectations are a lot higher. The bar has been raised. I was sitting in the audience early in the morning and somebody stood up and asked a question. I didn't know who that person was. So, I googled. My expectation was that this person must be on the Internet and, therefore, I should be able to find that person in less than a minute and figure out who he or she was. So, our expectations have changed tremendously.

Now when things break down today, I expect to be able to go on the Internet and be able to find information that gives me the answers that I am looking for. If you look at it from a different perspective, about five exabytes of information was created by 2003. One exabyte has at least 40,000 hours of television viewing. Today, we create five exabytes every two weeks. We are sitting over 100 exabytes of information. We get about three billion searches a day from around the world from 1.8 billion people. They are constantly looking for information.

The risk we run is that we will soon have an oversupply of

information and we won't be able to find it. We have a huge information challenge ahead of us. One of the big risks is that we are going to end up with a lost culture in many parts of the world. A lot of information is in libraries, old videos and archives but most of our kids are not going to want to go to a library. Their way of dealing with information is they are going to go to the Internet to try and find it.

The Internet is one of the world's largest information networks. It is also one of the world's largest communication networks. Today 250 million people are connected by Facebook. There are about 200 billion emails that cross the wires every day. There are over a billion people connected by instant messenger, Skype, some form of Google Talk, MSN, Yahoo or AIM. People use these networks to communicate with each other. It is one of the world's largest communication networks. This is going to change and shape the way we deal with the telecommunication world.

If you look at the characteristics of the distribution network, there is over $300 billion worth of commerce that is conducted on the Internet around the world. We use the Internet today to distribute pretty much everything: movies, music and any form of visual content. Over 60 per cent of the people who use the Internet say they have used it at some point in their life to look for information before they buy something. It is the world's largest distribution network.

I remember twenty years ago when I used to work – or even before that when I went to university in India – I had one PC XT in my university and one ICL 1904 mainframe. For those of you who are old enough to remember what an ICL 1904 was, you had to go, programme and punch a card. I went to the university and the punch card machine was broken during the semester I took the computer science course. So, we programmed without knowing what we were programming. We had to wait for the results to come.

If you look twenty years hence, my daughter does not understand how the world existed without computers. That's the revolution I am talking about. This is going to be the world's largest information communication distribution network going forward, and that is going to change the shape of pretty much everything that we deal with.

It is going to change the shape of business. Unfortunately, if you look outside of India at some of the emerging worlds, you will see a big shift in almost every industry. Look at the world of media where newspaper subscriptions are falling because people are going to the Internet to get information and content. Look at the world of television where twenty years ago there were 100 programmes in the UK which had 15 million viewers or more. Today there are three – and two of them are live football games. One programme has lasted out of 100 in terms of the audience that it generates.

People are beginning to use the Internet more and more as a way of getting their content, getting their information and as a way of conducting commerce. It is changing the cost structure of almost every industry. Perhaps, the commodity industry might be safe for a while. But you take any other industry – whether it is media, publishing or e-commerce – and it is going to end up being a very disruptive force.

In the modern world, about 50 per cent of the businesses are going to go through some serious transformation in the next ten years. I was in Japan, on my way here two days ago, and I met the minister of Telecom. He said they had won the election because of YouTube. All the politicians had actually been on YouTube canvassing with their constituents using online videos. Barack Obama had a very strong campaign where he had a Facebook manager and a team of people who managed his profile on Facebook. He had people who were creating networks on Facebook to be able to reach US voters. He had the largest online digital marketing campaign that any election in the world has ever had.

The world of social media is not just restricted to finding friends. It is a world where you are beginning to see the emergence of 'crowd sourcing' or engagement with almost everybody out in the street. That's what Facebook and that's what Twitter and the various social network platforms are going to allow us to do.

This is not only going to change the face of business. It is going to change the face of how society interacts. If we take that concept and apply it to other parts of the world, you will see it is creating a revolution in the world of advertising as well. Today we see roughly a billion views of videos on YouTube. We get twenty hours of video uploaded every minute on YouTube.

There is a $600 billion advertising industry, of which about $200 billion plus is with the television business. There is no advertising right now in the video world in the West. Over the next five to ten years, you are going to see a significant shift of the advertising money which is going to move from television to online.

People are asking where the Internet is going. What is going to happen? We have barely scratched the surface. We are just at the beginning of the phase. We are going to see a lot of change. If you ask where are we going to end up a few years from now, I would say that we are going to see a world where everybody is going to be connected to the Internet in some way, shape or form, whether with their PC or with their mobile phone.

If you follow the trend, you are going to see a tremendous shift in everything that we do. Within this context if you look at where we are in India, I am somewhat disappointed at the progress we have made. Our Internet penetration is equivalent to that of Kenya and other parts of Africa. China has 25 per cent Internet penetration with 340 million people. The US has 240 million people but China is the most connected country in the world. Rwanda, which in 1994 had no concept of where this world is going, is actually rolling out a national wireless LAN network and is putting in billions of dollars to build the best fiber network in Africa.

Twenty years ago, Korea mandated that it is going to have one gigabyte per second for every person in the country. Now it has mandated that by 2012 it is going to have 100 gigabytes per second and its GDP has tripled in that timeframe. Finland has just passed a law saying it is going to have universal broadband access for everyone in the country as a right.

There is a very clear correlation between investment in infrastructure, increase of broadband penetration, increase of access to the Internet and economic growth. For every 10 per cent increase in penetration, there is a one per cent increase in GDP. In this context, we have a long way to go as far as this country is concerned in terms of being able to invest in infrastructure.

I mentioned to you a short while ago about programming on an ICL 1904. Despite that, half of the people I went to university with are today creating software for some of the best companies in the world. We were able to create the inspiration and infrastructure for people to be able to do that over here.

The Internet is here to stay. I think it is going to transform pretty much everything we do around us. We are the transition generation. Our kids are going to ask us how we lived without the Internet.

I will end with one small story. I was at a dinner last night when somebody said to me, 'I love Google.' I replied, 'Thank you very much.' This gentleman was in his early 70s. He said to me: 'I was talking to my nephew last evening and he is five years old. His room is always a mess and I asked him how he ever found anything in it. He told me, "My Google mom does it". I asked him what he meant by his "Google mom" and he said, "My mom is great at searching for things in my room".'

Moderator | **Anubha Bhonsle**

Senior Editor, CNN-IBN

Q&A

Anubha Bhonsle: What in India are we doing that is wrong as far as the Internet revolution is concerned?

Nikesh Arora: I don't say that we are doing something wrong. We see tremendous amounts of usage of pretty much most of our products. I think the opportunity is still ahead of us. We have 60 million people connected to the Internet but only 20 million connected by broadband. We need to drive those numbers up.

Anubha Bhonsle: If you equate us to Rwanda...

Nikesh Arora: They are building a wireless network across the country.

Q: I wanted to ask you about Google's experience in China. One has read so many conflicting stories. On the one hand, you are telling us that it has the largest number of Internet users. On the other hand, there have been many restrictions by the Chinese government controlling the use of information by Chinese citizens. What did Google do to circumvent this and did you face any problems getting Google into China? Also, why is Google following Chinese maps on Kashmir and Arunachal Pradesh?

Nikesh Arora: The Internet changes a lot of things. It changes the notions of privacy, of copyright and of access to information. We at Google had a lot of conversation and debate within the company when we began our operations in China. To begin with, we began operations in China from outside of China. We were able to offer our services at Google.com to Chinese citizens when they chose to use Google. Then we decided to set up an operation within the country. We were not generating any revenue but once we had people in the country, then we had to make sure that we followed the laws of whichever country we operated in.

We follow the laws of every country we operate in. When we are faced with a particular challenge of trying to be transparent about information that the Chinese government wants us to be cautious about, we make that transparent to users. We make it transparent to them that some piece of information is not accessible to them because it has been restricted by their country.

So, when you search in China for something that is restricted, it would tell you that this piece of information is restricted and that you cannot access it. After that it is up to the users and their ability to convince the society they live in to provide them access to information. Having said that, this makes up less than one per cent of the information people are seeking in that country. The difficult choice we made was this: would you rather that people got access to 99 per cent of the information they are looking for, or would you restrict the 99 per cent on the basis of less than one per cent?

Anubha Bhonsle: I am wondering which is easier to do business with: India or China?

Nikesh Arora: I think every country has its nuances of doing business. India has its nuances of doing business. China has its own nuances. Western Europe has its own nuances of doing business. The same regulations exist in different parts of the world, whether on privacy or on copyright. The difference is that at least China has 340 million people who are connected.

Anubha Bhonsle: What about Google maps?

Nikesh Arora: The Google maps question is a simple issue. When somebody in India accesses Google maps, they get to see the map that the country reflects. When somebody in China accesses a map in China, they get to see the map as China reflects. If somebody from outside of India or China watches the map, they get to see how the world perceives the dispute that exists in the map. We are trying to satisfy people around the world. We are not going to take a particular position on what we believe is the right answer. We are going to take the popular notion in one country and what the notion in the other country is, and represent it the way it is.

Anubha Bhonsle: Is that true for all international conflict?

Nikesh Arora: It happens in the Golan Heights. It happens in Palestine. It happens in Arunachal Pradesh. It happens in other parts of the world.

Q: When such a large amount of data is available on the Internet, how do you regulate or provide the right kind of information, particularly when it comes to areas like healthcare? In India we call up a doctor and ask for medicine on the phone and very little attention is paid to clinical evidence. How are you going to regulate healthcare information?

Nikesh Arora: There are two parts. As I said earlier, Google is synonymous with the web. Most companies choose to put up their data there. What we do is to help you find it. We don't put the data up.

So, somebody puts up data on medicine – what it does, what are the side-effects and what are the other medicines. Healthcare is a very touchy issue. Healthcare is an issue where you don't want people to start self-medicating. You don't want people to start finding their own solutions. If you talk to people in the profession, the effect the Internet has is that the average individual has become more informed. People go to the doctor and ask, "Have you checked me for this, this and this?" The tendency is for people to assume the worst. If your hand itches you assume you've picked up some strange rash from Africa even though you haven't been there in the past one month. People go find the information themselves. I don't think anybody can particularly regulate that information. I think it is incumbent upon people who put up that information to be responsible for putting the information they put up.

Anubha Bhonsle: And no responsibility to the site that hosts that content?

Nikesh Arora: The answer is that Google does not host any content. It helps you find it. So, a medical website is responsible for the information on their site.

Q: Nikesh, you recently released the Éclair. There are rumours also that Google is coming out with an operating system next year. Without wearing your sales hat, give me an honest answer if you ever see Google replacing the installed base of Microsoft as an operating system? The second question: given that a lot of Microsoft devices today come prebuilt

with the Google search engine, do you still regard Microsoft as evil?

Nikesh Arora: There are a lot of presuppositions in that question. It is important to understand that we never sit around the table at Google to conspire to come up with a strategy to beat people out there. We spend most of our time trying to build the best product in the world. The whole idea is to try and create a technological revolution, whether it relates to handsets or whether it relates to PCs or operating systems.

Today as I was coming in here, the gentleman at security took my laptop and asked me to turn it on. Then he made me log in and show him how it worked. Then he said, "Now please take the battery out." I said, "Why should I take the battery out?" The more I resisted, the more compelled he was to believe that the battery needed to be taken out. I was resisting because I had to come in here and make a speech and my speech is on the computer. If I took out my battery it would take me five minutes to turn the computer on again and that's too slow. These operating systems were designed for a time when we didn't have connectivity. These operating systems are designed when you should be able to compute by yourself in a corner. The world of tomorrow is a world where you have difficulty in terms of access and you want most of the stuff done in the back-end. For that you need very thin, very light devices which mean you need the operating system. So, yes we are working on an operating system. We have announced it. We call it Chrome OS. Now whether that replaces the existing operating system, I don't know. That's for users to decide.

Q: We understand the overflow of information, especially when we want to seek a specific need for a specific purpose. Is there any attempt by Google to facilitate such a specific need?

Nikesh Arora: Ten years ago I would have been happy if I found the information somewhere on the Internet in some basic form. About two years ago, we used to trawl the web once every 24 hours. Three weeks ago we announced a deal with Twitter where you can basically get access to real time updates on the web. I would say that we now trawl the web within minutes.

Anytime anybody in the world around 100 countries makes a change, one of our spiders or crawlers would go find that piece of information and make it available for people to find. That requires a huge amount of computing power. That requires a huge amount of stuff to happen if we can get that result in sub-16 seconds. Wolfram Alpha does something very specific. They help us in trying to give you specific answers. We are trying to see if there are technological ways of solving this and being able to predict what you are looking for. We are going to try and a find more programmatic solutions towards finding the answer you are looking for.

Q: I would like to talk about online sales and its commercial viability in India compared to the West. I run a jewellery business in India. When we do online sales, we use high clarity pictures, offer guarantees and Hallmark certificates and ensure secure payments. But we do not see a big commercial viability. My research shows that women consumers prefer to go to the mall. They want to see the piece, try it on and then take a decision on buying it. Where do you see this transformation: do you see Indian women buying jewellery online?

Nikesh Arora: In my life I have never tried to predict what a woman is going to do. Having said that, in India we haven't been through the learning curve. If you look at the West, people started buying books first. People were comfortable buying books because they knew what a book looks like. It is pretty straightforward. Over time people got comfortable.

I remember not trusting my credit card in the West for many years after most people around me were buying books. But we have been through that learning cycle in the West. Over time people have chosen to order on the web for the sake of convenience.

I don't think we have been through that cycle in this country. In this country transactions are still based on relationship and trust. I think most people wouldn't buy anything expensive in this country without trust. Everybody says: "I know somebody who knows somebody and I can get you a good deal." The culture will take some time for trust to get to a point where we are comfortable for the sake of convenience to buy online.

Q: Are there any checks and balances within Google to avoid eventually controlling everything that moves on earth? I landed in Delhi today from Israel and as soon as I switched on my cell phone, I immediately got the Embassy number. This is a great power. Are they any security measures to avoid this great power that the Google controls today?

Nikesh Arora: The message you got must have been the mobile operator telling you where you are and where to call. I am constantly surprised by what we can do. The truth of the matter is that when you are going to live in the digital world, you are going to leave digital footprints.

I have been using a credit card for the last twenty years. Your credit card company has more information on you than you think. My credit card company knows when I got married, what I bought my wife, and when, who I had dinner with, how many people I had dinner with, when my child was born and when my child is sick. My credit card company pretty much knows everything I've done for the last twenty years because it can watch my spending pattern. But I choose to still use it because (a) they never abuse the data and (b) I trust they are not going to do anything with it.

Over time as we live in the digital world, we are going to begin to trust people who are not going to abuse the data and not going to use it to harm us. Over the last eleven years we have proven that we do not abuse people's data. Also, governments and regulators make sure that we delete all personal data after eighteen months. We don't hold any data on any individual. What we do is use data on a collective basis to find a way to make a better product. But we will never use data on an individual basis. We see no reason to, unless you explicitly choose to allow us to use the data.

When I checked into my hotel in New Delhi, the lady at the reception took a copy of my passport. I asked her: "Why do you take a copy of my passport?" She replied: "Sir, we are going to store it." I said, "For how long?" And she replied, "99 years." I actually want to go and talk to a lawyer and see if there is a Data Privacy Act in this country and if somebody can actually hold data on me for ninety-nine years.

Is Cricket, As We Knew It, Dead?

▪

Sunil Gavaskar

▪

Ravi Shastri

▪

Sir Richard Hadlee

▪

Moderator

Kadambari Murali Wade

National Sports Editor, Hindustan Times

Sunil Gavaskar

Former India Captain

One of the greatest opening batsmen of all time, and without doubt the finest India has produced, Sunil Gavaskar was a cricketing legend in every sense of the word. Statistically he was at the peak of the game for years with 10,122 runs to his credit. In terms of courage, he stood alone among Indians, defying the fiery pace of the mighty West Indies and succeeding consistently against them. Tactically he was a shrewd leader, piloting India to many of her early victories both home and away.

For almost two decades, from the early '70s to the late '80s, Gavaskar gave the Indian team the backbone it so badly needed. While the team as a whole wasn't always strong enough to win consistently, Gavaskar ensured that there was no lack of fight. If nothing, he waged a lone battle to ensure that defeat was averted.

While Gavaskar went some way to introducing professionalism in Indian cricket while he was still playing, his innings certainly did not end when he hung up his boots. Rather, a career as an analyst, columnist and commentator that has been as prolific as his playing days developed. Gavaskar also continued to serve the game through various roles in the Board of Control for Cricket in India (BCCI) and the International Cricket Council (ICC). A much-respected voice around the world, when Gavaskar speaks, he is heard with great attention, not just by fans and the public, but by administrators and players themselves.

Ravi Shastri

Former India Captain

That he began by batting at No. 11 and ended up opening the innings tells you pretty much all you need to know about Ravi Shastri. In the history of the game there are few players who have maximized ability and talent as fully as the Mumbai all-rounder. A thinking, wily left-arm spinner and a batsman who placed the highest possible premium on his wicket, Shastri played 80 Test matches for India and is among an elite group of players who managed 10 centuries and 100 wickets in the longest form of the game.

An astute reader of the game, Shastri was a valuable deputy to any captain he served. Tall, handsome and opinionated, Shastri was the poster-boy for Indian cricket through much of his career despite detractors constantly suggesting that he batted too slowly for the team's good.

It was a mark of Shastri's grit and determination that he averaged a massive 77.75 against the Australians, and no one will forget the unbeaten 206 he made in Sydney in Shane Warne's debut Test.

After giving up the game when only thirty, Shastri embarked on a career in the media that has gone from strength to strength. An instant success because of his tendency to be forthright when asked for an opinion, Shastri has, over time, become India' most dependable commentator. When the need has arisen, Shastri has stepped in to serve Indian cricket in various roles including cricket manager and director of the National Cricket Academy. He currently represents India in the ICC's cricket committee.

Sir Richard Hadlee

Former New Zealand All-rounder

Even at a time when the cricket world was spoilt for choice when it came to all-rounders – the era of Imran Khan, Ian Botham and Kapil Dev – Richard Hadlee was making a name for himself. In the big world of cricket, coming from a little country like New Zealand was a distinct disadvantage. All his life Hadlee played for a team that was not as good as he was, and he constantly had to lift it to great deeds against stronger opposition.

With the ball there were few fast bowlers who had the kind of control and metronomic efficiency that was Hadlee's trademark. Swing, seam, pace and accuracy combined to make a pretty deadly cocktail, one that Hadlee used to torment batsmen to the extent that his Test mark of 431 wickets stood for years before Kapil Dev surpassed it. Still, Hadlee will always be remembered as the first man to get 400 wickets.

Even when injury struck him down, Hadlee countered magnificently, going from being an out-and-out quick bowler to someone who extracted life from the most trying pitches with a near-perfect bowling action that has been copied world over.

As a left-handed batsman capable of both stonewalling and attacking, Hadlee would have achieved much more with the bat had he enjoyed some support with the ball.

When he finished up, Hadlee moved seamlessly into the media, writing trenchant columns and offering expert analysis on television. He also served as chairman of the selection committee in New Zealand, and in 1990 was knighted for his services to cricket.

KADAMBARI MURALI WADE: IS CRICKET, AS WE KNEW IT, DEAD? SUNIL GAVASKAR AND RAVI SHASTRI ARE MEMBERS OF THE INDIAN PREMIER LEAGUE'S (IPL'S) GOVERNING COUNCIL. SO, let me ask by asking Mr Gavaskar: you have been a great advocate of Test cricket and, with due respect to Sachin, perhaps its greatest Indian exponent. Will the IPL and all its riches kill the long form of cricket? And secondly, will technique become a thing of the past?

Sunil Gavaskar: To answer your first question, no, I don't think IPL or the 20-20 format will kill cricket as we know it. I believe there is enough space in the year schedules for all three formats of the game. What we saw when the 50-overs game became popular was that the number of Test matches got reduced. In the late 70s and early 80s, when a team toured another country, it played five Test matches and maybe just one one-day international (ODI). Within five or six years that changed. Instead of five Test matches there were three Test matches and five ODIs. I do believe that this is going to happen even with the T20 format.

The T20 format will have a lot more matches being played without Test matches actually being affected, except for their frequency. You could possibly have a two-Test series, five ODIs and five T20s as the schedule for all overseas tours, whether it is India touring another country or another country touring India.

Kadambari Murali Wade: So you think that the IPL and the expanded format of the IPL, which is going to come up, will not make a difference?

Sunil Gavaskar: It will make a difference in the sense that it will energize the 50-overs game, just as the 50-overs game energized Test cricket and made it a lot more result oriented. After the 50-overs game took root, you had more results in Test matches; a lot more shots being played in Test matches; a lot more runs being scored in Test matches in a day's play. The same effect is going to happen to the 50-overs game with T20.

In the last year or so since T20 became popular, the par score for a 50-overs game has increased. The par score used to be 250, now the par score is almost 300. If a team does not get to about 290 or 300, it doesn't feel secure that it has got enough runs on the board. You will see a lot more shots, and a lot of more new shots, being played thanks to T20. You will see a lot more new deliveries, which the bowlers have been looking to try and stop the batsmen from scoring runs. The overall game of cricket will benefit because we will see more different stuff than what we have seen so far.

Kadambari Murali Wade: Sir Richard, New Zealand has had a problem with players opting to play short-form cricket instead of the long form. Is that a danger? Do you have a difference of opinion here? Is there a danger for Test cricket going ahead?

Sir Richard Hadlee: First, I have to declare my position in the sense that I am a traditionalist. I am a purist in the game because that is my family background. Most of my cricket really was Test cricket with some ODIs. To me, Test cricket will always be the ultimate game. But New Zealand has had some recent problems.

When I was chairman of New Zealand cricket selection panel over a year-and-a-half ago, we had to choose the New Zealand cricket team to tour England. Because IPL was being played at that time, the New Zealand cricket team actually arrived in England without the captain, the vice-captain and three senior players. I was embarrassed that we had sent a team to England without those particular players. I believe it was fundamentally wrong.

Your country must come first. Decision makers must balance the game between 20-20, 50-overs, and Test cricket so that they can co-exist and not conflict with each other. This is most important, and it does affect New Zealand cricket more than most countries because we don't have a lot of depth and choices.

The players are starting to opt to play the one-day format and not the Test game. A prime example is Jacob Oram, a very good all-rounder with a very good Test record and a wonderful one-day player when he is in form. He has decided to give up Test cricket. The same is what Andrew Flintoff has done in England to pursue the one-day game, probably more 20-20 than 50-overs cricket.

The rewards are far greater in the one-day game than what they are in Test cricket. One could say it is an easier option: greater rewards for less effort. This is where the administrators have got to balance the game so that we don't have a saturation of one format ahead of the others and compromise the position of other games. This is the challenge that lies ahead for administrators and decision-makers.

Kadambari Murali Wade: Ravi Shastri, Jacob Oram made an interesting statement in which he said that it is difficult to have all-rounders today because of the amount of cricket being played. Is there a danger of players having shorter career spans and not being able to play enough because of so much cricket?

Ravi Shastri: It all depends on whether the player is good enough to play in all three formats. If he is, then yes, his career will be shortened because it will take a toll on his body. The travelling that goes with the amount of cricket being played will not help either. A batsman will probably last longer than an all-rounder or a fast bowler. It's not rocket science. It is common sense. The body is not a machine. Jacob Oram is right when he says that careers will be shortened. But it is up to the player to see what he is good at. He has got to be smart. If he thinks Test cricket suits him, then he should put all his energy into Test cricket.

Sir Richard Hadlee: An interesting development is that players, if they can, would want to play in all forms of the game. The problem this creates is they are going to be out playing with niggling injuries which can devalue their performance and the spectacle of the game. The other key thing I have noticed, particularly from New Zealand's point of view, is that if they are playing in all three forms of the game, different skills are required; different decision-making and execution of where you bowl the ball, for instance, and what shot to play. These can actually confuse a player. In a Test match, a 30-ball 50 would lose you a game, because you have got five days and you will have got into the game too quickly. But in the one-day game, it is the other way around.

Kadambari Murali Wade: What about the administrators? Is there no responsibility within the BCCI to create a pool that is large enough for the players to be able to rest and to give other players a chance while they rest?

Ravi Shastri: I think it will happen very quickly because of the amount of cricket that is being played. The amount of cricket that has been played in the last twelve months was not being played even two or three years ago. I am sure the selectors and administrators will be looking at getting a pool of 25 to 30 players. It is in their interest to do so, otherwise they will not have the best team on the park.

Balance is going to be the key for the ICC or the FTP (Future Tours Programme) that comes up in two years' time to get the three formats going. There is a place for all three formats, but you have got to get the right balance. The emphasis should be on Test cricket because you don't want the skill factor to go out of the game – strategy, skill, determination and guts – everything a young man growing up wanting to play for the country wants. He wants to play for India in a Test match and do extremely well. You go and ask any cricketer and you will get this answer.

Kadambari Murali Wade: Chris Gayle has said that he thinks Test match cricket is redundant.

Ravi Shastri: That's his opinion because obviously there are bucks in 20-20. He realizes how long he can carry on as a player. A young player growing up now will want to play Test match cricket. If he is not good enough, he will opt for 20-20.

Sir Richard Hadlee: Does a young cricketer want to aspire to play for his country in Test cricket and be measured by his skills by having a Test batting average of 50-plus or taking in excess of 300 Test wickets, which means you are obviously a very good player? Or do you want to be measured in the one-day format, particularly 20-20 cricket, by bowling 4 overs and conceding 40 runs every time you bowl or have a 10-ball innings with a strike rate of 200? Who would you rather be? Clearly you want to be a Test player, but the money is in the one-day game. Maybe the money is too much in the one-day game and needs to be pulled back or redirected into the Test game to create more incentives for the guys to play Test cricket.

Ravi Shastri: I don't think it needs to be pulled back. It could be monitored better. The emphasis should be on playing for your country first before you get picked for a club. The emphasis should be playing first-class cricket, which is very important, before you get picked or get into an auction for the IPL. Once you start laying down those rules, you will get some serious young players moving in the right direction rather than just thinking of making a quick buck.

Kadambari Murali Wade: Mr Gavaskar, you have been part of the ICC committee. When you ask them these questions they say that it is up to the respective boards. In a bilateral series, for instance, the ICC says we don't get involved. Is this a problem for the BCCI to sort out and is the BCCI going to do anything about it?

Sunil Gavaskar: Most tours are basically reciprocal tours. If you have played seven one-day matches in Australia, the Australians will come and play seven one-day matches in India. That is the way it has been working so far. But, as Ravi said, when the new FTP comes through in 2012, it may well be different.

It may well be that the cricket boards decide to have certain series or icon series – England versus Australia is an icon Test series – so, you may have five Test matches. India versus Australia might also be an icon series if the ICC and both boards agree to deem it such. So, you could have a five-Test series every time India visits Australia and Australia visits India. But right now, until 2012, we will probably have to go by the reciprocal way where it is a matter of revenue for both the boards concerned.

Kadambari Murali Wade: How difficult is it for a twenty-year-old cricketer, with the expectations of a billion people, to sustain himself through this?

Sunil Gavaskar: For a bowler it is going to be very difficult, not so much for a batsman. Every player, even at the early stages of his career, knows whether he has it in him to be a good player at the Test level. If he is not going to be a good Test player, he is going to focus on the limited-overs game, which is the 50-overs game and 20-20. He might actually opt to focus on what he believes is his strength. At the end of the day if you are going to spend the better part of your youth pursuing sport, you should be able to make a career out of it. That is why a lot of younger players might actually opt to do that, because they know in their hearts that they are not good enough to play at the highest level.

Kadambari Murali Wade: So you think the money doesn't matter? The amount of money that is paid in the IPL is tremendous. Is it possible for a youngster to say no to the money?

Sunil Gavaskar: Every youngster wants to play for his country at the Test level. As you grow, you realize whether you are good enough to play for your country or not. That's when you might say, "Look, I am actually better off in the shorter format of the game, so I will focus on that format of the game."

It is all right for Chris Gayle, Jacob Oram or Andrew Flintoff to say that they don't want Test cricket, because they have played enough Test cricket. They have got to that stage of their career when they are looking to maximize their earning potential and to prolong their careers. But if they were twenty-years-old, they would still want to play Test cricket.

Ravi Shastri: Why do players get money? Who decides how much money they get? It is market forces. Now, what makes market forces decide whether he should get 900 while another guy gets 300? It is how they perform for their country. To get the big bucks players will have to have played for their country and done exceptionally well.

Sir Richard Hadlee: We have seen a lot of one-day cricket – whether it is 50-overs or 20-20 – but not so much Test cricket. All youngsters are going to be motivated by the one-day format of the game, saying: "That's what I want to play. I don't want to play Test cricket." That is the danger, and that is why the balance needs to be absolutely right by administrators. Youngsters must be able to look at the various formats and make their choice. But there is so much one-day cricket that Test cricket will become irrelevant and devalued and could go out of existence 20 to 50 years down the track.

Kadambari Murali Wade: Do you think there is a danger of Test

cricket going out of existence, specifically with focus on India? In India you can still play for your country if you are playing T20 cricket and one-day cricket. But Test cricket gets empty stadiums. No one is coming to watch it and TV ratings are down for most, depending, of course, on the series. It is not like one-day cricket that is still popular if India is playing. Is there is danger for the Indian Test cricketer to become obsolete?

Sunil Gavaskar: I don't think so because, as Ravi said, playing for your country at the highest level, actually determines what sort of contract you will get for the IPL. If Ishant Sharma hadn't bowled that spell in Perth to Ricky Ponting, do you think he would have got the kind of money he got for signing up with whichever franchise that he did? I am not saying that it is the only reason, but it is the primary reason that he got such a big contract. You have to do well for your country at the highest level, the Test level, for you to come into the frame for consideration for the IPL.

Sir Richard Hadlee: You are almost saying that one performance can determine that. You would think that you need more than one or two or three performances to command 'x' amount of dollars in another form of the game.

Sunil Gavaskar: Yes, you would. But in India the moment a batsman plays his first game and scores 75 runs, he is termed a "batting sensation". If in the first game a bowler gets above four wickets, despite the fact those four wickets might have come when the batsman was trying to accelerate the score, he is termed a "bowling sensation". This happens only in India.

Ravi Shastri: You would want them to play three or four matches and three or four innings for them to be rated. Unfortunately, it doesn't happen that way. If you have one good series, a classic example as Sunny mentioned is Ishant Sharma or J.P. Duminy who had an outstanding series of Australia in Test matches and one-day games. When he came up for auction in the IPL, he was the front runner. Market forces decide that. But what market forces want to see is how well he does for his country.

Sir Richard Hadlee: Of course, his performance in the Champions League too might have upped the ante a little bit.

Ravi Shastri: But now he has got his money. He can wait for the next auction.

Kadambari Murali Wade: If you are talking about market forces, we will again come back to the fact that market forces are not interested in Test cricket. They were not particularly interested in the Champions League either. That is what I am trying to say. Isn't this going to be a problem going forward?

Ravi Shastri: Everyone realizes it is going to create a big problem in the future. This is where the administrators can protect Test cricket by emphasizing the fact that you must play for your country and balance it right. Cut down on the number of ODIs. A country must play a certain number of Test matches.

That is why this next FTP is extremely crucial. Seasons will start getting shorter. Each country will have a season of four-and-

Every player, even at the early stages of his career, knows Test level. If he is not going to be a good Test player, he is 50-overs game and 20-20.

a-half months. During their season, Australia and South Africa will have to start travelling outside. Say you fix a Boxing Day match. Now, India wants to play in India after Christmas because it pulls in 100,000 people in Kolkata. So India will say, "We don't want to move out of India." At that time we will say, "It is your turn to come here," especially when market forces suggest that India is the place which generates maximum income.

Sir Richard Hadlee: In New Zealand we don't get many Test matches. It doesn't really matter in a Test match whether crowds turn out or not. It is being televised and the sponsors get extra value because of the duration of the game. It shouldn't really worry the sponsors whether the grounds are full or not. Players, yes, love to have a lot of people in the grounds to help with their performances. But the Test game should still go on as it is. You are talking about reducing Test matches from five to four days and playing day-night cricket. In my view, you can't have day-night Test cricket because the conditions during the day and the conditions during the evening will vary considerably which will disadvantage one team or the other.

You also will have to introduce a different coloured ball. Test cricket is about the red ball. That is what statistics are all about. Now you want to introduce a new coloured ball. So, you will have new statistics. Then you are going to play four-day Test matches and you are not going to get as many results. Say you can play for a draw. Spin bowlers will get played out of the game simply because the pitch deteriorates more on the fifth day than on the third or fourth. We cannot allow these changes to happen in the Test match. Test cricket has survived 130-odd years. Why tamper with it?

You can tamper and play around with the one-day game or the 50-overs game. T20 cricket is marvellous, fun to watch, a

whether he has it in him to be a good player at the going to focus on the limited-overs game, which is the

– Sunil Gavaskar

wonderful game and a great spectacle. But it's pretty tough on the players, because very few of them get the chance to perform. In Test cricket you get a chance to perform, to grind out 300 or 400 runs for a player, to get eight or nine wickets in an innings. That's why I believe that 20-20 cricket is not real cricket.

Ravi Shastri: Spread Test cricket to smaller states and leave one-day cricket for the metros. You will get full houses in the metros. You try and take a Test match to the smallest venue and you will get 25,000 to 30,000 people easily because they are starved of cricket. They have not seen it. I will suggest this to the BCCI somewhere down the line. Take a Test match to a place like Cuttack and you are guaranteed to get 25,000 to 30,000 people. Make sure that you have good infrastructure and good stadiums and I am positive that you will see a lot of people watching Test cricket again.

Kadambari Murali Wade: From a technical point of view, there is experimentation going on about Test cricket in white clothes and day-

night matches with a pink ball. Do you think it is a realistic possibility? Or is Test cricket sacred?

Ravi Shastri: At the end of the day, it is a ball, not an orange or an apple. Pink, red, orange, what difference does it make?

Sunil Gavaskar: I think it is sacred. There will also be some experimentation. Some countries will try and do that, but they will not experiment with good teams. So if England is trying to experiment, it will be only when playing against Bangladesh, never against Australia. That is the way the ICC also looks to introduce different formats or rules in the game. It is first put to trial at the domestic and first-class level. Only then, does it come into the international arena. But I agree with Richard that that's not what we all know the game to be about.

Sir Richard Hadlee: In our country, I don't think anyone will even turn up at night during day-night Test cricket. It is too cold. So it would actually defeat the purpose of change. Test cricket is about tradition. It is about history and values. Let's preserve something that is special. Other formats are about entertainment but Test cricket does not need to be entertainment. It is the real battle.

Ravi Shastri: You mentioned the cold but there could be dew even in India.

Sir Richard Hadlee: In a Test match, if you are playing under lights at night-time and say you have got three slips and a gully with a new conker and somebody nicks it, they aren't going to catch it. So there are going to be some pretty annoyed fast bowlers around.

Kadambari Murali Wade: We are talking about change in the game, changes that are happening. I think one of the big changes really has been the way rules are basically skewed in favour of the batsman in the shorter version of the game. For instance, is the free hit really fair to the bowler?

Ravi Shastri: That is where the ICC has to think hard and make it a better contest between bat and ball. That is how the 50-overs game will continue to generate interest with a lot of people watching. What I find now with 20-20 cricket coming to the fore, is that the attention span for spectators watching a 50-50 game is reduced. If you have the matches that you had – India and Australia, two strong teams playing – you will more often than not have 50-overs games that go the distance. It's still very exciting. But if you look at world cricket all over, 60 to 70 per cent of the games get flat after 30 to 40 overs. So, you either want to reduce the number of overs from 50 to 40 to keep the interest going, or make it a better contest between bat and ball with something more for the bowler. There are some rules that can be added which give the bowler a better chance.

Sir Richard Hadlee: I think you are quite fair. But you can also, depending on pitch conditions obviously, see some very intense wonderful contests in a low scoring game, like even a 180. You can defend and even win, or struggle to get across the line if you are batting. That brings back the real contest, and an absorbing contest that can still generate interest and enthusiasm among spectators. You talked about the free hit, if a bowler penalizes himself by bowling a no-ball, it is absolutely fair. The bane of fast bowlers, in particular, is the amount of times they foot-fault; bowl a no ball. That's what they practice in the nets. They practice it and try never to do it in a game. When they do it in the game, they are penalized for it. I think that is absolutely right and fair. It is a good innovation.

Kadambari Murali Wade: There is a perception that all these changes have been happening because of the influence of the BCCI and money power. Is the perception of the BCCI being a bully correct?

Ravi Shastri: I don't think so. People have a very short memory. In my time when I played, we would call Australia and England the bullies. Why? It was because of market forces. The bucks came from there and they controlled the world game. Today, 75 to 80 per cent of the income for a world event comes from India. So, when India opens its mouth, you jolly well listen. What's wrong in that?

Kadambari Murali Wade: Do two wrongs make a right?

Ravi Shastri: I don't think they were wrong at that time. I don't think India is wrong at this time. Ten to fifteen years down the line, market forces might change again with another part of the world generating more income. We'll have to then listen to them. It is only sensible and fair.

Moderator | **Kadambari M. Wade**

National Sports Editor, Hindustan Times

Q: Ravi Shastri, will the successful completion of the Commonwealth Games in 2010 make India more determined in its journey to become a global superpower?

Ravi Shastri: The Commonwealth Games is a very prestigious event. If it goes well, it will do wonders for sport in India. It will portray India to the rest of the world as a place where you can hold major events and will spark off tremendous interest amongst the youth of India to take up sport. Don't forget the infrastructure will be tremendous after that.

Q: We see retired cricketers often getting into the commentary box or becoming members of cricket committees. But can they take up positions as ambassadors of the country and promote the interest of countries at various forums outside?

Sunil Gavaskar: The late Duleep Singhji was India's ambassador to Australia in the late 40s, I think. So, there is a precedent. But obviously he was of a completely different stature and the powers that take these decisions obviously don't rate former cricketers now that highly.

Q: IPL is a new phenomenon in Indian cricket. At the age of fourteen, youngsters have to make choices on which format of the game to follow. How would you motivate them, especially when IPL offers the kind of money it does. A player like Manish Pandey has not played a Test match for two years now. How do you motivate someone like him?

Ravi Shastri: You can ask Manish Pandey whether he wants to play for India or not. Let me tell you that he will do anything that is needed to play Test cricket for India. Yes, IPL has happened and one-day cricket has happened. It was a stage that he got to and he performed brilliantly. What has happened is that he is now in the reckoning. If he has a couple of good first-class seasons, he will be knocking at the door.

Kadambari Murali Wade: I think what the question relates to is whether at fourteen a player can be mature enough to make a decision about where his future lies? Will he not be seduced by the riches? And should there not be a system that helps players make that decision?

Ravi Shastri: It will happen. We are going to have not just zonal academies, but also state academies all over the country within the next three years that will cater to precisely this problem. But I don't see a problem because at fourteen you should enjoy yourself. You should enjoy the sport and take whatever comes to you naturally. As you grow older, you will realize what you are good at. You could be good at all three formats of the game and, as we discussed earlier, if you feel that are you are good only in limited-overs cricket, you can focus your energies in that direction.

Sir Richard Hadlee: A lot depends on the advice you give to a young fellow coming through the system. I assume you have player-agents here in India because they are all over the world. They might see a young sixteen- or seventeen-year-old who they will latch on to manage and control and steer in a certain direction that may not necessarily be in the best interest of the player. So, that's another problem for a young player.

Q: I want to pick up from what Sir Hadlee said about the game becoming entertainment. In India there is an emotional attachment to the game. It is a symbol of national pride. When we see movies like *Lagaan* or *Chak De*, in spite of the over-dramatization, they bring back memories of Test matches between India and Pakistan. Today, the game has gone into overkill. But I miss the old charm. Can it be restored?

Ravi Shastri: India-Pakistan, India-Australia and good Test cricket is what a lot of people want to see. Yes, there is overkill. That is why striking a right balance is important. Entertainment is needed; the sport needs it as well. Look at the positives of 20-20. It is important that it doesn't happen all the time so that you don't kill the goose that lays the golden egg. But it has brought a lot more people into watching the game than you can imagine. There are a lot more families watching the 20-20 game. You have a lot more kids taking to the game now.

Sir Richard Hadlee: At the end of the day, you and I and everyone else have a choice. If we love Test cricket, we will watch it. If we like 50-overs cricket, we will watch it. If we dislike the 20-20 game, we will turn the television off or we won't go and watch. So you do have that choice.

But if I take a poll on who loves Test cricket, 20-20 cricket will probably be liked by a majority of the people. You don't have to watch other forms of the game. But the point is that most people love the entertainment and the fast action-packed game.

Q: Sunny Gavaskar, twenty-six years ago you broke Don Bradman's record and there was not a greater moment in the history of world cricket. Can any other form of cricket recreate that magic?

Sunil Gavaskar: First, to set the record straight, I didn't break Bradman's record. I just got level as far as the centuries were concerned. I have always said that for it to be considered a record,

Test cricket is about tradition. It is about history and values. are about entertainment but Test cricket does not need to

a batsman will have to score 30 centuries in 51 Test matches and 70 innings. I played more than 50 Test matches, so really it was not a record. It was just a statistical achievement.

The highest level of cricket today is Test cricket. Speak to Yuvraj or Virender Sehwag or Gautam Gambhir, players who have played all formats of the game. They will tell you that they want to play well and do well at the Test level. They want to be recognized as great players at that level. Nothing they do in 50-overs and in the 20-20 format is going to make them great players. The only way you make great players is by playing at the highest level, which is Test cricket.

If a fourteen-year-old is thinking about money, then he doesn't have ambition at that stage and obviously has his priorities wrong.

At the age of fourteen, you are at the stage in your life when you are really not thinking about money but ambition. What is your ambition? It is to play well for the country. Your ambition is not to make money.

That's the reason why I feel that we really shouldn't be too fussed about this. There is a place in the cricket calendar for all three forms of the game. I don't think there should be too much of an issue. Test cricket is the ultimate.

Q: Are we also looking at 10-overs cricket?

Sunil Gavaskar: Actually, it has been played in different cities. I think there has been a league in Aurangabad, called the Aurangabad Premier League and there are other leagues where you have 10-overs-a-side games. Different versions of the game are coming through. The uniqueness of cricket is that you can have so many formats. Apart from Test matches and 50-overs and 20-20, there is also six-a-side and a double-wicket competition. There is a version for everybody's taste. It is all there.

Let's preserve something that is special. Other formats be entertainment. It is the real battle.

– Sir Richard Hadlee

But you ask the players themselves, they all want to play Test cricket. They might play a few years of Test cricket, realise they are not good enough to sustain themselves at that level and then start talking: "Oh, I want to concentrate on 50-overs cricket", or "I want to concentrate on the 20-overs version".

So, don't worry about it. The only people who say that they don't play for records are those incapable of setting records. If you could play for records, you will play for records because that is what is in your ability, mentally and temperamentally. A similar thing will happen with Test cricket, 20-20 and 50 overs. If you cannot play Test cricket, you will say, "Oh, I want to play only 20-20 cricket", because you know you are not good enough to play Test cricket.

Kadambari Murali Wade: There is just one thing which I wanted to ask Ravi specifically. This is to do with the Indian team management's written instruction manual for Indian players on a variety of subjects including the benefits of having sex, or masturbating, before a match. Is there a therapeutic benefit?

Ravi Shastri: That manual would have never come to me. I promise you, even if I was playing, whoever distributed that manual would have refrained from coming anywhere close to me. He himself would have said, "You know your responsibilities and you don't need to be told." This is something that happens naturally. I mean what is the big deal in what they have said? As a player you know your responsibilities the next day. You do what suits you.

Kadambari Murali Wade: So, it was not needed?

Ravi Shastri: Not needed at all.

When I played, we would call Australia and England the the world game. Today, 75 to 80 per cent of the income its mouth, you jolly well listen.

Q: What has the IPL done for cricket? Would the IPL be a medium to uplift other sports which are not very popular in India? And where do we see IPL in 2020?

Sunil Gavaskar: The BCCI, with the funds that it has generated through television revenue and the franchise auction for the IPL, has set aside a fair amount for other sports. It is making a pretty good contribution to other sports which they have identified as being Olympic medal prospects.

By 2020, I do see that the IPL will probably have double the number of teams instead of eight. By the year 2020, I think we could probably have 16 or even 20 teams. It could be pretty much like the football English premiership with divisions, like division I and division II.

Kadambari Murali Wade: You talked about the BCCI doing enough. Do you think that BCCI needs to allow a players' union in India on the

lines of FICA (Federations of International Cricketers' Association) for the worldwide body? There has been talk about players' rights and what players need. Is there a need for a players' union in India?

Ravi Shastri: You need it only if there is a total breakdown in communication. But I don't think that's the case now. I think the communication between the administration and the players is very good. A players' union will just complicate things more than anything else. Players, whether they are first class players, Test match players, ODI players or even Ranji Trophy players, have never been happier than they are right now. If you look at the monetary part of it, they are being looked after well. You play a good Ranji season, you win the Ranji Trophy title and you make a sizeable amount of income. You can take cricket now as a career.

Q: After the recent confession of Andre Agassi, is there an apprehension

bullies .... The bucks came from there and they controlled for a world event comes from India. So, when India opens

– Ravi Shastri

that because of the pressure of playing well drugs might be coming into the game?

Sunil Gavaskar: The pressure has always been there. You could say that there is probably a lot more media focus. But, the pressure has always been there. It's up to an individual how he deals with that pressure and if he chooses to take the easy and the soft route of going the drugs way, for whatever reason, then I think he has only himself to blame and, maybe, his upbringing.

I don't think what Agassi has confessed about can be generalized. Pete Sampras played under the same pressure, Roger Federer is playing under the same pressure and Rafael Nadal is playing under the same pressure. If you have had a really hard day at your sport, whether it's tennis or cricket, your physical tiredness makes you go to sleep straightaway. I don't think you will really feel the pressure and so I don't think it can be generalized.

Sir Richard Hadlee: It was certainly a big call on Agassi's part to admit to what he had done. One can say "well done". At the same time it is going to somewhat destroy his image and credibility. He is going to have to live with that, although his conscience is clear. All you want at the end of day is a fair and equal playing field for everybody, and if somebody is taking advantage by getting into drugs, then the penalties are going to be reasonably severe. It is important to set the example right for up and coming people.

Kadambari Murali Wade: Is there is a message that we can send out to youngsters? All of you have played the game. Is there a message that you want to send out to youngsters?

Ravi Shastri: I think it's a great time to be a youngster because there are so many options. You have sport in your bedroom or living room beaming in from all parts of the world. If I would want to exchange anything with my time growing up, I would say it is the opportunity to see live sport from all over the world. As a youngster you just watch and learn so quickly. You don't need a coach. You have so many options from football, cricket, hockey, athletics or whatever you want to play. By the age of fourteen and fifteen, once you realize what you are good at, you can pursue it. I think the opportunities are huge at the moment.

Sir Richard Hadlee: We have covered a lot of aspects in cricket. It doesn't matter who is right or wrong. At the end of the day, it is an opinion. But if I have a parting comment, then it is to issue an appeal to administrators, whether they are in the ICC or in countries around the world.

India will have a tremendous influence on the future of the game and, quite frankly, India leads the way in so many different fields, including cricket. But as a former player, watching what is happening in the game, we are slowly seeing it being dismantled. If it continues the way that it is going, with the success of the one-day format, particularly 20-20, the decision-makers could betray the game for all the players was have actually played it in the past.

I remember the words of the great Sir Donald Bradman. He said many years ago that we are all custodians of the game. So, it is up to us as players, administrators, officials, media, sponsors, spectators and whoever else is involved with the game, that we protect and preserve it. We talked about the balance of the game. I think that is one of the key things. We have talked about the balance today and if we can get that right, cricket will live forever.

The one sure way to stop terrorists is to use law enforcement and Intelligence and, when necessary, our militaries to find them, break up their networks and bring them to justice. In the long run we must defeat the terrorists by undermining their ideology and drying up their recruits. The best way to do it is advance our values of liberty, justice, tolerance and hope.

America Re-engaging with the World

Challenges, Opportunities and Risks

▪

George W. Bush

▪

Moderator

Vir Sanghvi

Advisory Editorial Director, Hindustan Times

George W. Bush

43rd President of the United States of America

George W. Bush was the 43rd President of the United States of America, serving from 2001 to 2009. During his eight years as president, he worked to broaden and strengthen the relationship between India and the US in many ways, from increasing bilateral trade and investment flows, to expanding defence cooperation and tackling environmental and energy challenges.

In 2008, these advances in US-India relations culminated in the historic civil nuclear cooperation agreement. This landmark agreement paved the way for enhanced cooperation on nuclear energy issues while reducing the danger of nuclear proliferation across the world.

Having developed into a strong strategic partnership during Bush's tenure, the US-India relationship is now a major source of strength and stability for both nations. Given his unique expertise, Bush is expected to address the future of that relationship, the challenges the two nations face today, and the importance of continued cooperation.

I AM DELIGHTED TO BE WITH SUCH A DISTINGUISHED AUDIENCE. I AM HONOURED TO BE BACK IN INDIA. ABOUT THREE YEARS AGO LAURA AND I CAME HERE AND WERE dazzled by India. It is a vibrant, diverse and modern nation built on an ancient civilization. I have been looking forward to coming back and saying *namaste*.

I have a different life now since the last time I was here. I have retired. I am an old, retired guy. So I do appreciate the opportunity to share some thoughts with you. It became evident that my life had changed when I went recently to a hardware store in Texas. They had advertised that since I had left office, perhaps I would like to become a greeter. A greeter is somebody who stands in the lobby of the store and says, 'welcome'. So, I went by just for the fun of it to say hello and a fellow walked up to me and said, 'Has anybody ever told you, you look like George W. Bush?' I said, 'Yeah it happens quite often.' The guy started to leave and then turned around and said, 'Gosh that sure must make you mad.'

Why is my life different? I suggested to Laura that she take up cooking. She suggested that I take up washing dishes. Nothing has happened. I am using my free time to write a book. I still hear people in the country, particularly those who live by my coast, say that I cannot even read a book, leave alone write one. I am building a policy institute at the Southern Methodist University in Dallas, Texas, and I am giving a fair number of speeches for which, incredibly enough, I get paid.

So, life has changed but some things haven't, starting with my great respect for India. America has respect for over one billion people who call India home as citizens of the world's oldest democracy. Americans feel a special kinship with the people of the world's largest democracy. Our nations are united by our interests and our values; our devotion to justice; a conviction that all should be free to speak their conscience and practice their religion of choice. This conference shows that we share a great appreciation for a robust and free press. Most of our people are bound together by ties of family, commerce and friendship. I have really, really liked your prime minister and am proud to call him a friend. Prime Minister Manmohan Singh is a wise leader and a really good man.

I was privileged to leave the United States during a time of extraordinary change. Think about it, when historians look back at the first decade of the twenty-first century, they will find a period of amazing change – the rise of new global powers, the forward march of freedom, the growing danger of terrorism, rapid economic growth that led to hundreds of millions out of poverty, followed by sudden financial crisis. Alongside these developments, historians will note another change of consequence: the new partnership forged between the United States of America and the Republic of India.

The early chapters of this story date back to 1991 when two fatal events took place. The first was the collapse of the Soviet Union and the Cold War that divided the world for half a century. The second: India, under the wise leadership of then Finance Minister Singh, liberalized its market and opened itself up to the world.

With time, the impact of both changes became clear. At the end of the Cold War, chilly relations between the United States and India began to thaw. And, India's free enterprise economy skyrocketed from $281 billion in 1991 to $463 billion in 2000 to $1.2 trillion today. India's rise was driven by the innovation of its private sector and the brilliance of its people, not central planning from the government. As the economy grew, quality of life improved and poverty declined, literacy expanded and hundreds of millions joined a confident middle class.

These changes were visible far from Delhi. When I ran for president in 2000, India was not a top issue in the campaign but it was a priority of mine. In one of my first major foreign policy speeches at the Ronald Reagan Presidential Library in California, I said this coming century will see democratic India's arrival as a force in the world and that the United States must pay it more attention.

My conviction grew stronger when I became president. When I looked at India from the Oval Office I saw a tolerant, peaceful, multi-religious democracy with a large and creative population, half of which is under twenty-four year old. I saw a dynamic economy with more than 300 million people in the middle class – which is more than the entire population of the United States. I saw an opponent of terrorism and a force for stability and peace in one of the most strategically important regions in the world. I saw the birthplace of 2.5 million Indian Americans who are one of the most successful immigrant populations in the United States.

I saw a country with extraordinary potential and a natural partner of the United States. Yet our relationship remained strained. I was honoured to work with two Indian leaders, Prime Minister Atal Behari Vajpayee and Prime Minister Singh to bring our partnership into the twenty-first century. We promoted commerce and trade by removing sanctions, opening up our markets, concluding an open skies agreement, and increasing the US-India CEO forum culture by a great Indian entrepreneur, Ratan Tata. As a result, trade between our countries doubled over the last five years. We brought in educational exchanges and issued more student visas. I am proud that America now welcomes more students from India than from any other country. We expanded high-tech cooperation and we deepened cooperation in science, space, and agriculture with the goal of helping India begin a second green revolution.

We increased counter terrorism and military cooperation after 9/11 and the 2008 attacks on Mumbai. We created the UN Democracy Fund, which is helping young democracies develop strong political institutions and civil societies. We expanded our diplomatic mission in India, including a new full-service consulate in Hyderabad. By the time I left office, our presence in India was our second-largest in the world after Iraq. These were important steps but yet the United States and India were kept apart.

On his visit to the White House in 2005, Prime Minister Singh and I agreed to pursue an agreement that would allow India and America to cooperate on civilian nuclear energy. We knew the negotiations would be complicated – and they were – but we worked through our differences. On my 2006 visit, Prime Minister Singh and I signed a historic accord. Under this agreement India gains access to peaceful nuclear energy technology from the United States and elsewhere. Businesses now have the opportunity to build a large civilian nuclear power industry. India gains the potential to generate huge amounts of electricity to power its growing economy and provide electricity in rural India without emitting pollution or greenhouse gases. The United States recognizes India's nuclear weapons' programme while India joins the international system of non-proliferation.

The agreement focuses on nuclear energy but its impact reaches beyond that. The deal has been called India's passport to the world. It is a sign that India has taken its rightful place as a great nation on the global stage. Since the agreement was completed, two major events have shaken our countries, both of which make our partnership even more essential.

The first was last Fall's financial crisis. My instincts are to avoid government intervention in the marketplace. If you make a foolish investment you should pay the price. However, Treasury Secretary Henry Paulson and Chairman of the Federal Reserve Ben Bernanke told me that if we did not act, America could face a depression greater than the Great Depression. So, I supported action to intervene in our economy. India moved decisively as well by allowing interest rates and cutting taxes and injecting liquidity into the financial system. The United States, India and other major economies learned the lessons from the past.

We intervened early, we intervened aggressively and we intervened together. I can't say that the actions we took would have prevented something from happening. That we will never know. But I believe that our intervention was necessary. I believe that the problems facing our economies today would be far worse had we not intervened.

The crisis also revealed how dramatically the global financial system has changed. The centre of the world's economic stage has shifted from West to East, from Europe and the Atlantic to Asia and the Pacific. An effective response to the crisis would not have been possible without the contributions of nations like India, China and

South Korea. That is why I decided to convene the G20 and not the G8 for the financial crisis summit in Washington in November 2009. Nations like India played a vital role in this summit and history will show that with your strong economic growth you are helping lead the world to recovery.

The second major event was a series of terrorist attacks on India's financial capital of Mumbai. I extend my deepest condolences to the victims and their families. We are mindful of the other terrorist attacks on India, including a strike on your Parliament and multiple bombings of your embassy in Afghanistan.

While 9/11 in America and 26/11 in India served as moments of clarity, both our nations are engaged in an ideological struggle against extremists who murder innocents to advance a dark vision of extremism and control. They attack our political, financial and diplomatic targets because they hate our way of life. They hate our vision for freedom and human rights; human dignity, prosperity and peace.

The one sure way to stop terrorists is to use law enforcement and Intelligence and, when necessary, our militaries to find them, break up their networks and bring them to justice. In the long run, we must defeat the terrorists by undermining their ideology and drying up their recruits. The best way to do it is to advance our values of liberty, justice, tolerance and hope.

The past year, both America and India held democratic elections. In America, voters chose the first African-American president in its history. That was an uplifting moment for our democracy. It ought to be clear to you that President Barack Obama was not my first choice. But I wish him every success. I am not going to spend a lot of time criticizing him. He has already got plenty of critics in the American political scene.

Here in India, hundreds of millions of people voted in the largest democratic election in the history of the world. I want to congratulate the Prime Minister and the Congress party on their victory and I applaud the Indian people on another remarkable democratic achievement.

President Obama has rightly said that the relationship between America and India is not only one of the most important relationships in the world, but should be one of the best relationships in the world. I wholeheartedly agree. It is not going to happen automatically. While we have laid a solid foundation, both our nations have important choices to make. America and India must work together to win the war in Afghanistan. The mission in Afghanistan has been long, difficult and costly but I believe it is necessary for stability and peace.

If the Taliban, al-Qaeda and their extremist allies were allowed to take over Afghanistan they would again have a safe haven. The Afghan people, particularly Afghan women, will face a return to a brutal tourney. This region and the world would face serious threats. I appreciate the $1.8 billion in assistance that India has provided to the democratic Afghan government. The United States and India must continue to stand together to support this young democracy for the sake of security, peace and decency.

As the world shifts its attention from weathering the financial crisis to manning an economic recovery, we should be guided by two principles: free markets and free trade. My hope is that India will continue its economic reforms and development by opening up more of its market to trade and foreign investment, by modernizing its agricultural sector, by expanding educational opportunities, and by openly confronting health challenges like HIV/AIDS.

My hope is that India will increase the use of nuclear power and other clean energy sources as a way to reduce dependence on foreign energy, especially from unstable suppliers. I hope India shows leadership towards a successful Doha agreement, which would create new opportunities for Indian business and Indian workers and help lift millions of people around the world out of poverty.

America has responsibilities as well. Government interventions that were intended to be temporary should remain temporary. We must smoothly but swiftly unwind federal ownership of the financial and auto sectors. The United States must avoid sending mixed signals about the openness of our economy. Americans should not fear trade or competition. Both will make my nation more efficient and prosperous. The United States Congress should pass pending free trade agreements and refrain from raising tariffs and other barriers to commerce. America must have a rational immigration policy, including expanding H-1B visas. We must continue to give nations like India a seat at the table of key government institutions. We must consider the possibility of a seat for India on the UN Security Council.

I support our president's decision to make the G20 the primary global economic body. America should ensure that India has a leadership role in talks on global climate change. We should focus on using new technologies to cut greenhouse gas emissions without inhibiting or cutting economic growth.

I have confidence in the future of both our countries because I have confidence in the values we share. Our nations are separated by half the globe but we have never been closer. This year marks the fiftieth anniversary of Martin Luther King's visit to India. When he arrived in Delhi he expressed his reverence for Mahatma Gandhi and the great traditions of this ancient land. 'To other countries,' he said, 'I may go as a tourist but to India I come as a pilgrim.' Twenty per cent more Americans than ever before have come to India. We come not only as pilgrims but as admirers, partners and, above all, as friends.

Moderator | **Vir Sanghvi**

Advisory Editorial Director,
Hindustan Times

Q&A

Vir Sanghvi: Thank you Mr President. That was a great speech. I am sure many people here loved the things you said. Can I now ask you slightly more awkward questions? Many people in India who are hugely admiring of, and grateful for, what you have done feel that, in some sense, America was conned by Pakistan. You gave it a lot of aid and support but it didn't actually do anything for you in Afghanistan. That battle continues. It didn't do a great deal in Waziristan either. It continues to send terrorists across the border, which 26/11 which you referred to, shows. Do you think that perhaps America should have been more sceptical?

George W. Bush: First of all it is in India's interests that the United States has friendship with Pakistan. I think you would want a friend of yours to be able to have a good, open and honest dialogue with a neighbour. Secondly, it is in the Pakistani government's interests to fight extremism and terror. After all, the current president's wife was killed by extremists.

One of the first phone calls that were made after the September 11 attacks was to President Pervez Musharraf. We asked, "Who are you with: the Taliban or the United States?" President Musharraf rightly chose the United States. There was a list of conditions we spoke to him about, which he has met.

It is unfair to say the United States was conned. To the contrary, the United States has worked hard to find elements within Pakistani society who are willing to go after extremists. One thing that has changed over the course of the last few years is that it has become apparent to the Pakistanis that extremists are a threat to their own democracy. I don't think you can negotiate with extremists. I think you have got to bring extremists to justice and replace the conditions that cause people to join their team with an education system and the creation of jobs. That is where America is trying to help Pakistan.

It has been tough. No question about it. On the other hand, it is important for our country to stay engaged with democracy. If I were you, I would be thankful there is a democracy on the border. History shows that democracies yield peace. There is no question that the countries have got challenges. But I do believe that it is in our nation's interests to stay engaged with them.

Vir Sanghvi: Do you believe that the Afghanistan conflict can end anytime soon and that the United States can get out of Afghanistan and restore democracy relatively soon?

George W. Bush: I think that it is a long and hard struggle. First of all Afghanistan doesn't have much money. It is a poor country. In 2001, their Gross National Product was the size of a city like Idaho. Society was completely suppressed by the Taliban. Young girls were not allowed to go to school. So they have got a long way to go. They have made some progress. They have written a Constitution. Secondly, people voted in a democratic government. Thirdly, girls do go to school. There has been a lot of progress. But there is still a long way for them to go.

The question facing us is: does it matter? It does matter. It matters for our own national security interests. It matters that we help societies where people have been completely suppressed. I hope that people in my country show concern about a society in which women are completely suppressed. I take great pride in the fact that for our own interests we liberated 25 million people. The work is hard and I hope we don't abandon the people of Afghanistan.

Vir Sanghvi: Let me turn now to a country to which you devoted more time and attention than India: Iraq. It is always easy to be wise in hindsight but do you think that perhaps you didn't devote as much time as you should have to a post invasion plan and to working out what would happen after the country was liberated?

George W. Bush: I think we devoted a lot of time to a post liberation plan. After all, democracy is taking hold in Iraq. It did not happen instantly, but this is how it works. I had a choice to make: do I replace one tyrant with somebody of our choice? My answer was to let the people of Iraq choose. Once the question was: do you go in and remove Saddam Hussain? Then the question was: who gets to choose the next leader? It would have been very easy for all of us to pick a person, put him there and then leave.

But I believe in democracy. I believe democracy is a fundamental right of every man, woman and child. I don't think that this is America's gift to the world. It is a universal right. Democracies lead to peace and I understand that democracy was essential in this ideological struggle.

I understand that some people don't think that it was an ideological struggle. But it was. I think when you find people who murder innocent people to advance an ideology, that's an ideological struggle. Make no mistake about it. These killers want to change forms of government to suit their view.

Then the question is: what do nations like the United States and others do about it? As I mentioned earlier, for our own self-protection I have to find these people and bring them to justice in order to prevent other attacks from taking place. You just can't sit back and wait.

After 9/11 the discussion in the United States was, 'Why do we sit back and not do something about it? Why didn't we get the information necessary to do something about it before the attacks occurred?' My view is when we do something about it – and that doesn't mean military action necessarily – in the long run these [extremist] ideologies will be marginalized with the advance of freedom and democracy. Imagine what would have happened if people hadn't supported Indian democracy years ago.

I am sure some people said that Indians can't possibly live in a democratic society. Well you did it and now you are important part of the world scene. It's important for people to see that India has a huge Muslim population living at peace with people of other religions. I am optimistic and I understand how tough it is to advance democracy as the source of peace.

Vir Sanghvi: Another Iraq question: many people think that while going into Iraq you radicalized global Islam. Islamists were able to say to ordinary Muslims that America is against Islam and, in the process, you actually created more extremists than were there before.

George W. Bush: The United States was not in Iraq when 19 kids killed 3,000 Americans. An estimated 10,000 people were training in Afghanistan prior to our going into Iraq. I refuse to grant these killers any excuse other than the fact that they wanted to advance their agenda and didn't need an excuse. They were doing it prior to the removal of Saddam Hussain and the advance of democracy in Iraq. What were we to do? Retreat and just let them have their way and not anger them?

It is for us to be proactive in protecting our countries. When people say our actions cause there to be more radicals, it is just an excuse for isolationism. I just don't buy it. If our action caused more radicals then is no action the answer? If we do that then what will happen is that all of a sudden these terrorists will strengthen their hands. That is one of the lessons of 11 September. The oceans no longer protect the United States of America. And the most important job of the US president is to provide security for our people.

Vir Sanghvi: Many people argue that in the euphoria of the rising markets, we took our eyes off the ball. Many governments, including yours, didn't worry enough about regulation. Do you think that is a fair criticism?

George W. Bush: Yeah, it's fairly okay though it's a little generalized. This is what I think. Wall Street got drunk and we got the hangover. How did they get drunk? First of all because of our trade balances there was a lot of capital coming back to the United States which is good. But there was so much capital that people started to invent products that they couldn't explain and were too complicated.

Secondly, there was an implicit government guarantee in Fannie and Freddie. These were entities that were flogging out money for mortgages. I don't want to say, "I told you so," but I did try to get Congress to regulate Fannie and Freddie because I thought they were getting beyond their charter. I couldn't get it done but there is no question that there was a case where there needed to be more regulation to bring sobriety into lending practices.

The bane of over-regulating is that we forget small businesses, entrepreneurs and risk-takers who will cause our economies to recover. It is one thing to work to help us recover, quite another to leave behind a regulatory scheme that will inhibit capital investment. I do not think governments are going to be able to spend their way out of this recession. I think the best way to recover is to encourage the private sector to expand and grow the job base of their respective countries.

Vir Sanghvi: A couple of personal questions. Many people who see you for the first time say, "Hey, he is taller than he looks on television." Do you get that a lot?

George W. Bush: Yeah, I mean I have been the same height since I was eighteen years old.

Vir Sanghvi: The second: "He is brighter and warmer than we thought." Do you get that a lot as well?

George W. Bush: Not in Texas, because there they know me. You get an image and it keeps getting reinforced by the filter and there is nothing you can do about it except not pay attention to it.

Vir Sanghvi: Does the image, the way you were sometimes caricatured and portrayed, ever worry you?

George W. Bush: As a president, you can't pay that much attention to it. You've got to just do your job. I never worried about the polls. I only worried about them on election days; the only time they count.

The problem is that in life if you chase popularity there is a temptation to sell your soul and compromise on principles, which is something I absolutely refuse to do. The important thing in life is that when I get home and look in the mirror I want to be proud of what I see. You know you have to make tough calls when you are the president, that is what you are paid to do. That's what I did. I didn't worry about history. There is no such thing as short-term history. It takes time for history to get a reach. It takes time for objective people to analyze. I am confident about this. I am confident that when objective historians analyze my administration and the administration of Prime Minister Singh, they will say that the change in India-US relationship created a strategic platform in order to help people realize peace. Fifty years from now I am confident of this even though there is no such thing as an objective short-term historian who exists this minute.

Vir Sanghvi: One final question before I open questions to the audience. You are still relatively young and energetic. If you were in Indian politics, you would be probably in the Youth Congress. So what does a former two-term president do when he has left the White House, reached the top of his trade and is still young and energetic?

George W. Bush: Go on cruise ships! I am writing a book that will be out hopefully next Fall. It's a book that will try to place you in my position as I had to make some pretty tough calls. I am going to recap history very anecdotally so that the reader today and the reader thirty years from now will be able to say, "Oh, okay that what was going through his mind", or "That's what the environment was like".

I am building a policy institute at Southern Methodist University which is where Laura went to university in Dallas, Texas. It is going to promote precisely the values I have just described here: free markets, free trade and freedom itself. One of the interesting things we are going to do is have a women-initiative front in the Middle East. We want to encourage women in the Middle East to work hard to advance democracy. So, all this is going to occupy a lot of my time. And then, of course, I am giving these speeches; what my dad calls "white collar crime".

Vir Sanghvi: Gender issues and women's issues are actually close to your heart, aren't they?

George W. Bush: I was raised by a very strong woman. I married a strong woman. And, I have raised two strong women. So, yes, they are. I am impressed by the number of women leaders I have met here in India. It's a tribute to your society. We have a lot of strong women leaders in our country as well.

Vir Sanghvi: And you appointed many women to positions of influence. Condoleezza Rice is just the most visible example.

George W Bush: I did. I had a rich administration; rich in opinion.

There were a lot of women in positions who could march right into the Oval Office and tell me what was on their minds.

Q: Do you think the economic recovery is an enduring one or do you believe it to be a bumpy ride? Without wanting you to become an economic astrologer, how do you think the Bush presidency would have handled this problem differently from the Obama presidency, recognizing that Ben Bernanke is your appointee?

George W. Bush: I remember getting briefed by my economists in the White House who would say, "On the one hand this," and "On the other hand that." If they had a third hand, they would have said, "And on the third hand..."

It's an inexact science. You are asking me to make a prediction and I am really not well positioned to tell you with certainty what the economy is going to do. I think it's going to take a while to get out of this recession. The job picture in the United States is slow in recovering, which is too bad. We want people working and until jobs pick up, the US economy is going to be sluggish but not negative. I say that because 70 per cent of our GDP is consumption. Therefore, when people aren't working, it's going to be harder for them to purchase goods and services.

I hope the world makes rational decisions that will help accelerate growth. I am deeply concerned about protectionism. Protectionism seems like an easy solution during tough economic times but a protectionist world would really inhibit the flow of capital and cause our economies to stagnate. Policy-makers have certain choices to make during this year and the next. I hope we don't wall ourselves off from each other. As for comparing myself with President Obama, I am not going to do it.

Q: Why is India, the largest democracy in the world, being denied a place in the United Nations Security Council?

George W. Bush: Because the politics is difficult.

Vir Sanghvi: That's a good answer but it's a bit general.

George W. Bush: It is. First of all, the threshold question is: should the UN Security Council be changed? I think the new realities of the world say that yes, we should seriously consider it. I am not the guy anymore so I am just giving you a point of view. But if I were the president I would be much more definitive. I don't want to speak for the current administration but I do think it ought to be considered.

Q: Secondly, the question is: should the second-largest democracy in the world be considered? Japan is a permanent member of the UN Security Council. Should there be a regional consideration? Should Brazil, a major economy, be considered? Who in the Middle East should be represented in the UN Security Council?

George W. Bush: The reason why I say this is because I want you to understand how complicated the issue can be. If the UN Security Council permanent members expand beyond five to fifteen or ten, then what's the rational size of the committee? If it gets too big will it become unwieldy? Will things get done? Do you have a veto power given to more than five members? In other words, it is a complicated issue. But there's no question that the world's second-largest democracy ought to be in the mix. Yet, I repeat, the threshold question is: should the UN Security Council expand at all and, if so, how big should it be? Once that threshold question has been answered, then obviously India ought to be seriously considered.

Vir Sanghvi: When you were President for eight years did you seriously consider pushing India's case for permanent membership?

George W. Bush: We seriously considered expanding the issue. But when you get into the discussion with nations who get to make the decision or have a big influence over the decision about the diminution of their powers, you sometimes get blowback. In other words, you say to a person, "You are no longer one of the five who will get to veto". In effect we dilute that power. What sounds clear on paper may not be in my interests. So, yes, we considered it seriously in 2006, if I am not mistaken. Condoleezza Rice handled it for our administration. There were serious discussions about how big the UN Security Council should be.

Once the decision to expand the Security Council is in place, then obviously India will be in the mix. But it's the expansion issue and not only the expansion issue, the governance issues at the UN Security Council: who gets the veto, who doesn't. It's complicated. It's rational to say that India ought to be in the mix. What makes it difficult is deciding what composition the UN Security Council would like in the first place and what are its powers.

Vir Sanghvi: I am glad you cleared that up because in India this issue comes up again and again. The view in India is that if we agree on climate change we will be made a member of the Security Council. If we sign the nuclear deal, we will be made a member. But it's not actually that simple.

George W. Bush: I don't think it is in India's interest to try to get people to change the Security Council. But what's difficult is the politics of change, not India itself. People are not going to say, "Let's not expand because India will be in it." To the contrary people say, "We want India to be at the table." It's the threshold issue that creates complications. India is not going to try to promote itself into the UN Security Council and do things that are not in its interest. That doesn't make any sense. I suspect this government won't do that. This government is going to represent the Indian people in a way that advances India's interests.

Vir Sanghvi: There is a subtext to all the Security Council stuff which you probably realize. When Indians talk about the Security Council it is partly about India becoming an emerging superpower. But, it is partly also about how the world sees India and China. There is a great sense in India that although we are a democracy, the other big boy on the block, we are sometimes unfairly neglected by the West in favour of China.

George W. Bush: Well you have just to get over that. There are other ways for India to be players on the world stage. One is through the G20. Another is through the discussion on climate. India's voice will be heard.

You are not the first person who has brought up the relationship between the China and the United States or China and India or India and the United States. From a foreign policy perspective, it is in your interest that the United States has a working relationship with China and Pakistan. I have already talked about it. If you are friend and an ally, you want your friend and ally to have some influence on people with whom you may have disagreements. It is very essential for the United States to keep strong bilateral relations in this part of the world and that we not fall prey to this notion that we can conduct our business through only multilateral organizations.

Bilateral foreign policy lays the foundation for peace and security. It has for fifty years and it will for the next fifity years. What has changed in the equation is that now the United States has got a very strong relationship with India. We are good friends and good allies. That's what has changed. That is going to create a strategic balance in the long run. That will make it more likely that the area is prosperous and peaceful.

Q: I want to ask you a broader question about Iraq. If you were forced to rewind and think back what would you say were your three or two major regrets during your presidency?

George W. Bush: Removing Saddam Hussain was not one of them. I think the world is much better off without Saddam Hussain. I firmly believe that the people of Iraq are better off without Saddam Hussain.

Let me explain this very quickly. After 9/11, it was important for the United States to take a look at all threats before they materialized. There was no question in my mind that Saddam Hussain was a threat to the United States. He was a declared enemy of the United States. But what is interesting is that prior to my arrival in Washington, the United States Congress by President Clinton allowed that regime change in Iraq was the policy of the United States of America. I wasn't the first person to show up and say Saddam Hussain was a threat. What worried me with Saddam Hussain and with weapons of mass destruction – which everybody in the world thought he had – was the danger of the use of these weapons in conjunction with terrorism which was a huge threat for stability in the world.

My hope was that we would disarm Saddam Hussain peacefully. That is why I went to the United Nations Security Council for the seventeenth time. The Security Council said, "Disarm, disclose or face serious consequences". Now the question is do words mean anything in the international world? I happened to think they do. The decision was Saddam's to make, not the free world's.

I was hopeful that he would disarm peacefully. But he denied inspectors. So what does that tell you? He was not letting inspectors in. It's got to tell you that he is trying to hide something; that he is a dangerous person. He was shooting at our airplanes, using weapons of mass destruction against his own people and was a brutal dictator. He had invaded a country. I am sorry that we had to use the military but I had to because it was his choice.

It wasn't just me. At one point in time there were 41 nations who had joined us; 42 in Afghanistan and 41 in Iraq. It was a multinational effort to remove him. I believe if he were in power today, you would see a nuclear arms race between Shia Iran and Sunni Iraq in the Middle East which would have been incredibly dangerous. I believe you will see nations using surrogate extremist forces to advance their agenda like the Shia Iranis at Hezbollah. But I regret some of my language.

Vir Sanghvi: What in particular?

George W. Bush: Like "dead or alive". I am a pretty straightforward guy. I said some things that sent messages that got people confused. But in expressing my determination to go after the enemy, which I believe all of us free nations ought to continue to have, I used some phraseology when I probably should have been a little more sensitive. By the way, I am reminded of it by my wife on a constant basis.

Vir Sanghvi: You raised the question: so is Osama bin Laden dead or is he alive?

George W. Bush: I would guess he is alive. But you know, we will bring him to justice. I will tell you one thing he is not leading any victory parades. He is not on television espousing his views. He is hiding. The definition is when and if. The answer is yes, he will be brought to justice. He deserves to be.

Q: The US has always argued for free markets and free access. You

talked about the issue of capital being an important resource. But we also believe that in addition to capital, the most important resource is human resources. What to us is alarming is when a country like the US starts advocating and thinking about policies and bills internally that will limit the movement of professionals from one country to another as well as force Indian companies to hire domestically in the US. So how does the US tend to cope with this dichotomy, if I may call it that, of an inward pressure on protectionism and outward advocacy of openness?

George W. Bush: That is a great question. In our country's history, we have isolationism, protectionism and bad immigration policy that have gone hand-in-hand in the past. The United States has obligations and one of them is to have a rational immigration policy.

I tried to work with Congress to expand H-1B which affects India directly, because of Indian students who want to stay in the United States but cannot because of visa expiration. It is short-sighted for the United States not to allow H-1B workers – high-tech, smart people capable of contributing to our society. I tried to reform immigration as president. But it's a tough issue in the United States.

But your question is very legitimate. It is a legitimate concern and I hope our Congress and president address it over time. The president has got his hands full right now. But I do believe that at some point in time, the issue will be revisited; the issue being immigration reform that is rational and fair and represents the interest of the United States.

Q: You are in a country which has the third-largest Muslim population in the world after Indonesia and Bangladesh. There has been a perception that you are seen as a hate figure in the Muslim world and among Muslim communities. How would you like to reach out to them? How would you like to reach out not just to Indian Muslims but Muslims across the world? What would you say to them now that in you are in a reflective mood and are writing a book?

George W. Bush: I would say that I respect your religion. You all live in a society where you can practice it freely. And I would say, "Please don't let the propagandists tell you that George W. Bush or America doesn't respect you". What we don't respect are people who hijack a great religion and murder innocent people to advance their ideology. I don't believe murderers are religious people.

I understand there is a notion about George W. Bush not liking Muslims. To me that is just an excuse for us to do nothing. They were trying to make us back off. But there is something meaningful when you liberate Muslim women and give them a chance to realize their dreams. So, I totally reject the notion that advance of democracy is anti-Muslim. To the contrary, I think it is pro-religious feeling. I think democracies are respectful for people's rights and people's different points of views.

People tell me that I am idealistic about the advance of freedom. One of the great ironies of my presidency was my relationship with the prime minister of Japan. Right after 9/11 he called me on the phone and said, "The Japanese people and our government stands with the United States. To enhance our mutual security we will together advance freedom and democracy as the great alternative to the ideology of the haters and killers."

What's ironic about this is that sixty years ago my father fought the Japanese. Now, sixty years is nothing in the march of history; sixty years is nothing particularly if you are sixty-three. It's a snap of the fingers. So an eighteen-year-old navy fighter pilot Bush fights the Japanese and sixty years later his son is working with the former enemy to advance security, peace and freedom.

Something happened. Let me just say that in 1945, if people in America had said the Japanese will be the great allies of the United States, people would have said they are hopelessly idealistic. But democracy is transformative. Japan adopted a Japanese style of democracy and as a result an enemy became an ally.

The same thing is going to happen in the Middle East, if free nations do not lose their nerve and become weary and tired of doing the hard work. So I leave here as an optimist. But I am optimistic. I am also incredibly optimistic about the relations between India and the United States. I am confident that this relationship will not only benefit our people but will benefit the world.

Is the Global Economic Recovery for Real?

▪

Anshu Jain

▪

Chanda Kochhar

▪

Moderator

R. Sukumar

Editor, Mint

Anshu Jain

Head of Global Markets and member of the Management Board, Deutsche Bank

Anshu Jain is Head of global markets, Joint Head of the corporate and investment bank and a member of Deutsche Bank's management board. He is globally responsible for Deutsche Bank's 6,000-person sales and trading operations, including government and corporate bonds, commodities, emerging markets, equities, foreign exchange, money markets, interest rate and credit derivatives. From a standing start in 1995, Deutsche Bank has grown to be among the largest firms active in global markets, ranking among the top two by earnings in 2007.

Previously at Deutsche Bank, Anshu had been Global Head of fixed income sales and trading, Global Head of derivatives and emerging markets as well as the Global Head of institutional client coverage. Anshu joined Deutsche Bank in 1995 to set up and run a specialist unit focusing on hedge funds and institutional derivative coverage. Prior to this, Anshu was a Managing Director at Merrill Lynch in New York where he founded and led the securities industry's first dedicated hedge fund coverage group. Between 1985 and 1988 he worked in derivatives research at Kidder Peabody.

In addition to his Deutsche Bank commitments, Anshu is a Non-executive Director of Sasol, South Africa's leading oil and gas company. He has also served as a member of the Prime Minister's Working Group on Inward Investment in India and more recently on the Working Group to advise the UK Treasury on financial stability, with a broad mandate across all elements of the bank rescue package and other financial issues. Anshu is also a member of the Financial Services Global Competitiveness Group, asked by the Chancellor of the Exchequer to consider the UK's long-term approach to international financial services.

Anshu is a 2005 recipient of the American Indian Foundation's Achievement Award for philanthropy and ongoing involvement in India's development. He was the 2003 winner of *Euromoney* magazine's Capital Markets Achievement Award.

BANKERS DON'T GET MANY INVITATIONS THESE DAYS SO I AM REALLY DELIGHTED TO BE UP HERE. THERE ARE MANY ADJECTIVES WHICH HAVE BEEN USED FOR us lately. Avid cricket fan is but a nice compliment that I will take.

Is this recovery for real? Let's focus on US GDP numbers in light of the preceding speaker, George W. Bush. The numbers tell a story. In June 2008, the US economy contracted by 0.7 per cent, shrank a further 5 per cent in the third quarter, 5 per cent again in the fourth quarter, and 6 per cent in the first quarter of this year. If there is any doubt in your minds as to how big this crisis was, let me tell you, having sat at the helm of one of the ships which was being tossed by those turbulent seas, things truly did look dire.

Then suddenly in the second quarter this year, minus 0.7 and in the numbers that were just released, a growth of 3.5 per cent. The forecast over the next three quarters hovers between 2 per cent and 2.5 per cent positive. Now, if someone had asked us six to nine months ago what was the forecast on this same year's GDP numbers, there was a contraction of 2 per cent assumed for 2008 and a contraction of 2.5 per cent for 2009. Frankly, a depression loomed ahead of us of truly epic proportions.

It was a crisis of confidence. People had lost confidence in the financial system. Inventories were being torn down and the economy was basically in significant reverse. What happened? Were those predictions wrong? Were things not as dire as they appeared back then?

No, things were truly terrible. We had to tip our hats to global central bankers who threw a massive coordinated and unprecedented set of steps, injecting 16 trillion dollars of liquidity in the US alone. A set of measures were taken across the board to stabilize the banks. Terms like TARP (Troubled Asset Relief Programme) and TALF (Term Asset-Backed Securities Loan Facility) became household terms in the US.

This was done on a global basis. China created more credit in the first half of this year than the entire contraction in the US and Europe combined. Guess what? It worked. The US housing market which was the source of turbulence in the first place has now stabilized. The Case-Shiller index, which is the index which is used as the best gauge of how US residential housing is faring, has actually appreciated for four months in a row. Even in the UK, residential housing has expanded by 6 per cent of the bottom and, most importantly, confidence is back.

So is the crisis behind? Are things going to be fine? Are there no consequences?

Unfortunately, far from it. The very acts which have stabilized the economy and have turned things around are now likely to create an autoimmune response which needs to be very carefully analyzed. There are a few things in particular which concern us. The first and the foremost is the size of the deficit which has now been created. In the West, we are going to go from deficits, which were running at between 2 per cent to 2.5 per cent of the GDP on a running basis, to something which is now approaching 12 per cent to 12.5 per cent.

The debt-to-GDP ratios have now skyrocketed to about 80 per cent. The dollar is under severe stress. Most important, the US is now at the mercy of international countries. Fifty per cent of the US deficit is now funded by other countries, principally but not exclusively by China.

That fatal embrace between the US and China has some very scary risk factors for the global economy. Step away from the dollar and look at the taxation system, which is now going to be required to actually cut this deficit. Marginal rates in the UK have shot up by a full 10 per cent from 40 to around 50. In the US, in New York particularly, federal, state and city taxes are up at about 52 per cent. All of a sudden, a lot of what the Western economies took for granted is now being questioned.

Commodity price inputs have to be watched very carefully. Any time you watch the dollar come down as rapidly as it has, the price of oil and the price of commodities in general can create inflationary impact which could then lead to a dreaded combination of high unemployment, which is what you have today plus rising inflation.

These combinations do not worry me as much as the questioning of the very fabric of the West which is taking place. As a child with faith in socialism, I grew up in the city in the 70s and 80s. There is no doubt in my mind that free enterprise and capitalism is the only way forward. In the twenty years leading to the breakdown of the Soviet Union and the collapse of the Wall, there was a differential of 50 per cent in the per capita GDP growth rates of the US and Russia. Yet the very system that brought that much power and that much wealth to the West is now being questioned, which for me is really astonishing to watch. As a regular reader of *The Financial Times* to actually read weekly columns titled 'The Future of Finance' with a question mark is stunning.

My kids who go to school in the UK are now being taught that the entire edifice of Western capitalism needs to be questioned. That to me is stunning. The price that one will have to pay from that questioning is going to be significant and long-lasting. If you take a step backwards, the tremendous bailout which has happened is through taxpayers and the way taxpayers get their own back is via politics.

So in the West something which has not been seen before is the involvement of policy and politics in business decisions. This is something which is happening on a daily basis. Globalization is being questioned. George Bush spoke about the perils of tariffs and intervention. There is no debate in my mind that that price is being paid today. When local taxpayers bail the economy out, the response that comes is in the form of very direct pressure on specific sectors of the economy which is very regional in tone.

If you look at the banking industry, global banks have been saved by regional taxpayers and the pressure which is upon them at this point is to keep lending going along very specific regional lines. So the impact of this bailout itself has some risk factors in it. We have talked about the dollar. We have talked about the deficit. These are things which will constrain the bounce back.

The West is going to have to live with sub-par economic growth for a long time to come. We could have a decade of growth between one and 2.5 per cent with taxation running well above 50 per cent.

I was in Beijing a month ago and in my opinion the optimism and surge towards free markets that we see in China and India now exceeds that of the West. Having spent the last two decades in the West this is truly astonishing to watch.

Does this mean all is lost? No. I think the inherent flexibility dynamism, our store of wealth and the best-practice traditions in the West are going to hold in very good stead. I think they will make a comeback but they will have to do something which they haven't done in a long time: practice austerity.

Just to provide the contrast from an outside-in perspective, if

The debt-to-GDP ratios have now skyrocketed to about important, the US is now at the mercy of international funded by other countries, principally but not exclusively

you take a look at the things that have gone wrong in the West and the things that the West is battling with and then apply the same template to India, you get a very different set of answers; 25 per cent dependence on exports. Does this mean that India is completely firewalled? No. But nor is it as allied to Western fortunes as China is, for example. Thirty-five per cent savings rate gives India a very stable platform with which to finance its own growth. It doesn't need foreign capital in nearly the same quantum that other countries do.

Our best of all, 56 per cent of the GDP is coming from domestic consumption. Again, does it immunize you from global cycles? No. But it provides a very comfortable buffer against it. That gives India some very strong structural positives to be able to combat the headwinds that we will see over the coming few years. In my mind that process of channelizing savings back into investments always happens through domestic banks. And Indian domestic banks – here we have to tip our hat to the Reserve Bank of India and very strong local management – are the envy of the rest of the world. Indian banks are in good shape.

If you put all of that together, India starts this next ten-year period from a very strong vantage point. It has to make sure again from an outside-in perspective that the investment which is made, is made wisely. To me there are three sectors which stand above all. Infrastructure is the obvious one and enough has been said on this, and will be said on it, for me to add much at the margin.

Literacy is one which doesn't get the attention which it deserves. A year of secondary schooling adds 1.2 per cent to our growth rates. Nothing could be as important. Yet among the BRIC (Brazil, Russia, India and China) countries, India spends the least as a percentage of its per capita income on literacy. That's a crying shame and that

80 per cent. The dollar is under severe stress. Most countries. Fifty per cent of the US deficit is now by China.

is something which has to be tackled. Literacy rates have moved from 60 to 80 per cent in the last fifteen years. We could have universal education. That has to be a major priority.

I have to talk about my pet cause, which is the environment and deforestation. There is a very strong view that this is India's decade, that we should not be slowed down and that efficiency of energy is the most important question. Well, I beg to disagree. If the price you pay is an irrevocable price which takes away an asset over the next thirty, forty and fifty years in terms of species gone, top soil destroyed, the annual cycle of floods and droughts chasing each other, that's way too high a price to pay.

Putting all of these together, even a mediocre implementation on these three fronts, allied to the tremendous structural advantage that the country has, puts India in a very strong position.

For the first 1,800 years of the last 2,000 years, India and China contributed 50 per cent of the world's GDP. So the coming of age that we talk about is actually a restoration of the old economic order. In that spectacular period between 1750 and 1950 their share of GDP plummeted to 8 per cent. India went from contributing 16 per cent of the world's GDP to 3 per cent by 1973. We are at 16 per cent today and, according to our analysis, by 2020, we could be back up 50 per cent; India and China making up 50 per cent of the world's GDP.

That's a spectacular bounce back within 250 years. In summary, yes, the recovery is for real. But as George Bush pointed out, most economists and financiers will not conclude that statement without saying 'Yes, but we can spend more time on it during our session.'

Chanda Kochhar

Managing Director and Chief Executive Officer, ICICI Bank

Chanda Kochhar is the Managing Director and Chief Executive Officer of ICICI Bank. She began her career with ICICI in 1984 and has thereon successfully risen through the ranks by handling multidimensional assignments and heading all major functions in the bank at various points in time.

In 1993 when ICICI decided to enter commercial banking, Chanda was deputed to ICICI Bank as a part of the core team to set up the bank. When ICICI set up the Infrastructure Group in 1996 to create dedicated industry expertise in the areas of power and telecom, she was handpicked and made in charge of the Infrastructure Industry Group. In July 2000, she was chosen to head the retail finance division of ICICI and has been instrumental in scaling up the business.

In April 2001, Chanda was promoted as an Executive Director, heading the retail business in the bank. In April 2006, she was appointed Deputy Managing Director with responsibility for both the corporate and retail banking business of ICICI Bank, and from October 2006 to October 2007 she handled the international and corporate businesses of ICICI. In October 2007, Chanda was appointed Joint Managing Director and Chief Financial Officer.

Chanda was ranked 20th in *Fortune's* 2009 list of 'most powerful women in business'. She was awarded 'Business Woman of the Year' by *The Economic Times* in 2005 and in 2004 was awarded 'Retail Banker of the Year' by *The Asian Banker* amongst prominent retail bankers in the Asia Pacific region.

IN MY VIEW RECOVERY IS ALWAYS A RELATIVE TERM. WHEN WE LOOK AT THE SITUATION TODAY VIS-À-VIS SIX MONTHS AGO, THE RELATIVE TERM LOOKS VERY DIFFERENT. IF WE look at it eighteen months ago, again in relative term things look very different. But instead of just looking at numbers and relative terms, it is important for us to look at the last one year. What is the impact of this one year on the world economic order?

As recovery takes place – and some signs of recovery, and that they would be sustainable, are clearly there – we have to realize that we would now emerge into a new world economic order. The world that would emerge from this crisis is going to be different. The economic order is going to be different and the balance of power in this economic order is going to be different. For us in India that's a very important point that we need to ponder on.

If we look at the US, the numbers over the last four to five quarters on a quarter-on-quarter basis show contraction. Now we are seeing a positive growth rate. There are other signs of stability. Housing prices have stabilized. Financial markets have stabilized. Foreign flow of funds into India are increasing. These are some very positive signs. But, even as these signs look stable, what is going to be the growth rate and the fundamentals of growth rates of some of these countries as we go forward?

If you look at the US, growth was really dependent on consumption and, of course, consumption on the back of high indebtedness. Today if we turn customer behaviour into an economy where the consumers are not likely to consume as much and the banks are not likely to lend as much for that consumption, then we really have to adjust the estimates of growth rates for that country.

A few challenges still remain for Western countries. One, consumers are not going to consume as much. Earlier there was no real savings rate but today the consumer in the US is saving 5 per cent. It's going to change consumption behaviour and, of course, saving is going to be very good for the structural stability of the economy. But in terms of growth rate, it's going to be a different story.

Similarly, while the financial markets have stabilized, we have to still look at the impact of high unemployment rates in those countries, again in terms of future growth rates. The unemployment in some Western countries is still 9.5 per cent and 10 per cent. It is estimated that if unemployment in the US has to come down to a more stable rate of 5 to 6 per cent, the US economy will have to grow at 6 per cent year-on-year for the next four to five years.

That is a slightly optimistic estimate. But even by local estimates there, unemployment levels will continue to remain high for the next two to three years. Clearly, if unemployment rates remain high then it will impact future growth rates: there are less people who are going to be able to change cars and less people who are going to be able to consume.

The third, of course, is the entire cost of the stimulus package in terms of fiscal deficit and inflationary pressures and how they are going to be managed.

So, if you look at Western economies, a lot of action has taken place both in terms of stimulus and structural adjustments. We are clearly seeing signs of stability which are very positive. But as those economies emerge, their growth rates are definitely going to be very different from what they were in the past.

Contrast this to Asian economies which, to start with, were structurally better suited to handle the crisis. The saving rate-to-GDP was much higher than that of Western economies. In India it was close to 38 per cent. In China it was close to 51 per cent. That is one big strength.

The debt-to-GDP ratios of Asian economies were also much lower than that of Western economies. Our banking system was much more conservative. These were some of things that were inherently and structurally the strength of the Asian economies.

As we move forward, emerging Asian economies are going to capitalize on these structural strengths and play a larger role in the world economic growth order. Some signs point towards this. Look at the number of car sales. In emerging economies, the total car sales in the year 2000 were about 8 million. This is now

60 million annually. In the US, in the year 2000 the number was 20 million. It has come down to 12 million now.

These figures are telling us what the new world economic order is going to be. In this context if we look at India, the last one year has shown us that the inherent strengths of the Indian economy are really playing up to keep the growth momentum strong. The first inherent strength, of course, was the strong reliance on domestic consumption rather than exports. This domestic consumption strength comes to us from our inherent demographics. As a young country we add millions of people to the working population every year. These people have purchasing power in their hands. Domestic consumption gives us the basic driver for growth in the current year, and as we go forward.

But we will have another driver of growth, which is going to be growth driven by investment. As the per capita income increases

Broadly, for India, the question is not whether we will fast we take the growth rates to 9 per cent and 10 momentum to continue to grow at these rates.

and as more and more people get added to the working population, the country needs to create manufacturing and infrastructure capacity. We are at a point where we will see investment in manufacturing and infrastructure. That is going to be the next driver of growth and that is what will accelerate the growth rate for the Indian economy.

The third strength is that the structural advantages of savings and investment as a percentage of GDP on a year-on-year basis gives us the ability to keep financing as much of that growth internally as is possible. We do not have to rely only on foreign flow of funds.

The fourth advantage: during the last one year the Indian corporate sector in particular has emerged even more efficient and productive. There were always inherent cost advantages in certain sectors in India. But the last one year has made most corporates look internally to emerge more efficient and more productive. As the growth rates come back, the Indian corporate sector would capitalize on these growth rates being more efficient, fitter and, therefore, being able to actually get better advantages.

The final advantage is the fact that the Indian banking system has been so safe and sound; a very conservative leverage ratio. There is no presence of subprime kind of lending, no presence of very complicated products which created some amount of financial crisis. So if you look at the economy as a full body, the banking sector is the heart of the body. In the Western world, the crisis really started from the heart and, therefore, impacted the other parts of the body. But in India the banking sector continued to pump; the heart remained strong. Whatever little impact that was felt was felt on some of the manufacturing sectors because of exports and so on.

grow at the current growth rates. The question is how
per cent. Domestic consumption will provide enough

These are some of the ways in which structurally the world economic order will change. That does not mean that Asian economies or the Indian economy will not have some challenges. We will have to keep an eye on inflation. We will have to make sure that we do not make infrastructure investments a bottleneck in our growth. There are things we will have to keep working on. But broadly, for India, the question is not whether we will grow at the current growth rates. The question is how fast we take the growth rates to 9 per cent and 10 per cent. Domestic consumption will provide enough momentum to continue to grow at these rates. But the better we do on infrastructure, on investment, the better we capitalize on some of these opportunities, we can, with multiplier effects, keep adding a half per cent or one per cent through each of these steps to our growth rates.

Clearly a large part of the financial instability and crisis that the global world faced is behind us. We are seeing stability in the financial markets. But that is not enough. Last year's impact on the world economic order is going to be a shift in economic powers. The Asian economies and emerging economies because of certain inherent structural advantages that they started with and because of their demographic base and domestic consumption are now going to drive the next phase of growth.

Over the next decade, world economic growth is going to be driven by countries like India. We should make it a point not just to participate in that growth but to catalyze that growth.

Moderator | **R. Sukumar**

Editor, Mint

R. Sukumar: Anshu, what are the risk factors for the recovery from the global point of view? What could stop this recovery from continuing?

Anshu Jain: It's a bit like an autoimmune reaction. The patient had a serious disease, Chanda used the heart analogy, I will go along with that. What happened was this: global policy makers realized within three weeks of letting Lehman go that they had made a titanic mistake. Because of that incredible feeling of humility, they responded together. President Bush talked about the G20 summit in November. I remember it well because we were all sitting over there wondering what was going to come out. Our fear at that time was that they wouldn't take it seriously enough. That was the wrong fear to have. In hindsight, you can actually say that they perhaps acted with too much vigour.

The amount of liquidity which has been pumped into global systems is something we now need to worry about. Quantitative easing, a term that you hadn't heard before, has led to trillions of dollars being pumped into the market. So the number one fear you should have is that there could be a second bubble forming.

Chanda and I have talked about the significant risk factors which are still out there. The US dollar is something we have to watch very carefully. Inflation is something which the US needs to watch carefully, and so does India. Food and energy inflation galloping out of control is something we need to watch. Recession is losing something which you could have. Fareed Zakaria spoke last week at an event where he memorably said, "Inflation takes away what you have today, and yet we are creating perfect dynamics for runaway galloping inflation."

Our markets are not reflecting these risk factors enough. I

think there are a number of things for us to watch very carefully. But the chief one for me is the Western questioning around free market enterprise, capitalism, free trade and globalization – the very things which have made the West powerful. These are being questioned without a clear solution. If I were to talk about the one thing which I worry about the most, it's the thing India battled with for thirty years. The US is battling with it for the first time and it's a very alien feeling for it.

R. Sukumar: And, they're doing it without an alternative in sight.

Anshu Jain: Without a clear alternative. These geniuses out there, these prominent, eminent economists are saying that perhaps the free market system doesn't work; perhaps capitalism has its flaws, and of course it does. But I have yet to hear any of them come out with a system which is superior or replaces it as opposed to saying that we have the best system which happens to have flaws like every other system. We move on with our faith reaffirmed. There is a questioning of the very preset of these important concepts which I think is too high a price to pay.

R. Sukumar: That kind of questioning doesn't seem to be happening in India. I don't think anyone is questioning those fundamentals, or are they?

Chanda Kochhar: I think even Indians would get impacted with this kind of questioning. There is clearly a trend. In fact, I would use a stronger term to say that it is getting to be a nationalistic kind of trend. In the financial world, in some of these Western countries, there is a feeling that if you are raising money here then you must utilize the funds in this country itself. Now clearly, as Anshu said, this is not a good trend because in the short term it may look like a trend that would probably be helpful for those countries but in the long term it is not going to be helpful for those countries either. The world has to finally emerge as a global world. So clearly I think this is a very strong trend that is emerging which is not going to be good for the world as a whole.

R. Sukumar: Do both of you see this in some way affecting Indian financial sector reforms? A lot of things need to be done, both in

terms of allowing Indian institutions to go outside, and in allowing multinational financial institutions to come into the country and operate with the kind of freedom with which they should ideally operate in a free market. Do you see this affecting us?

Anshu Jain: There are two ways India can respond to what has just happened. We have all exhibited optimism, starting with President Bush. India has come out of this very well. In fact, there is a thought that this reordering of the world economic order is going to be accelerated by the crisis. Hence the crisis may bring forward India's arrival on centrestage. I believe that. We can see that those estimates of BRIC economies overtaking the West have been brought forward by five to six years. China is going to now overtake the US eight years sooner than what the BRICs report had estimated. India is going to be a bigger economy than Japan by 2020. Those estimates have been brought forward.

We can reach one or two conclusions. Either we believe that there are some fundamental structural advantages which India enjoys which were not created through policy – at least not most of them – but just happen to be the natural contours of the Indian economy. This has held India in very good stead. But instead of basking in that glory one should take advantage of what has happened and over the decade embrace the changes with confidence. Go after the world economic order; embrace capitalism just as the West starts to question it. That sets up the best possible platform.

Alternatively, you can turn around and look at the specific policy steps we have taken in the last ten years. Unquestionably, restraining the leverage in the banking sector, particularly keeping a lot of leverage entering real estate, have been some very wise moves made by Indian policy makers. That's terrific. But it is in the past. We now need to look forward.

The most fatal mistake India could make is to take the trend of the last five years and have that strengthen the hands of the recidivists, perhaps even going as far as saying that we should continue to shun foreign influences; that 56 per cent domestic consumption is so good and we can bank on it for so long that perhaps we are fine where we are in our cocoon. I don't see a lot of it in business thinking. But we have just to make sure the policy makers, don't for too long enjoy the strong position that we have. They must acknowledge it as the historical contour of this country and do the things that need to be done to move India forward.

Chanda Kochhar: It is not going to be an advantage for India to assume a role sitting in its cocoon. We should learn from whatever good has happened in the past. But at the same time we must understand that for future one has to have open policies. One thing India would keep in mind, I hope, is to avoid the two extremes and operate on the basis of reciprocity. Even if you look at just the banking world or the financial services world, it is going to be more advisable to say, "Let's take a country-by-country approach". With countries that are more open, we will have to have policies that are more open. Where we don't see so much reciprocity, we will have to devise our policies accordingly. In the current scenario, that would be a wiser move.

R. Sukumar: Reciprocity is a good way to go about it. Both of you mentioned inflation and part of the recovery is because of the fiscal and monetary stimulus that governments and central banks around the world undertook in the wake of the events of 2008. We see a lot of those central banks now thinking in terms of moving away from that. The Reserve Bank of India's recent monetary policy was definitely hawkish. It clearly hinted that the easy money policy might be coming to an end, which is understandable given that inflation is a concern. But could this really crimp the recovery? That's really the dilemma, isn't it? How do you strike a balance?

Anshu Jain: You have to be extremely concerned about inflation. One has to understand the central banks and their history. If you look at the composition of the Fed, most of them are students of post recession era economics. All the analysis that we have read in the West talks about the lessons of 1929. One of those lessons was that the easy monetary condition which was created to protect Western economies was withdrawn too early, leading to a second recession. Post 1929, there was a ten-year slowdown.

The errors that the West is likely to make, in my opinion, are skewed heavily towards letting this easy monetary policy continue for too long. What are the perils of that? Effective interest rates in the US right now are zero. They are targeting 0.25. Effective overnight rates are zero. That's a very perverse set of circumstances. You don't have natural economic conditions when you can borrow money at close to zero on an overnight basis. The equity market rally that you are seeing, and which we are all enjoying and basking in, is the credit rally that we are saying is not efficient.

Now to an extent we needed those healthy doses of antibiotics to cure the horrible disease we contracted last year. But at some point this needs to be reversed. There is no text book on this reversal of artificial liquidity because the scale of this intervention is unprecedented. There is no rule book on it. If they get it wrong by leaving things too liquid for too long, the inflationary consequences, particularly on food and energy inflation, is something developing countries will have to be very careful about.

There are vast inequalities of wealth in countries like India. Food and energy inflation affects the poorest the most. Take a look at the bottom 40 per cent of the population and what it spends on food and energy. If you wind up with a system where artificial overnight injections of liquidity create uncontrollable inflation, the political and social ramifications of that in the form of very high food and energy inflation can be something that developing countries will have to worry about and, frankly, have very little control over. So compared to everything else that India can influence, this is one area where India will be a hostage to global demand patterns.

R. Sukumar: Chanda, how do you see the inflation growth equation?

Chanda Kochhar: Inflation is definitely a concern. Inflation in real terms is really a bigger concern than what the numbers show because we normally measure WPI (Wholesale Price Index). But if you see on the consumer side, inflation is already much higher. Some of the numbers even on WPI today are looking smaller because of the base effect and so on.

But clearly there is a huge challenge here as far as inflation is concerned. In an economy like ours what is going to be important is how we manage the right balance between inflation and growth. For India, part of this inflation can only get cured as we create capacity and supply. Creation of supply and creation of capacity, in a way, also breeds inflation. This is a very complex equation that we are living with and it's really going to be very important for us to manage this equation well.

So far, I should compliment regulators, policy makers and the government for taking a very balanced approach. Even if you look at RBI's statements on monetary policy, it has said that it is looking at both. While inflation is a concern, while the policy may sound like a very hawkish policy and while there are indications of an exit from the soft policy, the actual exits that have been made are the ones which will not destabilize liquidity and prevent growth from taking place.

So far we have been taking a very balanced approach. It's not a very easy equation to solve. But how we manage it, is going to impact our growth process. The only comfort I can derive is that so far we have been managing it pretty well.

R. Sukumar: I am going to throw the field open for questions.

Q: This question is to you, Anshu. Being a big part of a large multinational, conventional planning processes have been set aside this year. We have really been managing quarter-on-quarter and the focus is cash. Cash is king. How do we plan for the next year? There are two schools. The first says, "The optimists say the recovery is a V or maybe a U, so let's factor it into the planning process and get back to investment mode." The second, to which you have alluded, fears the double dip, which is a W and says, "Continue to navel gaze, manage quarter-on-quarter and this could become self-fulfilling where we don't plan for investments." I want to have your views as you move around in the world. How many people you meet are optimistic and how many continue to fear another big crash?

Anshu Jain: Your question allows me to tackle the implied opinion which is not right. I am not calling for a W at all. I think this recovery is for real. I think GDP growth rates in the West are unlikely to go back to negative any time soon.

However, positive GDP growth by itself is not enough. It's a jobless recovery. We have very significant political intervention in banking. So while the heart has stabilized, as Chanda says, it is not functioning as well as it normally should. Credit creation isn't back. Securitization is being tampered with by excessive intervention from the outside. My advice to a multinational is: continue to do what you are doing. Your inventory is on the rise. But for that, recovery would not have turned as quickly as it has. The 3.5 per cent that we have just seen in the US is thanks to multinationals. The best way to measure that is rising inventory levels.

The second part of your question was how do you finance it? Cash continues to be king. So to an extent holding liquidity and making sure you have contingency planning around capital would be a wise thing to do.

So, I am not calling for a W. I am calling for a square root, which is a long bumpy ride back up.

Q: Anshu, India needs about $400 billion of infrastructure equity in the next ten years. The expectation is that 30 per cent of this will come from foreign capital. When I speak to private equity investors in the US and elsewhere, the returns they are getting in their countries in railroads, for instance, is 16 to 18 per cent. They say, "Why should we go to a new country where we don't understand the risk; we don't understand the regulations and then, maybe, get one or two per cent points more of return?" If infrastructure is indeed important for us to get back on the 9 per cent growth path, what are the sources of private equity capital globally?

Anshu Jain: India saves 35 per cent. It invests 46 per cent already. There is a gap between savings and investments today and that's without making the infrastructure investments which are so crucial.

Let's take a look at a negative example of poor infrastructure investment. Argentina spent much more than they could afford. It built things which it didn't need. With India, infrastructure is badly needed. This is investment that is going to be highly productive. It will come back in the form of rapid GDP growth. The macro case for infrastructure could not be stronger and this is well recognized by the West.

Interest in India is back. I was in New York three weeks ago talking about the West and they wanted to talk to me about India. That has not been the case for the past eighteen months. The chief positive that India offers is the reciprocation for all the reasons that we have just talked about. It offers a different set of bets than the Western bets which they have already invested in.

Gone are the days when India's 14 per cent to 15 per cent looked good. Western economies, because of depressed valuations, are offering mid-teens again. Two things are crucial. India will have to rely on public-private partnerships. The government will have to play a very important role and this investment will need to be made using proper implementation of the rules of law. People need to feel that long-term infrastructure contracts are sacrosanct, important to the government and will be well-protected. Otherwise, the cost of capital will be around 25 to 30 per cent which India cannot afford.

R. Sukumar: Chanda, what are your comments? Where is infrastructure funding going to come from?

Chanda Kochhar: The Indian domestic savings rate is one source but, capital markets and foreign inflow of funds are an important source too. The more of those we get, the faster our investment in infrastructure can take place. What we have to look at is how do we move from 6.5 to 9 and 10 per cent? The more we can accelerate infrastructure investment, the faster we can get to that growth rate.

What is important is for the government to create a facilitative environment that enables people to come in. Interest in India is there. The growth story of India is well known. But even today there are concerns in certain sectors of infrastructure: Is the policy environment going to be conducive enough so that the investment will continue generating returns for the next 10 to 15 years?

I see a lot of intent on the part of the government to make this facilitative environment. But, look at the roads and highways sector. Everything in the contracts and agreements -- in the way termination clauses and dispute settlement clauses are defined – would prevent people from putting in money. They don't know how disputes will be settled, if they arise two years down the road. If we create that kind of facilitative environment, I think we will indeed see money coming in.

Q: We have been hearing a lot of talk about review of the stimulus package in India. What do you think are going to be the short- and medium-term impact on consumption and the investments that we talked about? Secondly, it is good to hear that car sales are going up in India. But do you think it is the right way to go? Without proper infrastructure, will it inhibit growth that requires a pollution-free environment?

Chanda Kochhar: The stimulus package that happened in India actually made sure that growth continues and that liquidity doesn't get tightened. But we must remember that even other initiatives, which may not so apparently look like a stimulus package, gave more people purchasing power that kept consumption going. For instance, the increase in salaries under the Sixth Pay Commission and NREGA (National Rural Employment Guarantee Act) gave more people more purchasing power. It was that purchasing power that kept consumption going.

It is the impact of so many measures that helped move the Indian economy in the way it has moved in the last one year. It is important, of course, that domestic consumption continues to be strong. We will have to watch what impact the monsoons will have on rural consumption. But, broadly we will be able to keep the momentum if domestic consumption continues to be strong.

If we look at the past ten years in India, we have seen that people are changing cars much faster than they previously did. People are buying homes at a much earlier age than previously happened. That is what has driven the economic growth of India for the last ten years. The good part of that growth was that people were not buying cars or homes in excess of their repayment capability. The difference is that ten or twenty years ago, people used to save for their entire working life so that by retirement they had enough money to buy a home. Today, people prefer to buy a home while in their early 30s, if they can, through EMIs or other means. They would rather buy their homes in their 30s, not 50s. But they never went to the extent of being like US consumers, where they used that home like an ATM machine, going every year to the bank and saying: "The value of my home has gone up, so I can borrow some more and use that money to pay off last year's debt."

The point is where do you take your consumption? In India we took consumption and accelerated it based on affordability, not on excessive leverage. That has worked well for the Indian economy.

In Conversation with Vir Sanghvi

▪

Kareena Kapoor

▪

Saif Ali Khan

▪

Moderator

Vir Sanghvi

Advisory Editorial Director, Hindustan Times

Kareena Kapoor

Indian Actor

Kareena Kapoor is the only actress to feature in the *Filmfare* power list. This makes her the number one actress in India and also the most powerful. Kareena wears her status lightly and believes that success does not come from chasing numbers or power but from doing her best at all times. Her mantra is: 'To be the best, you have to do your best.'

She chooses her projects with care, whether it is the movies she signs or the brands she endorses. Her roles as Pooja in Karan Johar's *Kabhi Khushi Kabhie Gham* and as Geet in Imtiaz Ali's *Jab We Met* are two of the most iconic performances in contemporary Indian cinema.

Pooja and Geet symbolize urban and small-town India respectively, while also showcasing Kareena's versatility and her appeal across both India and Bharat. Chips manufacturer Frito-Lay leveraged this to its advantage in a commercial for Kurkure Desi Beats where Kareena goes from playing a spoilt urban brat to a hearty *desi* daughter of the soil. Other brands in Kareena's portfolio include Airtel, Anne French, Gitanjali, Head & Shoulders, Chronotech watches and Vivel.

Kareena had four movies in 2009. *Kambakht Ishq* was a commercial blockbuster. *Kurbaan, Main Aur Mrs Khanna* and *3 Idiots* followed. The movies conveyed her range, going from romantic comedy to intense drama, from the gregarious to the introspective. They also convey how this actress is a magnet for big studios and production houses. While most actresses vie to work with one Khan (Aamir, Saif, Shah Rukh and Salman), she has worked, in a single year, with all four: each is a legend in his own right.

Her forthcoming films include the action thriller *Agent Vinod* and the Indian remake of *Stepmom*, where she plays Julia Roberts' role.

You could say Kareena is India's pretty woman: youth icon, fashion icon and global icon all in one.

Saif Ali Khan

Indian Actor

In a country where the two biggest passions are cricket and cinema, Saif Ali Khan combines both. He was born to Mansoor Ali Khan Pataudi, the dashing and celebrated cricket captain of India, and Sharmila Tagore, Hindi cinema's legendary beauty. Not that Saif took fame for granted. He chose to forge his own path and has spoken in a voice and sensibility that is uniquely his own.

Saif's stellar performances have included his work in *Dil Chahta Hai, Kal Ho Naa Ho, Hum Tum, Parineeta* and *Omkara*, to mention but a few. Far from resting on his laurels, he has continued to take risks with edgy films like *Ek Hasina Thi* and *Being Cyrus*, which was one of the most successful English language films in India. With *Love Aaj Kal*, Saif turned producer with Illuminati Films and chose to mount an ambitious movie that straddled love across two generations. Once again, he was rewarded with both box office success and critical acclaim.

Saif's unique appeal has endeared him to brands as diverse as Airtel, General Motors, Head & Shoulders, Lay's, Asian Paints, Seagram's Royal Stag, and Taj Mahal Tea.

VIR SANGHVI: LET ME START WITH THE OBVIOUS QUESTION. DID YOU KNOW YOU WERE GOING TO BE AN ACTOR WHEN YOU WERE GROWING UP?

Saif Ali Khan: No, most certainly not. I had dreams of being a cricketer following in my father's footsteps. I think I also thought about the army.

Vir Sanghvi: Why the army?

Saif Ali Khan: I do not know. A part of my family lives in Pakistan. My cousins used to play army games and we would get very distressed when we thought that we might have to shoot each other. Then I realized that I don't have to join the army.

Vir Sanghvi: You can fight with them in cricket.

Saif Ali Khan: Yeah, and it was all very pleasant.

Vir Sanghvi: Were you a good cricketer when you were young?

Saif Ali Khan: Comparatively, no.

Vir Sanghvi: Compared to whom?

Saif Ali Khan: Compared to other kids, I was decent. I played for school. But in the family I belong to, I would be called a rubbish player.

Vir Sanghvi: Was there a stage when you said to yourself, "I am never going to be good enough to play for India or be as good as my father, so I should do something else?"

Saif Ali Khan: Yes, I think it happened very early, before public school. I must have been about twelve or thirteen-years-old when I realized that being good at cricket is a gift from God. It's not just a question of what you want to do or how much you work on it. It is something you need to be born with. It's what Sachin Tendulkar has. Abba [father] played with one eye.

Vir Sanghvi: He was really, really outstanding.

Saif Ali Khan: Yes, he would have been another story altogether with both eyes.

Vir Sanghvi: That's right. He would have been like a Bradman someday. Both your parents are famous. Were they role models when you were growing up? Which did you like more: the world of Bollywood and acting or the world of cricket?

Saif Ali Khan: I actually liked the world of cricket more. When I was growing up, there was not much television in India except for Doordarshan and they used to telecast films only once in a while. I saw my mother's movies when I was very young and I remember watching *Mausam*. It distressed me a lot.

Vir Sanghvi: Why?

Saif Ali Khan: The kind of roles that she would play would be quite often those of tormented women. I didn't like to see her cry. I found her films to be slightly troubling to me and I did not watch them.

Vir Sanghvi: Was there a phase when you said, "It is going to be movies for me," or did it come gradually?

Saif Ali Khan: I have always loved films. I loved American films and I watched all the movies in the video shop, particularly Clint Eastwood films and action movies. I knew as a child that I wanted to be part of a moment in cinema with the right background music and the right shot and something immortal which I could watch later on DVD.

Vir Sanghvi: Kareena, you, of course, grew up as a Kapoor, which brings with it many responsibilities. When did you know that you would be an actress?

Kareena Kapoor: From the time that I was in my mother's womb I knew I wanted to face the camera.

Vir Sanghvi: Really? Why?

Kareena Kapoor: Apart from movies running in my veins, everything around me was about movies when I was growing up. All I would do is watch my grandfather's films, watch Nargisji and all the olden day actresses – Saifu's mom and Saira Banuji. For me it was just unbelievable: the dancing, the singing and the different roles. I wanted to do that since I was nine or ten-years-old.

Vir Sanghvi: Did you have any favourites? You don't have to be politically correct and say Sharmila Tagore was your favourite.

Kareena Kapoor: Actually, earlier it was Madhubala and more recently, Sridevi.

Vir Sanghvi: Between Madhubala and Sridevi there is a huge gap. What about the in-between generation?

Kareena Kapoor: I am not just saying this because Saifu is sitting here, but I identified most with Sharmilaji because she mixed glamour with great cinema like *Apur Sansar* and *Mausam.*

Vir Sanghvi: She was the only one who could make the jump from Satyajit Ray to dancing roles.

Kareena Kapoor: Absolutely. She was stunning in *An Evening in Paris.* I want to follow that path.

Vir Sanghvi: You've said that the nice part is that you have talent. The bad part was that you were like a filmy child growing up.

Kareena Kapoor: Not a filmy child because mom and dad actually made an effort to see that we grew up in the Bombay side, on Nepean Sea Road. We were sent to Cathedral school. Mom always encouraged me a little bit but she was strict about things like reading and no TV after 6 o'clock. But I would find a way to sneak out of bed and flip channels desperately trying to find a Hindi movie.

Vir Sanghvi: Were you good in studies or were you like a filmy child?

Kareena Kapoor: No. You are repeatedly asking me I was a filmy child but, no, I was not. I was actually quite a bright student.

Vir Sanghvi: That doesn't surprise me but often people don't have an interest in studies.

Kareena Kapoor: Well, I don't read many books. My interest level is not that of Saif's. But I was a good student. I did pretty well, averaging 70 to 75 per cent which is not bad.

Saif Ali Khan: Which is more than mine, by the way.

Vir Sanghvi: So, you've inherited your brains from your mother's side of the family on the whole. Karan Johar has said that your character, 'Poo' in Kabhi Khushi Kabhie Gham was in many ways a reflection of your personality. Is that accurate?

Kareena Kapoor: In *Kabhi Khushi Kabhie Gham*, Poo was bratty but at the same time a very lovable cute girl.

Vir Sanghvi: You were happy with the character then.

Kareena Kapoor: I was happy then.

Vir Sanghvi: I remember I interviewed you when the movie came out and you said it was so easy to do the role because it just fit in. I asked if you really looked at yourself in the mirror and said, "How dare you be so beautiful." You gave me a very vague answer to that question.

Kareena Kapoor: Well, ten years ago I wouldn't look in the mirror and say "God, you're so beautiful," because I was.

Vir Sanghvi: Really.

Kareena Kapoor: But now...

Vir Sanghvi: ...But now you're actually much better.

Kareena Kapoor: Of course I am better. I am thin and glamorous.

Vir Sanghvi: Saif, did you think you are good looking?

Saif Ali Khan: No.

Vir Sanghvi: Why not?

Saif Ali Khan: My mother had a very movie-style dressing table with her brushes and things lying around on it. I was sitting in front of it one day admiring my hair and my father walked in and asked me when I was planning on getting it cut. So, I never thought of myself as good looking. I hoped to finally grow into a swan. Actually, I wouldn't say that I was an ugly duckling but I was a slightly gawky teenager.

Vir Sanghvi: I may be betraying family confidence here, but your father told me that when you were growing up he was constantly evicting woman from your room in the evening. So, what was it: women like ugly guys?

Saif Ali Khan: Ugly guys look for reassurance a little too much. Yes, he was evicting women.

Vir Sanghvi: So, you were a sort of sexy guy, much sought after?

Saif Ali Khan: Yes, in the sense that I did a lot of seeking and once in a while people were pliable.

Vir Sanghvi: When you did join films, you did okay in the beginning and then you went through a really bad patch. How many flops in a row was that?

Saif Ali Khan: About seventeen.

Vir Sanghvi: Did you want to say, "Forget this. I am not good at it and I need to do something else?"

Saif Ali Khan: Right from the start there was something about this job that was the only thing in life for me. I have a problem of not being able to concentrate too much on the same thing for too long. This was a problem in school and a problem that everyone thought would affect my career. Basically, I was not very academically inclined.

When I got my first film offer, I was living in Delhi. I was so excited to go to Bombay and actually move into my own apartment and get a job that entailed meeting new people, doing different things, playing different characters, working different hours, and not being fixed into any kind of routine.

Vir Sanghvi: But it was a very different world for you. I remember meeting you in those days.

Saif Ali Khan: I had burnt every bridge. There was nothing else I could possibly have done. I hadn't gone to college. So my options were severely limited when it came to getting a job. I knew that somehow or the other I had to become a successful actor. I told myself, "I love this world and even though I am not very good at it and am alien to it, I am going to give it everything I have."

Vir Sanghvi: I remember you had just come back from England and still spoke with a slight English accent. Your mannerisms were very different from everybody else in the industry. In many ways, even though you were Sharmila Tagore's son, you were a misfit in the industry.

Saif Ali Khan: Absolutely. It is only because the films changed that I was able to survive.

Vir Sanghvi: So, 17 flops. What was that like?

Saif Ali Khan: It was a crazy time because there was such a big disconnect between the directors and the people I was working with. The time was also different. This is about seventeen years ago when an average actor would have about eighteen films on the floor at the same time, running from one studio to another. The barometer of success was not how well a film did, but how many films you were doing. Shashi Kapoorji, Kareena's uncle was nicknamed Taxi at one point because he was doing so many.

I don't understand how people play different characters when they are playing six characters in a day. I didn't really understand the people I was working with. The concept, the idea of a film director or producer was some *paan* chewing, white-clad person; not the most intellectual or respectable figure.

That has changed now. Whether it is Karan Johar or Farhan Akhtar, there are many people who you would be proud to have conversation with about the art and cinema that represents our country. Of course, I was rubbish as well. I mean we both didn't understand each other.

Vir Sanghvi: Was there a struggle to keep finding work as the flops accumulated?

Saif Ali Khan: No. We make so many films that it was always possible to get something and I always chose the best of what I was offered. But there were some pretty dark days. I would think, this has to get better. I mean, there was a time when I had to pull a big white rat out of my trousers as a part of something called the rat song.

Vir Sanghvi: Was it a real rat?

Saif Ali Khan: Yes.

Vir Sanghvi: You put a real rat down your trousers?

Kareena Kapoor: You did not tell me this.

Vir Sanghvi: Would it have made a difference?

Kareena Kapoor: No. Yes.

Vir Sanghvi: This is a rude question, but why were you required to put a rat down your trousers?

Saif Ali Khan: It will take me a long time to answer that question. It goes back to the time when you couldn't show onscreen kissing and so we had a lot of songs with double meanings. Fortunately, it was a rat and not a mouse. I was playing a dance instructor and was dancing in Essel World in the heat with a beard and suddenly

I had burned every bridge ... I hadn't gone to college. So getting a job. I knew that somehow or the other I had

there was this line, "*Tumhare peeche mera chuha bhagega (*my rat will run after you),"– or something like that.

They have all done it. Every actor has a *chuha* story. I think Amitji has done it with a rooster in *Jadugar*.

Vir Sanghvi: Kareena Kapoor, your years of struggle are not going to make a very long book, right?

Kareena Kapoor: No. For me, it was too much because I had added responsibility. Everything I did was put under microscope: what is she doing? What role is she playing? Why is her film not doing well? Why is she acting in this movie?

Vir Sanghvi: But did you have a lot of flops?

Kareena Kapoor: Of course I had. In fact, in my short career, there are about 16 to 17.

Saif Ali Khan: But they are much better looking flops than mine.

Vir Sanghvi: And no rats. Did they happen in a row? Was there a phase when people said she does not measure up to her sister's record?

Kareena Kapoor: There was a phase definitely. The media kept writing me off before *Jab We Met*. But I was choosing the best from what I was getting. I think films also have changed from what they used to be. I have been working for ten years. Today, women in Indian cinema get very different roles from what they used to get when I started out.

Vir Sanghvi: Were there days when you would worry when your films were about to be released or were you quite cool about it?

Kareena Kapoor: Initially there were days when I would be really stressed out and have sleepless nights. There was an article once in a newspaper that said, "Kareena Kapoor is finished". I cried all night when I read it. In the morning my mom asked me why had

my options were severely limited when it came to to become a successful actor. – Saif Ali Khan

I been crying. I showed her the article and she got so upset with me. She said, "I cannot believe that you are succumbing and just giving in to all this. You should be working harder. Just do your work, and be true to yourself. Believe in yourself and your dreams." From that day onwards, I really don't take what anybody writes seriously.

Vir Sanghvi: Was your sister a role model?

Kareena Kapoor: Of course. I owe 60 per cent of what I am to her. I would hang around her sets, looking at her behind the camera all the time, absorbing, trying to realize what I want to do.

Vir Sanghvi: And she is actually a good role model to have because she was always very sensible. She never let success go to her head.

Kareena Kapoor: Absolutely. I have yet to see any other Indian actress have the kind of dedication and perseverance that Karisma had. I lived with her. I know what kind of woman she is.

Vir Sanghvi: She has no airs and graces. She is a very normal person, which is very unusual in your business.

Kareena Kapoor: Absolutely.

Vir Sanghvi: Saif, was your mother a role model or was her career too far back in time to have made an impact on you?

Saif Ali Khan: When I was younger I came to the realization that I had the worst qualities of both my parents, which worried me. Now, I think I am trying to imbibe the best qualities of both of them because I know them so much better.

Vir Sanghvi: You have your mother's brain surely as an actor. You can do *Omkara* and you can do something quite light.

Saif Ali Khan: I respect Amma's work tremendously. But I am a totally different kind of actor.

Vir Sanghvi: One of your distinguishing characteristics, as Kareena said, is range. You have shown that in your career as well.

Saif Ali Khan: Unfortunately, cinema seems to be divided into two. I don't know why it is so, but you have what they call art cinema and you have commercial cinema. It should just be cinema. One thing that I have learnt from Amma is that doing more thoughtful cinema increases your span, your lifespan and your longevity. You are taken more seriously and the benefits are tremendous too.

Vir Sanghvi: Your generation has it easy in many ways: you can do commercials and live shows. You don't have to do crap films only for the money. Older actors had to do that. You guys still make a lot of money.

Saif Ali Khan: Nothing really changes. Names change, things get a little funkier, the colours get brighter. But the basic thread remains the same. There are still people who will at some point in time do films basically for the money, depending on their circumstances or how much money is offered.

Vir Sanghvi: You make an average of how many films?

Saif Ali Khan: Two to three; one to two.

Vir Sanghvi: That's a very small amount, isn't it?

Saif Ali Khan: It has become that way because films take a lot of time. It also depends on who is the producer.

Vir Sanghvi: Which is what you are trying to become with a big hit, *Love Aaj Kal*.

Saif Ali Khan: Yes, and I am very thankful for that. But I also realized the amount of work that goes into a movie before it goes onto the floor and after it's done. I see Kareena working. She has three films coming out and she is trying to dub, shoot and promote all at the same time. It's insane. I can't do it anymore. I would like to pre-produce a film or get involved in it before I shoot it. After that I would try and sell it. These are three different areas that require a lot of concentration. You can't be in three places at the same time. They take a lot of work and a lot of time. Your life is on hold while you are doing it.

Vir Sanghvi: Also as a producer you have to manage people, make arrangements, which as an actor you don't necessarily have to do.

Saif Ali Khan: Certainly being a producer entails much more responsibility. I would be lying if I said I do it all myself. I have a partner who does most of that. But the creative responsibility is mine. Very often on a set you are sitting around wondering why nothing is happening because you have to drive it. It needs to be organized.

Vir Sanghvi: Kareena, are you ever going to produce your own movies?

Kareena Kapoor: No. Saif is going to produce them and I am just going to act in them hopefully.

Vir Sanghvi: You are not a business-minded person?

Kareena Kapoor: No. I don't think I can handle the full financial aspect.

Saif Ali Khan: But she does know more about the business than most people, at least more than most girls. She also knows which cameraman shoots how, with which lens, she knows what kind of lighting pattern is better.

Vir Sanghvi: So, it's not just the business side. It's the actual creative side.

Saif Ali Khan: It is a creative side. She is deeply committed and an intelligent actor, which I think is genetic.

Kareena Kapoor: I am interested in what the director is doing or the angles of photography; how am I going to look. We have to raise the bar ourselves. It is important and I am interested in that. I want to look good. I want to know how a scene is going to be edited and what is going to come out of it. So many times you read a script and it doesn't really turn out like that on screen. So I think an actor needs to take an active interest to be involved

I am interested in what the director is doing or the We have to raise the bar ourselves. It is important

and to know whether it is an advertisement or whether it is in the show or on screen.

Vir Sanghvi: Do you see yourself moving behind the camera at some stage? You are Raj Kapoor's granddaughter after all. Not many would remember that your father also was an excellent director.

Kareena Kapoor: As of now, I don't see myself doing that at all. The roles that I am getting are really exciting. I just want to get totally involved in them right now. But in the future, who knows?

Vir Sanghvi: When you were growing up, were you very conscious of being a Kapoor, of the whole Kapoor legacy?

Kareena Kapoor: I wasn't really conscious of it. But my parents kept drilling in us that we have certain responsibilities. But I think

I am quite a rebel in the family.

Vir Sanghvi: Give me an instance. You don't drink a lot, but apart from that?

Kareena Kapoor: I am a pure vegetarian. That's completely against the legacy.

Vir Sanghvi: Hot tempered?

Kareena Kapoor: No, not really hot tempered. Saif, am I hot tempered?

Saif Ali Khan: I am wondering how to get out of this question.

Vir Sanghvi: So, I take that as a yes.

Saif Ali Khan: She is very patient.

Kareena Kapoor: I have pretty much lived my life on my own terms.

angles of the photography; how I am going to look. and I am interested in that. I want to look good.

– Kareena Kapoor

Saif Ali Khan: There are obviously many things that would probably be private about the way she feels and the things that she will do. But I don't think anyone can really get Kareena to do something she does not want to do.

Vir Sanghvi: So, you are a free spirit in that sense?

Kareena Kapoor: Absolutely.

Vir Sanghvi: You don't take kindly to being dictated to?

Kareena Kapoor: Only from my directors. Not from anyone else.

Vir Sanghvi: Since your success, many things have been said about you. One of them most notoriously has been about your weight. Are you a size zero?

Kareena Kapoor: No, I am not a size zero.

Vir Sanghvi: Were you ever?

Kareena Kapoor: No, I never was. The fact is that everyone else termed my weight loss as a size zero.

Saif Ali Khan: I have been shopping with her and she has never bought a size zero.

Vir Sanghvi: He would know, right?

Kareena Kapoor: He buys my dresses and shoes. What do you think?

Saif Ali Khan: There was never size zero.

Kareena Kapoor: I lost a lot of weight for my role in *Tashan*. It was required.

Vir Sanghvi: How much weight did you lose?

Kareena Kapoor: From about 58 kilos, I came down to about 50.

Vir Sanghvi: Pretty much on the edge of malnutrition. Did you have to lose that much weight?

Kareena Kapoor: No, not at all.

Vir Sanghvi: They wrote about you being fat in *Don* and that really did it?

Kareena Kapoor: No. There were people who said I looked a little overweight in a song. I took it badly.

Vir Sanghvi: And decided to lose weight? That is the real reason?

Kareena Kapoor: That and the fact I wanted to do something that would get people around me to say that I lost weight for a role. In the same way I could probably gain weight.

Vir Sanghvi: Like Robert De Niro?

Kareena Kapoor: I would love to gain weight for a role but...

Vir Sanghvi: ...but there are no such roles?

Kareena Kapoor: There aren't those roles especially for women.

Saif Ali Khan: The dietician has become a superstar.

Vir Sanghvi: Thousands of copies of her book [Rujuta Diwekar's *Don't Lose Your Mind, Lose Your Weight*] have been sold on the basis of an interview that she made you a size zero.

Kareena Kapoor: It is a number one bestseller.

Vir Sanghvi: It is a number one bestseller with a quote from you on the cover. What was that diet all about?

Kareena Kapoor: Cheese, *parathas*, *paneer*...

Saif Ali Khan: It was a pretty sensible diet: eating light every two hours. A healthy breakfast, and then a couple of hours later eat something else – six meals a day.

Kareena Kapoor: Earlier I would eat four *parathas* with butter. On the diet it was more like two the first week, and then just one the week after that. But she didn't stop me from eating them. The first two to three weeks were tough.

Saif Ali Khan: It was incredibly tough. She would be passing out by 8 in the evenings. It is not easy to change your body type. Habits are engraved in your brain. To change the smallest thing in your lifestyle takes a monumental amount of strength.

Kareena Kapoor: I also did a lot of yoga. I have not entered a gym since the last one and a half to two years. I do lots of *surya namaskars*. There was a time when I would do 100 every day. When I first started with my trainer, I could do eight or ten.

Vir Sanghvi: And you eat normally now?

Kareena Kapoor: I eat a healthy diet. Not many people know this, but I don't enjoy regular vegetables. I like *doodhi ki sabzi* and *daal*. When Saif and me are sitting down to lunch, he says: "What's for lunch? I'm not going to eat *tinda* and *doodhi*."

Vir Sanghvi: You are a non-vegetarian and she is vegetarian? Can you eat out and not have a problem?

Kareena Kapoor: I go to restaurants and eat everything. I eat asparagus and broccoli and mashed potato.

Saif Ali Khan: The point is not being judgemental. You can eat around her.

Vir Sanghvi: How did you guys meet?

Saif Ali Khan: She doesn't remember. I first saw her when she was fourteen-years-old sitting outside her sister's makeup room, staring into space. She gave me an odd look. I asked somebody who she was and they said, "That's Kareena Kapoor. She is going to be a movie star." I replied, "Yes, she probably is."

She looked like a movie star. After that we'd run into each other periodically, at parties. I didn't speak too much. Then, we did a film together where she was very outspoken. She said such funny things which I can't repeat here because they are politically incorrect. But she was very disarming.

I just thought that was refreshing and that was that. We went our separate ways. Then we were signed to do *Tashan* and somebody – he was giving me a foot massage – asked me, "Are you and Kareena seeing each other?" I said, "It is absolute rubbish. I have never met her and I don't know what you are talking about." So, when I saw her on the sets of *Tashan*, I remembered this guy and I told her, "Apparently in the foot massage circle, they are talking about us." She gave me this look and smile, and I thought: "Oh, okay."

Kareena Kapoor: Please, this is embarrassing.

Saif Ali Khan: I am not embarrassing you. So, we spent some time together shooting for the film and we just became more and more friendly.

Vir Sanghvi: One thing led to another?

Saif Ali Khan: Very slowly.

Vir Sanghvi: Slowly is – what – a couple of weeks?

Saif Ali Khan: A little longer than that. Maybe a month or so; maybe a bit longer than that.

Vir Sanghvi: You guys didn't comment on the speculation for a long

time. And then you went to a film premiere together and somebody asked you a question and you replied: "Yes, we are together."

Saif Ali Khan: That was the first time anyone really asked me. I don't know if this is the right place to say this because it's obviously so personal to her. But it was a sensitive time. She had just come out of a relationship. At the same time, I have always believed, and she has too, that to deny a relationship is not the way either of us would really want things to be. If you expect respect from other people, then you have to respect your relationship first. So, the first time somebody asked me on camera at Fashion Week, I stammered my way through a sentence saying, "Yes, ah, yeah, ah, yes, I think we are seeing each other."

Vir Sanghvi: Kareena, is that your version of how you two met or is there a significant variation?

Kareena Kapoor: There is always something about Saif right from *Parampara* that I have liked. In fact, I saw *Parampara* quite a number of times because I thought Saif was actually very, very charming and cute.

Saif Ali Khan: That was my gawky phase.

Kareena Kapoor: But I liked your gawky phase.

Vir Sanghvi: Charming and cute or sexy and good-looking?

Kareena Kapoor: Sexy and good-looking in some. When we were shooting *Omkara*, he was very charming, cultured and chivalrous. He was always very sweet. I was in a relationship and he was in a relationship, and whatever people were saying about him, painting him out to be a big Casanova, he never, ever crossed the line. It was always, "Hello ma'am," "Goodbye ma'am."

Saif Ali Khan: Never gave you The Look.

Vir Sanghvi: You called her ma'am?

Saif Ali Khan: Not ma'm. Did I say ma'am?

Kareena Kapoor: Yes, you always say ma'am. Even today on the sets you called me 'ma'am'.

Saif Ali Khan: We save the pet names for the bedroom.

Vir Sanghvi: So, you gave him The Look that started all this?

Kareena Kapoor: Now, it is coming on to me that I gave Saif The Look. Very convenient!

Vir Sanghvi: That's his version.

Saif Ali Khan: We did have a romantic chat under a tree in Ladakh. I would like to see that tree again. And we went for a little walk. We weren't really sure. She wasn't sure what was going in my life. I wasn't sure with what was going on in her life. But we went for a walk, which is unusual for both for us, and we sat under this tree and I was stammering my way through trying to explain that perhaps I shouldn't be getting into a relationship.

Kareena Kapoor: No, actually that's not the word. Under the tree, Saif just looked at me and said, "Listen, I think you and me will be great together." And I said, "What?"

Vir Sanghvi: That doesn't sound like stammering.

Saif Ali Khan: I remember she doesn't like dogs much and suddenly she grabbed me and I thought, "Okay. This is going well." But then I saw that there was a dog behind us. She said, "The dog, the dog."

Vir Sanghvi: So, he said, "We'll be great together." And you said?

Kareena Kapoor: I said that we don't know each other well right now.

Vir Sanghvi: You said demurely and then?

Kareena Kapoor: We continued shooting the film and we got to know each other better and became good friends gradually.

Vir Sanghvi: And when did you get the tattoo? It's still there, right?

Saif Ali Khan: The tattoo? Yeah, it is still very much there.

Vir Sanghvi: Is it a permanent tattoo?

Saif Ali Khan: It's permanent.

Vir Sanghvi: So, you are stuck. Nothing can go wrong.

Saif Ali Khan: I am committed. That was the idea behind getting it. We were sitting in the car in the afternoon in Bandra and talking about, I don't know why, David Beckham. And then the tattoo came up and then I said, "Maybe, I should get one on my shoulder. Would it look cool?" And she said, "Why shoulder? Put it on your arm." I thought maybe a nice 'K' but she said, "It's a bit ambiguous."

I knew under that tree in Ladakh that if I was to take this further it would be very serious. Our families know each other and this was not going to be a fling of some sort. After a point I realized that this is pretty much it for me and the tattoo was my way of saying it.

Vir Sanghvi: So this is it? You guys are going to get married?

Kareena Kapoor: We have not really addressed that issue.

Vir Sanghvi: You must have talked about it.

Kareena Kapoor: We've talked about it. But right now I think Saif wants to set up his production company and I want to do some great roles.

Vir Sanghvi: Which you can't do after you are married?

Kareena Kapoor: Of course, I can.

Vir Sanghvi: His mother worked for many years after she was married.

Saif Ali Khan: There is no rush to get married. And secondly, in today's age, what exactly does that mean. I mean there is legitimacy to children. But the important thing is to be connected, close, have a relationship. We are working; the focus right now is different. Let's face it. I believe that Kareena is at the top of her profession working as an actress in this country. No matter how open-minded we are, I think your career does get impacted with marriage.

So, to take someone who is doing so well and is working so hard and to try and turn her into a housewife is not a very constructive thing to do. I love her for what she is. I enjoy the fact that she is deeply passionate about acting. We manage to get a lot of time together. We are doing very well considering many things. As far as marriage goes, in our profession somehow people will put you into a box and say, "Okay that's done, then." It's more exciting when people ask us when are we going to get married.

Vir Sanghvi: So, it will happen at some stage.

Kareena Kapoor: God willing.

Vir Sanghvi: God willing. Insha'Allah. What does it feel like to be asked these questions and to live your life as the Brad Pitt and Angelina Jolie of India in the constant glare of publicity? Everything you do is talked about, photographed.

Kareena Kapoor: It is very, very tiring. I can't even go to a friend's house without makeup. The last time I got photographed without makeup, everyone went, "Oh, look at Kareena Kapoor. Why can't she wear makeup?" Do they expect me to be in makeup 24 hours a day? Am I not allowed to attend a party without makeup in jeans and t-shirt?

I went to Hrithik Roshan's party in jeans and t-shirt and there was a huge article that said I had no time to put on my makeup. I mean this is my personal time and I might want to go and visit a friend with or without makeup. So for me, it is really exhausting and tiring. We just cannot handle it anymore.

Saif Ali Khan: There has to be a certain amount of disconnect. There is a vast sort of spectrum within media from yellow to slightly more serious colours. We have to just take things with a pinch of salt. There are a lot of publications out there. And if we look at the West, we are still better off. I am waiting to see if the paparazzi will actually arrive in my bathroom. I am surprised they haven't shot somebody there already.

Vir Sanghvi: It will happen. There will be telephoto lenses and all that.

Saif Ali Khan: Not like America when you go on a holiday on a beach somewhere and you are being stalked. I can't believe some of the stuff I read in the *National Enquirer.*

So, yes, some of this goes with the territory and you have to be a bit careful. But part of being a movie star is to find normalcy in your mind.

Kareena Kapoor: Now that *Kurbaan* is releasing, which Saif and I have done together, the question always is, "What's it like to work with each other?" Nobody asks about the film.

Saif Ali Khan: It's the same when we have a press conference to announce a brand endorsement. The questions always are: "Where are you going on holiday?"

Vir Sanghvi: But by now you surely have standard answers for these questions.

Saif Ali Khan: Yes, but I hate that. There are some standard answers but now the time has come to start saying, "Listen, let's focus on our work." The press also realizes that enough is enough. So, you say, "Look, let's not ask personal questions today and let's stick to why we are here."

Moderator | **Vir Sanghvi**

Advisory Editorial Director,
Hindustan Times

Q: Kareena, my kids are very big fans of yours. What are your views as an icon for youth in terms of social challenges and awareness? How do you plan to work around these issues?

Kareena Kapoor: Ever since *Jab We Met*, little girls have been looking up to me. My niece is like that. She just looks at me all day, looking for my picture in the newspapers. So, that does put a lot of responsibility on me. I am answerable to society for whatever I do. But what I really want to do is leave my mark through my roles or in terms of public appearances – what I wear, how I speak. I am definitely more aware now of what I do on screen. I have definitely done films in the past which now make me cringe. Now, I am more conscious about the roles I play.

Q: Saif, where do you see yourself in time to come: more as an actor or as a director-producer?

Saif Ali Khan: I don't think I will direct because the commitment level is something I don't know whether I can do. I like to go home at some point and I don't know if directors do that because when they are not editing, writing, creating, shooting, they are busy inspiring everybody from the spot boy to the main star. You have to pump everybody up and then drive everybody with that vision. I don't know if I can do that. But as far as production goes, I love the creative aspect of being involved and developing ideas for movies. I would like to carry on doing this for a while and when I feel the time has come to shift, I would like to make movies in which I would love to cast other people. Even now I would like to cast other people. Already I am not young enough to play college love stories, which is a staple of Hindi films. So, we would be happy if we get a great script to work with other actors and that's how I see my future.

Q: Kareena, to get to the number one position for any heroine in Bollywood, does she have to pass the size zero milestone?

Kareena Kapoor: Well, it is a challenge that I face. I can proudly say I did it and I think I did it pretty well. But I do not believe in numbers and whatever I am and wherever I am today is thanks to my body of work and not just my body.

Q: When you take on an assignment or endorse a brand, what goes through your mind? Do you see your personality blending with the brand and hence take it up or is it just the size of the commercial offer?

Kareena Kapoor: When I'm endorsing a brand and when I meet the agencies and people who offer us these things, I basically have three conditions: I will not endorse a non-vegetarian product like McDonald's or Burger King. I will not endorse an alcoholic product and I will not endorse tobacco. Apart from that, yes, there is a temptation to earn a little bit of money and, yeah, have fun too.

Saif Ali Khan: I don't think you are allowed to advertise alcohol openly in India. There has to be some kind of surrogate advertising. I actually endorse Seagrams. My take is that it is a question of freedom. But I would draw a line somewhere. I have been offered vast amounts of money to promote tobacco products and Kareena forced me to say no, though I was very tempted. It was a big offer. I could have bought an apartment.

It's not always just the finance. The money can be a barometer of your success. Brands do a lot of research before they come to sign you. If someone like Pepsi wants to sign Kareena or somebody like Lay's wants to sign me, it means that we represent something and there is a fit and a complementary kind of benefit to both the brand and to us. It also helps to do ads for visibility. But the first point that comes to my mind when I am signing an ad is the class of the brand. When you say Head & Shoulders, that is a brand. When you say Lay's or Taj Mahal tea or Asian Paints, there is a connect. But there are some things you don't want to be associated with.

Vir Sanghvi: Such as?

Saif Ali Khan: Underwear.

Vir Sanghvi: So, no VIP *banyan* ads?

Saif Ali Khan: *Banyan*, I might do. But no *chaddies*.

Q: Five years down the line where do you see Indian cinema internationally and intellectually? How would you contribute to it?

Saif Ali Khan: I think we have to stop using that word 'international' in cinema. We have to start focusing on Indian films again. We have to start looking within. We have a different palate. You cannot serve the kind of food that we like to feed to every Westerner. They won't like it. They won't understand it. We have a different rhythm. So, instead of looking to the West, we have to start focusing on our identity. Only when that identity is fully developed, will our films be international.

I see my role as a filmmaker in five years to try and do my best to make the best movies that I can; looking inward, looking at us and to develop that. That is an important lesson that we all need to learn. I hate the word Bollywood. I don't know how it stuck. I don't know how we have allowed to stick. This is the Indian film industry. This is not something that sounds like Hollywood, but has a 'B' instead of an 'H'.

Q: Kareena, after *Jab We Met*, you could have done any role. Why did you pick *Kambakht Ishq*?

Kareena Kapoor: Because I wanted to be glamorous and I wanted to wear those clothes.

Q: Just for the clothes?

Kareena Kapoor: No, but sometimes you do films like that.

Q: You had no role, nothing substantial. Your job was to look pretty.

Kareena Kapoor: But I had something substantial in my bank account and sometimes I do films for that reason.

Q: Saif, I live in Delhi and have seen you around in different places as a teenager. I have seen a tremendous transformation in you over the

last twenty years. So, beyond commercial success, what have been the important milestones in your life? What caused the transformation?

Saif Ali Khan: I think this is something that grows and comes slowly and is still happening for me. Maturity is actually a good word for it. It takes time and then imperceptibly it becomes something else. I think that is what has happened. It comes to everybody with a certain amount of age. Obviously there should be a massive difference between a nineteen-year-old and a thirty-nine-year-old. Also, I have had great influences around me: my parents, for instance. With age you start confronting the fact that all this is going to end one day and you figure out what your responsibilities are, who you are answerable to, what kind of life you want. There has been a slow and steady kind of growth where one is ready for more.

Q: Kareena, you had critically acclaimed roles in three movies, *Omkara*, *Chameli* and *Jab We Met*. Which one did you find most challenging?

Kareena Kapoor: I would say it was *Chameli* because I think I was twenty-three-years-old when I did that role. I had no idea of what the Indian Kamathipura sex worker would be like because what I had seen was English movies and *Pretty Woman*. I did not know the background of a sex worker on the streets of Mumbai. For me, the challenge was getting the lingo and body language right. Also, it was the story of what happens over a single night. That was a new format for me because nobody in Hindi cinema had made a movie based on a conversation that happens between two people. This was the first time that I was working with a director like Sudhir Mishra who is considered very much a part of art cinema. But *Chameli* somewhere did break grounds because it did do well commercially too.

Vir Sanghvi: You want to add to it?

Saif Ali Khan: Not to what Kareena is saying. I suddenly realized that we are talking to so many dignitaries here at the Leadership Summit. I just wanted to say that what has contributed most to my maturity has been actually been success, being a father and being a producer. I am a leader in my own small world, in my little office. All of you are leaders. So, obviously with that comes great responsibility and a maturity where people look up to you, almost as a parent at times, and, of course, we have to then behave accordingly. While we were children we had fun and made a lot of noise.

I think everybody in this room, us in cinema and you in your respective fields has a responsibility to move forward into a new era. We have been talking about it for a long time. We have ads in the airport saying "Incredible India". It is not really that incredible sometimes. But when you are talking about 2020 vision and we have heard all the slogans, please, actually do your best to make us proud.

Between Brickbats and Bouquets

Role of the Opposition

▪

Sukhbir Singh Badal

▪

Sitaram Yechury

▪

Sushma Swaraj

▪

Moderator

Sagarika Ghose

Senior Editor, CNN-IBN

Sukhbir Singh Badal

Deputy Chief Minister of Punjab

Punjab's Deputy Chief Minister Sukhbir Singh Badal joined mainstream politics when he was elected to the Lok Sabha in 1996. He was re-elected to the Lok Sabha in 1998 and served as the Union Minister of State for industries in the Atal Bihari Vajpayee government from 1998 to 1999.

Sukhbir was also Rajya Sabha MP between 2001 and 2004 before being elected again to the Lok Sabha in May 2004.

The president of the Shiromani Akali Dal, Sukhbir wants to make his party a national one. A management graduate from the California State University in Los Angeles, USA, Sukhbir believes in prompt decision-making and aspires to transform Punjab into a modern state with a focus on infrastructure development and big power projects.

The forty-seven-year-old Akali leader is the son of four-time Punjab chief minister Parkash Singh Badal who has been at the centre stage of the state's politics for five decades. Sukhbir who is gradually stepping into his father's shoes has been effectively handling party affairs after he was appointed party president.

His wife, Harsimrat Kaur was also elected as Lok Sabha MP, from Bathinda, in the 2009 elections.

Sukhbir is now focusing on implementation of administrative reforms, setting up power projects and mega infrastructure projects in the state, and strengthening his party for the 2012 Assembly elections.

I WOULD LIKE TO CONGRATULATE THE *HINDUSTAN TIMES* FOR ORGANIZING THIS SUMMIT AND FOR INVITING LEADERS AND DISTINGUISHED PERSONALITIES OVER THE last two days to express their views on various topics.

Today's topic is *The Role of the Opposition*. As Sagarika said, we need to look at the challenges before the Opposition in the year 2020. But before we get into the role of the Opposition and the challenges before it, let us look at our past. India is the largest democracy in the world. The role of the Opposition is critical. The success of our democracy means that the voice of dissent needs to be heard. But if you look at the past, voices of dissent have been historically crushed.

The political scenario of India since Independence can be divided into three phases. During the first phase – the first thirty years – we had a single-party system with a very weak Opposition. The Opposition was fragmented and it was the Congress party all the way. Then came the phase of a strong Opposition, where the Opposition formed a strong party alliance and came to rule. The ruling party became the Opposition. This phase continued for fifteen years. The last phase is what we are going through now, where we do not have strong national parties or national Opposition parties, but there is an emergence of strong regional parties and regional groups.

If you look at the situation, one thing has been clear throughout: the Opposition has always been suppressed whether during the Emergency or while removing Opposition governments. The basic thing we need to understand now is what we need to do and where we have to reach.

What has occurred over the years is the emergence of regional parties and regional groups. Why has this happened? Why has coalition politics come in? Basically, it is because some regions felt their aspirations, views and dreams could be better looked after and expressed with regional parties. That is why you have seen a lot of regional parties come up in the last fifteen to twenty years. The role and power of regional parties has dramatically increased.

Let's look at another question. There is a difference in the role of a national Opposition and the role of regional ruling parties and regional Opposition parties. A regional party or regional Opposition will look at one issue which is important. The national party may not think that issue is important. Some issues which national parties might think are important will be regarded as less important by regional parties. That is why regional parties like us, the Shiromani Akali Dal, have to fight differently and have to raise issues differently.

For instance, in our state, Punjab, the problems faced by the farming community is a priority. We produce more than 50 per cent of the nation's food grains. We are treated as the food producing machine of our country. But, the result is that we are depleting our land, our soil and our rural infrastructure. Our water table levels have gone down. According to NASA, Punjab

With the emergence of regional parties, national politics number, the more power you have.

may become a desert in fifteen years. So, when we present a case to the Central government either as the ruling or Opposition party, we focus on things that might not be a priority of other national-level parties.

Since Independence, no ruling party has got more than 45 per cent of the vote – and that's the highest level of votes. Except for 1984, where the ruling party got 48 per cent of the vote, that percentage has been coming down. The average is more likely to be in the 30s. The majority of people have voted against the ruling party. That is why the role of the Opposition has become important.

Another area which I feel does not get the attention it deserves is the youth of our nation. The population configuration twenty years ago was very different. Today, 60 per cent of the population is below the age of thirty-five. Obviously, the role of the Opposition and the ruling party has to change accordingly.

The roles have changed. Opposition parties no longer have the standard opposition role when there was only one single party. With the emergence of regional parties, national politics has become all about the numbers' game. The bigger the number, the more power you have. Parties that have 85 MPs in Parliament have a very significant role in the government, or even within the Opposition. Parties which have only 5 or 4 or even 3 MPs are much less relevant, even if those MPs represent a state.

The smaller states now have a lesser say because their numbers are smaller. Today, every policy of the Government of India is designed keeping in view the major states. Unfortunately, certain policies may suit one state but not another. So, we have to oppose it. Regional parties can understand that. Policies should not be made across the country. Allocations can be made to the states.

has become all about the numbers game. The bigger the

These things are very important keeping in view the role of the Opposition. But what I want to repeat is that even if you feel that the Congress has emerged strong, it remains very weak if you compare it to what it used to be and what it has now become. It controlled the country for thirty years with no opposition. Then came a situation where it got a strong opposition and lost, despite using all kinds of methods during the Emergency. It has now reached a stage where it has to depend on regional parties. In the future, things can go in any direction. Regional aspirations are increasing. Regional parties are merging and maybe more new regional parties will come up and the scenario will change again.

It does not look like we will have a single-party government in the near future. I think, coalitions are here to stay with regional parties or groups and associations of parties. Obviously then, the role of the Opposition will change accordingly.

Sagarika Ghose: Are you saying there is not going to be a national Opposition and that regional parties will provide the Opposition?

Sukhbir Singh Badal: No, it is not that. There will be a national Opposition but regional parties will act very strongly. They have a say now.

Sitaram Yechury

Member, Rajya Sabha & Leader, CPI (M) Group in Parliament

One of the most visible faces of the Left in the country, fifty-seven-year-old Sitaram Yechury represents the new-age CPI (M) leadership, willing to talk to the world about the once closely-guarded party. Known for his crisp one-liners to waiting television cameras, Yechury is the star negotiator for his party in an era of coalitions.

During the UPA government's first tenure, with the Left supporting the government, the Congress leadership looked up to Yechury in times of crises before both sides snapped ties in 2008.

He joined the party as a student in Delhi's Jawaharlal Nehru University, where he was elected the students' union president thrice in a year starting from 1977. With the old guard making way for the new, Yechury, along with party general secretary Prakash Karat, is now among the senior-most leaders in the Politburo, the highest decision making body of the CPI (M).

Yechury has authored five books on the Left movement in the country, and has been editor of the CPI (M) weekly *People's Democracy* since 1996.

He also heads the party's international department and is one of the rare leaders in the country to have met such international figures as Fidel Castro, Nelson Mandela and Yasser Arafat, other than the leadership of the Chinese Communist Party.

Yechury was nominated by the party to the Rajya Sabha in 2005, where he is now the party's Parliamentary group leader.

I ALSO THANK THE *HINDUSTAN TIMES* FOR BEING GRACIOUS ENOUGH TO INVITE ME HERE, AT LEAST TO PROVE THE POINT THAT THE LEFT IS NOT LEFT OUT.

This is a very, very important subject not only in the Indian context but in the general context of democracy. Let me pick up from where Mr Badal ended: the question of coalition governments and multiple parties and the era of single parties having ended, at least for the time being.

This is a process of the maturation of Indian democracy. I do not see this as a regression of Indian democracy, where so many people bemoan the fact that five-member parties can hold the government to ransom. We have to go through this phase because of the simple reality of India. A country of such diversity and plurality in its social order, cannot have a monolithic political order. This diversity will reflect naturally in the polity and it is only through

A country of such diversity and plurality in its social only through the process of coalitional arrangements

the process of coalitional arrangements that the maturation of Indian democracy will take place.

In this situation, the Opposition has a very important role to play in the sense it is the sentinel of democracy. I say that it is the sentinel of democracy because it can prevent the ruling party from grossly abusing its power. We have seen that happen in the past. Sagarika reminded us of the significance of today, twenty-five years ago. You have the legacy of the Emergency attached with it. Terrorism, the Frankenstein that the ruling party created, has consumed many of its own leaders.

To contain the abuse of the ruling party, the role of the Opposition is important. But it is more important in another sense, that is, the ideal in a democracy should be that the rights enshrined in the Republic must match the capacity of individuals to exercise those rights. The mismatch between granting rights and not granting the capacities to exercise rights has to be bridged. To bridge that mismatch, the Opposition has an important role in setting the agenda for the government. The real role of the Opposition is to push the government into an agenda. This is what we in the Left have always sought to do right from the time of Independence: whether it is a question of linguistic reorganization of the states, whether it is a question of land reforms, abolition of *zamindari* through the various struggles that took place or whether it is a question of uniting the princely states into the Republic of India.

Likewise in the more recent period – and I am treading on dangerous ground now – we prevented the earlier government from taking at least four steps of financial liberalization for which Bills had been drafted. Had we not done this, we would have felt a much worse impact of the global recession than that we are feeling today. These Bills relate to the full convertibility of the Indian Rupee, bank reforms, reforms in the insurance sector, and the privatization of

order, cannot have a monolithic political order ... it is that the maturation of Indian democracy will take place.

pension funds. Had we passed these, our integration with the world financial markets would have been much deeper and, therefore, we would have been hit much harder. So there was a role even from within the government as the Opposition. I know this is a contentious issue, and that's why I said at least give the devil its due.

In this situation, the Opposition's role is very important and in that context comes up the whole question of disruptions that have been taking place in Parliament. Many people have said that each minute in Parliament costs Rs 24,632. Is the Opposition playing its role properly when it continues to disrupt Parliament? Is it in the national interest?

This term, national interest, is very ambiguous. You have general sermonizing saying the Opposition should keep the nation's interest in mind and not oppose for the sake of opposition. But how do you define the national interest? Yes, in times of war, in times of terror attacks, in times of national calamities, there is a national interest which cannot be negotiated and cannot be compromised. But today, for instance, I will just leave this thought with you: you have two Indias in the making. You have a shining India, which is young, and you have a suffering India which is outside.

When you talk of national interest, which India are we talking of? If you are talking, like the Prime Minister, of inclusive growth to bring the shining and the suffering Indias together into one India, then what are the policies that will allow you to achieve this job? On this naturally there will be, and there ought to be, differences of opinion. When you raise an issue as the Opposition and try to force the government's agenda to move in a particular direction, you are doing it according to your understanding and definition of what is the national interest.

National interest per se, except for the categories that I have mentioned earlier, has to be defined through the perception and the vision that people may have for the country as a whole. The Opposition will have to make an important contribution in creating that vision. The Left has always wanted to create the vision that there is a hiatus between the shining and suffering India that must be bridged. This is talked about in a different language by the Prime Minister – inclusive growth and so on. But the question is: what are the policies that you are going to adopt for that? On that there will be differences in opinion.

To address another question of fragmentation of the Opposition and smaller parties, the time has come in the interest of our democracy to move towards a proportional representative system. Mr Badal is right. There has not been a single government at the Centre which had more than 50 per cent of people support. In fact the majority of the people vote against the party that forms the government. That is true for both the Congress as well as during the NDA government.

If you define democracy as majority rule, you need to think seriously about moving towards a proportional system in which case the potential blackmail capacity and problems created by smaller parties can, to a large extent, be met. Secondly, the ills ailing our electoral system – the use of muscle power, money, caste considerations, in which constituency which candidate will you put up depending on the social composition of that constituency – much of this can also be eliminated if you have people voting for political parties and their programmes rather than for individuals. But in India's context, we will have to have a mixture of both. That is something we will have to discuss but I think it is necessary for India's future.

Finally, since there is a great deal of distress about the manner in which the Opposition – and I include the Left Opposition – behaves in Parliament with disruptions and so on. I would seriously want the country to consider banning direct media coverage of Parliament at least for the question hour period.

Sagarika Ghose: But then how will the country know what you people are doing?

Sitaram Yechury: We will tell you what we are doing because a lot of disruptive activity takes place only to look a certain way in front of TV channels. Secondly, there is a serious point involved: the presiding officer can take a decision on expunging certain remarks from the proceedings because they are anti-Parliamentary. But when you have a direct telecast, then what is the meaning of this law? It loses all sense. Publicity should not be an element of Parliament's disruption. That is not good for democracy. Media would also have to cooperate. We will work out methods: defer live proceedings or show it after a certain period of time. Let the country know what is happening but not to provide the outside stimulus of disruption through publicity generation.

Sushma Swaraj

Deputy Leader of the Opposition, Lok Sabha

Sushma Swaraj, deputy leader of the Opposition in the Lok Sabha, was born on 14 February 1952. She started her political career as a student leader in the 1970s. A lawyer by training, she took up the cases of political leaders detained during the Emergency.

Swaraj was a member of the Haryana Assembly from 1977 to 1982 and from 1987 to 1990. As a Janata Party MLA, she was Minister for Labour and Employment from 1977 to 1979. She joined the BJP in 1980. From 1987 to 1990, she was Minister for Education, Food and Civil Supplies. She was adjudged Best Speaker of the Assembly for three consecutive years.

In 1990, Swaraj was elected to the Rajya Sabha. In 1996, she was elected to the 11th Lok Sabha from South Delhi and was appointed Union Minister for Information and Broadcasting during the thirteen-day Atal Bihari Vajpayee government.

In 1998, she was re-elected to the 12th Lok Sabha, retaining the information and broadcasting portfolio with additional charge of the Ministry of Telecommunications.

Swaraj left the Union Cabinet in 1998 to serve as the first woman Chief Minister of Delhi.

She returned to Parliament in April 2000, once again as a Rajya Sabha member, and was re-inducted into the Cabinet as the Minister for Information and Broadcasting. Later, she was made Minister for Health and Family Welfare and also held the post of Minister for Parliamentary Affairs.

In April 2006, she was re-elected to the Rajya Sabha and served as BJP's deputy leader there. She won the 2009 election to the 15th Lok Sabha from the Vidisha constituency in Madhya Pradesh.

FIRST OF ALL, I WOULD LIKE TO EXPRESS MY THANKS TO THE *HINDUSTAN TIMES*. AT A TIME WHEN EVERYBODY LOOKS UP TO THE GOVERNMENT, IT HAS THOUGHT OF the Opposition parties and invited me here to the summit as a leader of the principal Opposition party.

The subject before us is *Between Brickbats and Bouquets: Role of the Opposition*. Whenever we think of a democratic country, along with the ruling party we necessarily must think of the Opposition and give equal weightage to it. In the elections, the electorate entrusts the mandate to rule to one party or to an alliance of parties. But equally, the other party or the Opposition alliance, is entrusted with the responsibility to act as a watchdog that will safeguard the people's interests.

I am happy to admit that barring the six years that the BJP was in power, it has been entrusted with the responsibility of safeguarding the people's interests. We have acquitted ourselves well in this role.

When people's issues are raised in Parliament and when the Opposition buttresses its criticisms and allegations with hard facts, it is always appreciated.

But I would like to pick up from what Sitaram Yechury said about disruptions in Parliament. The media is very critical whenever proceedings in Parliament are disrupted, when the House is adjourned or when MPs rush to the Well of the House. I would like to clarify this issue here today. This summit has been organized by a media house and there are many journalists present. I would request you to please take a look at the record of all disruptions of Parliamentary proceedings to see why they took place.

Have we ever disrupted the House or caused adjournments because we wanted our salaries and allowances increased? Have we ever caused disruptions because we wanted quotas and permits for our family members? Have we ever disrupted proceedings because we wanted better perks and privileges? You will find that whenever there has been a disruption, it has always been in order to raise issues concerning the public good.

If thousands of farmers are committing suicide and we call for a discussion on the issue and the government is not prepared to face that discussion, then what are we supposed to do? If we want to raise in Parliament the plight of housewives reeling under the price rise and the government tells us that the Budget session is on and that we should discuss the issue only during the debate on the Budget, then what are we supposed to do? If the prime minister of India agrees to include Baluchistan in a joint statement with his Pakistani counterpart and we demand an explanation but the government tries to avoid giving it, then what are we supposed to do?

So, I would like you to carefully examine the issues on which the House has been adjourned or disrupted before you jump to

Today every Opposition party is ruling in some state is in the Opposition in those states.

conclusions. We are not fond of rushing to the Well of the House. If we are compelled to do so because we have no other choice then I would request you to please decide on who or what is to be criticized. Should we be criticized for causing adjournments or should we be praised for focusing attention on people's issues from the Well of the House?

The second thing I want to talk about is the way media covers Parliament nowadays. When Sitaram Yechuryji said that he wanted live telecasts to be stopped, you [Sagarika Ghose] wanted to know what the media was doing wrong. Firstly, I will say that Sitaram Yechury is perhaps mistaken: there is no problem with the reporting of the question hour. There are problems only with the reporting of zero hour. If I were to reply in one sentence to your question on what wrong is the media doing, then I would say that the media's entire focus of your Parliamentary coverage is limited to zero hour.

If we make a detailed, forty-five-minute speech on an issue of public interest, peppered with facts and figures, it is reduced to a single sentence, if at all, in the next day's newspaper. In fact, we consider ourselves fortunate if even one sentence is published. Otherwise what is reported is that so and so MP spoke on this issue. But if we rush to the Well of the House over that same issue or if we get the House adjourned over that issue, then we are assured of front-page headline news.

I want to tell you about the last session in Parliament. It was the first session after the formation of the 15th Lok Sabha. The BJP performed very well in the House and for the first time I am grateful that the media gave us good coverage and praised our performance. However, I must also relate an incident when I was sitting in the Central Hall with some journalists. One of them said to me, 'Sushmaji, the speeches from your MPs are very fiery but are you going to continue to allow Parliament to function smoothly? Why don't you make a little noise so that we get some good stories?' Now this tendency that only spicy, controversial stories make for good news reports and constructive opposition does not have news value has contributed to the negative image of the role of the Opposition.

government somewhere and the ruling party at the Centre

We are passing through a phase in Indian politics where you cannot call any one party the ruling party or a single party the Opposition. Today every Opposition party is ruling in some state government somewhere and the ruling party at the Centre is in the Opposition in those states. Yechuryji's party is part of the Opposition at the Centre but rules in West Bengal. Sukhbirji's party is in the Opposition at the Centre but is in the government in Punjab. My own party is in Opposition at the Centre but is in power in Gujarat.

I would like to repeat something I said in my speech on

the motion of thanks to the President's address. I had told the government: 'If you work for the public good, we will support you. If there are delays, we will remind you. If you make mistakes, we will caution you. And if you still don't understand, then we will oppose you.' This, I feel, is the role of the Opposition that we have played in the Lok Sabha.

Moderator | **Sagarika Ghose**

Senior Editor, CNN-IBN

Q&A

Sagarika Ghose: Sushmaji, you have spoken with your usual eloquence and passion. Before I turn the discussion over to the floor, let me ask you a question. In 2004 and 2009, the BJP suffered what many have described as a shock political defeat. After 2009, particularly, we had seen a kind of unraveling to some extent of the BJP, both in terms of leadership and in terms of ideology. The BJ P seems to have gone from crisis to crisis. At this stage in your existence, do you seriously fear single-party dominance because the Congress party compared to the BJP looks much more cohesive at the moment?

Sushma Swaraj: Not at all. First of all, in 2009, it was not a shock defeat. We got 116 seats. I would like to remind you that the Congress got 114 in 1999 and it was only after that it came to power in 2004. So 116 is two more than 114. If the Congress's future was not bleak after 114, how can the future of BJP be bleak after 116?

Secondly, as far as unraveling goes, you are forgetting what happened in Maharashtra and Haryana. Do you think that the Congress became victorious in Haryana? They could not reach the majority mark. They were five short. They got only 40 and they could form the government only with the help of independents. What happened in Delhi? In 2009, they won all seven Lok Sabha seats from Delhi. Three months later, there were seven by-elections – five for the Corporation and two for the Assembly. They lost all seven. So I don't think there is going to be single-party dominance nor do I think that the Congress is on the rise.

Sagarika Ghose: Let's leave that for the house to debate later. But before we take questions from the audience, let me get in another question to Sitaram Yechury. The same principle could also be said of the Left where in 2009 there has been what many have called a drubbing for the Left parties, particularly in your bastion of West

Bengal. Your cadre has revolted against you. Now, that's a generalized perception. But, you left the government because of your opposition to the US Nuclear deal. This issue found no electoral relevance within the voting public. So, do you feel you are missing out on generating fresh ideas and that you don't have fresh ideas within the Left to attract newer, younger voters?

Sitaram Yechury: No. The number of votes that we polled in 2009 and the number of votes we polled in 2006 are not very different: 1.85 crore then and 1.85 crore now. It is not that people have deserted us or that my cadre has gone away. In Bengal, what has happened is that the index of Opposition unity has been very strong. The same people polled more votes this time from the same constituencies. The same candidates who won last time with a margin of one lakh votes, lost this time with a margin of one lakh votes. You have to analyze why things are happening and it is because of the index of Opposition unity which has always been the case in Bengal.

The press attributed us with mighty strength even in 2006 when we got three-fourths of the Assembly that we had won. Our voting percentage was 50.4 per cent and the Opposition's voting percentage was 49.6 per cent. They were divided and we got three-fourths majority. Today, they are united and this is the result that you have got. So the question is not a lack of fresh ideas or a lack of the work that we are doing. In Indian politics, we have a first past the post system – and that is precisely why I am a great votary for proportional representation to remove these abnormalities.

I don't know if the BJP continues to support us on this issue but that is the actual issue. Otherwise, the general impression of a drubbing on the national scene, if you want, that is a different reason altogether. The alternative that we tried to project to both the BJP and the Congress was an alternative that did not find credibility nor was it seen as a viable alternative by the people. The more this alternative was being projected, the greater was the desire for the people to have a stable and a secular government.

Sagarika Ghose: But do you fear that the Congress has taken over your

constituency? The Congress has taken over aam aadmi. The Congress has taken over inclusive growth. The Congress has taken over growth with equity, NREGA, karza mafi (loan waivers), all this is now in the Congress realm. You are left with very little now to sell to the public.

Sitaram Yechury: No, we are not afraid of that at all because right from the days of Jawaharlal Nehru, the entire socialist rhetoric has been taken by the Congress, but the results among the people are there for all to see. It is the people who will respond from the basis of those realities. Just by mouthing slogans, these concerns do not get appropriated by the Congress. That has been the history of most of post-Independent India, and that is what it will be even now.

Q: Mr Yechury, I feel both distress and disgust when I look at the Indian Left. Whatever you have touched in terms of economic policy has turned to dust around the world. You wrecked Cuba. You wrecked Russia. You are wrecking Kerala. In Kerala, the one thing the Left used to be known for was honesty and now even that is under serious doubt with proven allegations of corruption against one of your leaders. You have repeatedly broken from proceeding on the path of reform by hanging on to some obscure ideology which has not succeeded anywhere in the world. Why should you not learn from the Chinese Left and reform yourself or else be confined to the dustbin of history?

Sitaram Yechury: Thank you, sir. Thank you very much for your prophecy. I hope you are not an NRI.

Q: I am not an NRI. I am an IAS officer. I see this happening in five years.

Sitaram Yechury: Thank you very much for your prophecy. But next time I suggest you join politics and take a political position and let the people decide. You and I cannot decide. There is nothing to answer. This is your observation and your comment. We are doing what we are doing. If you are not satisfied, then that is your view point. You please stick to it. You are most welcome.

Sagarika Ghosh: Many would call Buddhadev Bhattacharya the Deng Xiaoping of the Indian Left. But unlike Deng Xiaoping who reformed the Chinese Communist Party and made it acceptable to the masses, the Indian Left has failed perhaps to come up with an equivalent to

what Deng called socialism with Chinese characteristics. Maybe we would have socialism with Indian characteristics, which could mean something very different from socialism.

Sitaram Yechury: You are right but do not simplify these issues. Deng Xiaoping was ruling a country under unified command. Buddhadev Bhattacharya is ruling one of the 28 states in India. In our Constitutional scheme of things, the state government is a glorified municipality which has certain limitations. Secondly, remember that Indian communists are the only communists in the world who, within a capitalist country and within a democracy, have been elected and formed governments. Show me any other country in the world where this has happened. Is this not reform? Have we not responded to specific Indian conditions?

What would have happened if the last government had privatized pension funds, if we had allowed foreign banks to take over our banks and if we had allowed foreign insurance companies to come and take over Indian insurance companies? If we had we would have fully converted the Indian rupee, India would have had to face a tremendous impact of the global recession and the financial ruin would have been much worse.

Who stopped the government? Today, very happily we can sit back and say we have been cushioned from the economic crisis and recession. Why? Have the courage to face reality. Instead of having ideological blinkers to go on batting for somebody else, face the actual Indian reality and then tell us what you think.

Q: Why is it that when the Opposition comes to power the assets of its members suddenly increase? Has there been any introspection among us on the issue of corruption in this country?

Sitaram Yechury: Yes there is introspection. We are looking inwards. Today we in the Left are accused of corruption. Nothing has been proved and nothing will be proved. But that is not the issue. The question is about the system, and if we talk about the system then what you are saying is absolutely right.

Q: Why is that there are no minimum qualifications or retirement

age required for people in government and those who head the government?

Sushma Swaraj: As far as the issue of minimum qualification and retirement age are concerned, we need a larger public debate. This is not the forum to discuss this issue. But we have seen that sometimes an absolutely illiterate person has done extremely well as a representative of the people because what you need more than education is sensitivity. There are certain IAS officers sitting here who after having worked with such people have reached the conclusion that there hasn't been a better chief minister or minister. But this issue needs to be discussed on a national forum where we can try and reach a consensus.

Sitaram Yechury: Sushmaji. I would like to add that a lot of educated people have turned out to be really bad administrators. So don't set such conditions. This issue has already been resolved during the debate in the Constituent Assembly on the Universal Adult Sufferage Act.

Sagarika Ghose: Let's come back to the theme of the Summit which is leadership. Sushmaji, we have been hearing about the leadership change in the BJP and that Mr L.K. Advani is going to step down as leader of the Opposition and you will take over from him. Is this going to happen soon? Now, is it time for it happen because at least it will put the BJP out of its present confusion?

Sushma Swaraj: I don't want to respond to speculation.

Sitaram Yechury: Sushmaji I want to speak in yor favour_

Sushma Swaraj: Don't speak in my favour. Speak in my party's favour.

Sitaram Yechury: The question of the BJP's leadership is their internal matter. And we will respect their decision. Don't ruin Sushmaji's chances by taking her name.

Sushma Swaraj: That is what I am saying. All this talk is mere speculation and guess work. I don't want to respond.

Q: My question is for all. What are your views on the Nuclear deal, now that it has been signed? And, second, what are your views on getting back black money from Switzerland?

Sitaram Yechury: Let me begin with black money. We are all for it being brought back into the country and have raised the issue. It is a technical matter. Whether we raised it before Advaniji raised it or after is not the issue. This is an issue that has serious consequences for India. Our point is very simple: if the US and other European countries can extract this information from the Swiss authorities then India should also do so in the interest of our country and to get those monies back. Ownership can remain, the monies can remain with the owners, but at least the money will be back in our economy.

On the Indo-US nuclear deal, the deal has been done but nothing has been delivered.

Sushma Swaraj: All our apprehensions have come true.

Sitaram Yechury: Worse are the pressures that are coming, saying that unless we sign on NPT (Nuclear Non-Proliferation Treaty), CTBT (Comprehensive Nuclear Test Ban Treaty), etc., they will not part with the technological transfers. This is something we had apprehended and warned against.

Q: Sushma Swarajji, how can the BJP, which is facing differences among its leaders, reclaim a leadership position in Indian politics?

Sushma Swaraj: As in human lives there are bad phases, in the life of political parties also there are good phases and bad phases. These phases are not permanent. We will come out of it very, very soon. You can take this as a prophecy.

Q: While I do understand the Opposition's role in criticizing the government's agendas and policies, why can't we ever see a united front when it comes to dealing with terrorism? There have been terror strikes during the NDA regime as well as during the UPA regime. But every time, the politics kick in within 24 hours regardless of which alliance is in power. Shouldn't all parties issue a joint condemnation?

Sitaram Yechury: I said right at the beginning that as far as issues like terrorism, war or national disasters are concerned, there should be no differences. We should all be guided by national interest. If this does not happen then it is the media's duty to inform the people about who is being irresponsible and to pin responsibility.

But this allegation cannot be made about us.

Sushma Swaraj: After the 26/11 terrorist strike, Advaniji went to Mumbai and said that this was not just a terrorist strike but an attack on the nation. At such a time, he said, the Opposition and the entire nation must stand behind the prime minister like a rock. Whatever course of action the prime minister wants to follow, we must all support him. So when such a situation arises, the Oppostion will be not be found wanting.

Q: Madam, what are your views on proportional representation that Sitaram Yechury has mooted?

Sushma Swaraj: The question of proportional representation has been thrown open today by Sitaramji. We have not discussed it within our party as yet. After we discuss it, we will give you our very well-thought out answer.

> The foundation of real, inspired leadership is to make sure everyone knows you are doing the right thing and that you believe that you are doing the right thing upfront. Then it is easier to re-inspire people when things get tough which, if it is a big project, they will.

Leadership Lessons from Shakespeare's Henry V

Richard Olivier

Moderator
Suhel Seth
Managing Partner, Counselage India and Founder, Equus

Richard Olivier

Artistic Director and Founder, Olivier Mythodrama

Richard Olivier is the artistic director and founder of Olivier Mythodrama, a unique leadership development consultancy. He works internationally as a leadership development consultant, keynote conference speaker and workshop leader.

Olivier was a leading theatre director for over ten years, directing *Henry V* for the re-opening of Shakespeare's Globe Theatre in London in 1997.

He is the founding voice within Mythodrama – a new form of experiential learning which combines great stories with psychological insights, creative exercises and organizational development techniques to explore issues faced by modern leaders. He has worked extensively in the fields of organizational and personal development and his work today is at the leading edge of bringing the world of theatre into the development of authentic leaders.

From 1998 to 2003, Olivier was the Master of Mythodrama at Shakespeare's Globe Theatre. He is an associate fellow of Said Business School, University of Oxford. He was a guest speaker at the World Economic Forum in Davos both in 2003 and in 2009.

He is the co-author (with Nicholas Janni) of *Peak Performance Presentations: How to Present with Passion and Purpose* and the author of *Inspirational Leadership: Henry V and the Muse of Fire.*

I HAVE BEEN WORKING WITH *HENRY V* NOW FOR TEN TO ELEVEN YEARS. I WAS WORKING ON IT AT THE END OF MY FIRST CAREER AS A THEATRE DIRECTOR, TO DIRECT IT for the re-opening of the Globe Theatre in London after 400 years of closure. For the opening season we wanted a play that encapsulated the struggle and the journey that it had taken to get that building to reopen. We could not find anything better than the story of Henry V, a great struggle in medieval history.

I then took the story as a bit of personal inspiration. We began doing workshops with some business leaders, actually extrapolating some of the core leadership lessons from this 400-year-old myth and applying them to modern-day business. That is my second career, which I have been engaging in for the last 10 years.

Inspired leadership is of another order that can be added into any effective management system, adding a higher purpose, bigger picture and ultimate sustainability to that purpose. I invite you to suspend your disbelief, as we do in all theatrical engagement, for the next one hour and imagine that *Henry V* has something that could perhaps set light on another stage of leadership that is a possibility for all emerging nations and, indeed, for all emerged nations.

Without more ado, I will introduce you to the story of Henry V, which like many myths has a number of plot points. The plot points in this particular myth are as follows:

In the beginning, there is a call to imagination to get people engaged with the story and with the myth that we are living. As we move into Act 1, we see people assessing the past – where we have been and where are we now, of course, can effectively help us to envision the future. Where do we want to go and why do we want to go there?

If we survive Act 1, we move into Act 2 where we have to prepare for that new desired future. We have to allocate resources to make sure that the future is manageable but also deal with the traitors. There will be some people who do not want to go where you want to go. If we get the right people on the ship and the wrong people off the ship in Act 2, we will be ready to set our foot into the new desired territory.

At the beginning of Act 3, we take the first steps into the new future. But inevitably, we meet the first blocks to success. We, as leaders, have to change behaviour first, tactics second. Often if that does not work, we have to come up with strategy to be able to overcome the first blocks to success. In any big meaningful projects, the first blocks are not the final blocks. What we almost always find is that any big enterprise, or meaningful change, hits a crisis point; what I refer to cheerfully as the long dark nights of the soul.

Shakespeare shows us that if, in the midst of crisis, we are first able to re-engage ourselves and then go out to re-engage the hearts and minds of our troops and all those who started despairing even before we did, then we will give ourselves the best chance of victory, even against apparently overwhelming odds. This is what happens at the end of Act 4 where Henry wins miraculously the Battle of Agincourt in 1413. But that is not the end of the play.

In Act 5, we see Henry as a leader, attempting to change his stripes from being a very successful warrior leader to becoming a leader who can sustain the peace. Tony Blair and George Bush did not manage quite so well. Turning the battlefield into a garden requires a different style of leadership than getting into the next battle. It takes really wise leaders to be able to know how, when and where to change their character; to change the kind of characteristics that they use.

This is where we work. We work with the idea that leaders are performers. The CEO in any organization is the leading actor and the leading players are the leadership team. In order to engage with your audience you need to be an effective communicator. You need to know who you are, you must be authentic. This is more and more important in leadership. You cannot fake it. You also need to be able to communicate in many different ways with many different people at many different times. And that takes a performance ethic. So what we try and work with is a notion of authentic performance – knowing who you are and what you stand for but knowing also how to deliver that, how to communicate it, and how to get across to different stake-holders.

Henry V starts with a call to imagination. The chorus comes and says, 'Oh for a Muse of fire, that would ascend the brightest heaven of invention.' The 'Muse of fire' in Renaissance times was the spirit of imagination, creativity and inspiration that not only the great artists but also the great leaders in the Renaissance were looking for. Looking beyond the 'brightest heaven of invention' simply means looking into the as yet unknown future. So, beyond everything we know of those invented under the sun, what else could we or should we be doing?

This is very similar to something that Albert Einstein said towards the end of his life when he said: 'Imagination is more important than knowledge. For knowledge is limited to all we now know and understand, while imagination embraces the entire world, and all there ever will be to know and understand.' The prime task of inspired leaders is to be in touch with their creative energy, to be able to imagine a better future and then to engage their people's collective imagination in order to co-create that desired future together. The call to imagination sets the story off.

We move into Act 1, scene 1 where we meet the Archbishop of Canterbury and the Bishop of Ely who are acting as Henry V's internal strategy consultants, only much cheaper. They are assessing the past; telling us about the past of the nation and the past of the new leader. They tell us a couple of interesting things. One, the nation has recently emerged from a time of civil war: there has been lots of infighting between all the different noble factions, or executive teams, as you might like to think of them. Those factions have been brought to a temporary truce under the auspices of King Henry IV who has died and left his throne in a fragile peace to his young, untried, untested son, Prince Hal or Prince Harry.

As a lad, Prince Harry suffered from what in England we call a dodgy past. This means that he was hanging out with all the wrong kinds of people in the wrong kinds of pubs. It could not possibly happen to our prince Harry nowadays obviously. This was 400 years ago; there was a chance. So his first challenge is perception management: how do my people see me and will they trust me to lead them forward?

I was in Davos a few months ago when an Indian professor was speaking before me and had a wonderful phrase that he claims he got from his grandmother about leadership which was this: human beings and chimpanzees have one thing in common, the higher you climb the more of your ugly bits everyone else gets to see. I'm afraid this is a truth about leadership and so we have to be very careful. This is another bit of what I call the performance ethic – how do people see me? How do I need to adapt my behaviour, style and personality in order to affect what I need people to see in me?

Henry decides to change mentors. He has been hanging out with the fun-loving criminal called John Falstaff who has taught him the ways of the people, how to drink and various other very important leadership skills. However, this is not enough. As Henry steps into a much more formal position of leadership, he embraces the Lord Chief Justice who can teach him a lot more about law and strategy. The willingness and ability to take on new mentors as we transition into more effective and influential leadership posts would seem to be a little clue here from William Shakespeare.

As we move into Act 1, scene 2 we see Henry with his nobles for the first time. He is now trying to build consent around a collective mission and vision. The mission is to reclaim the lost territory of France. Being in the middle of the Hundred Years' War, this was a fairly popular mission in fourteenth century England. But he still has to make sure he can get enough engagement from his key stake-holders, all the most important nobles there, and he has to be able to give them a compelling reason why France is the right place to go.

He just asked the Archbishop of Canterbury to make sure this as just not an ambitious target but actually the right thing to do. This is one of the things that separates inspired leaders from other categories of successful leaders: they always have one eye on the right ethic of what they are doing, not just the success rate. So, Henry says to the Archbishop: 'God forbid, my dear and faithful lord, that you should fashion, wrest or bow your reason...not in native colours with the truth; for God doth know how many now in health shall drop their blood in approbation of what your reverence shall incite us to. Therefore take heed how you impawn our person, how you awake our sleeping sword of war.'

This is a very clear instruction: do not sex up your documents for war. Tony Blair did not listen to this one. I was working with the International Atomic Energy Agency at that time. I happen to know as a fact that he was not listening to what he was being told. If you are then spinned right at the beginning of the project, how on earth are you going to inspire people to keep going when things begin to go wrong? The platform, the foundation of real, inspired leadership is to make sure everyone knows you are doing the right thing and that you believe that you are doing the right thing upfront. Then it is easier to re-inspire people when things get tough which, if it is a big project, they will.

At the end of Act 1, Henry has to sell his vision. He has to stand up with his AGM and say: 'We are going to France. We believe it is the right thing to do and we need your help to get there.' In my experience of over ten years, this is an area where some managers and leaders fall down. They are very good at building consent and doing all the strategic analysis but very often they are tempted to stand up at the end of Act 1 and give everyone a 350-slide PowerPoint presentation of a very detailed risk analysis of why they cannot go to Germany, Spain or Italy that year. That may be important information for the financial analysts in the room. But as a leader you need to really consider when your people need to be informed – in which case IT is of course a great vehicle – and when they need to be inspired – in which case, the instrument is you. This is inspiration technology. Do you know how to turn it on, tune it up and deliver on demand as a leader? That is one of your performance targets in this performance ethic way of looking at leadership. That is Act 1.

We will move into Act 2. You are not quite sure who the enemy is. You really decide where you are going and it brings out a few hidden traitors in the camp. Henry was lucky. He had a very effective traitor management system known as the Tower of London. He was simply able to separate the traitors' heads from their necks by the simple whip of a blade. Many HR managers are extremely jealous of this particular management tool. But we do, of course, have to develop some political intelligence to make sure we are getting the right people on the ships that we want to go to France with.

The other piece has a bit more to do with emotional intelligence. As leaders emerging into new challenges and new targets, we have to be prepared to adapt our style. We work with a little archetypal model of leadership. It talks about four characters that exist in all cultures. We call them the 'good king', the 'medicine woman', the 'great mother', and the 'warrior'. The good king is in charge of strategy. The medicine woman is in charge of vision, dream and imagination. The great mother is in charge of emotional intelligence, team-building and empathy. And the warrior is the one getting out there and getting it done.

If you can get the right mix in yourself – because these are all potentials we have – and the right mix in your team for that particular territory or target you are approaching, you will ease your way through Act 2 and Act 3. It's not just external traitor management. There are some traitors inside. If you get addicted to one of these roles, it will be very difficult to change. Winston Churchill, a notoriously amazing wartime leader, could not make the transition to peace. Nelson Mandela could become a gardener leader after having been a warrior for many years. So, the ability to change as necessary to the situation is what Henry adapts himself to in Act 2.

In Act 3, he sets out with the simple strategic target to leave the port town of Southampton in the middle of July, which was good fighting weather in those days, with 10,000 troops, mainly archers, which was a good mobile force in those days, to arrive at a surprise strategic pinpoint: the small walled town of Harfleur, to take this town in one week with all his modern siege warfare techniques and then march on through France and be in Paris by Christmas. This is what is popularly known as Plan A.

As many of you know, when you put plan A into action, it often changes. Henry's Plan A is no exception. When we next meet him in Act 3 scene 1, we realize that it is now near the beginning of October but he is still standing outside the gate of Harfleur.

In the last three months, he has lost 2,000 of his 10,000 troops. Another 3,000 are calling in sick with dysentery having lived in a mess for three months, leaving the remaining 5,000, as you might imagine, not particularly impressed with the current state of leadership. So, his leadership challenge changes again. Henry's task now is to motivate his de-motivated troops.

Motivation is interesting because usually you need to motivate people when you cannot change the target. Henry Kissinger said: 'The task of the leader is to get his people from where they are to where they have not been.' When you cannot change what they are doing, how do you change how they do it? This is one of the real affects of effective motivation.

Henry delivers one of the best motivational speeches in English literature, which starts with the words: 'Once more unto the breach, dear friends, once more; or close the wall up with our English dead.' And he goes on for 20 or 30 lines, injecting energy and images into his people so that they feel different at the end. This makes enough of a difference that after the next attack, the governor of Harfleur holds out a white flag and invites him in for a peace parley. Now Henry has a chance to negotiate his way into Harfleur, which he takes through another very effective influencing technique that we call painting negative pictures.

There are many times in the story that Henry paints positive pictures with words. He talks and people see a future state with some sympathy. Here, he uses reverse psychology. He paints such a negative picture of the future that the governor opts to change his mind about what he is doing at the moment to stop the negative future from coming to pass. The colloquial way of saying this is:

some people will see the light, others need to feel the heat. If you don't have a literal burning platform, can you as a leader talk the heat? This is a very important technique because not everyone will see the light that you are showing.

With these two influencing techniques in place, Henry gets through the first block. He re-engages his strategic intention, realizes when the winds are coming on, signals to his troops that it would not be sensible to push on with plan A and comes up with plan B: a five-way move to the port town of Calais, which was still in English hands in the earlier part of the Hundred Years' War. Here he can get more resources, rest his exhausted troops and continue in the spring.

Plan B is put into operation at the end of the Act 3. Plan B lasts about five days. Something happens. Something comes over the horizon that his forecasting unit could not possibly have predicted. In his case, it is five French lords from the Southwest of France who were normally fighting the Spanish or each other but have managed to unite under Constable. They rent a huge bunch of Swiss mercenaries because the Swiss were known to be the best mercenaries and the best fighters at that time.

But the Swiss have not actually fought since the Middle Ages. They are experts in their field, rented and Henry's 8,000 retreating, exhausted troops find themselves being chased by 40,000 fresh-mounted troops. They are trying to outrun them but cannot and end up surrounded outside the little town of Agincourt. Montjoy, the herald of the French king goes to Henry with a very simple message: give up now and pay a huge fine, or fight us tomorrow when we will kill you all. It's really up to you. Henry has to take this to his nobles and his troops. Now he has to really ponder some of the big leadership questions: what am I doing? Am I still doing the right thing? Is this still the right thing to do? Do I have the right to ask my exhausted troops to continue making a sacrifice?

Warren Bennis, the American leadership writer, has one of those little catch phrases which go: 'Managers are people who do things right, while leaders are people who do the right thing.' That crisis is one of the times you really need leaders who are prepared to think about what is the right thing to do. This is Henry's dilemma that sends him into the long dark night before the battle. He does not have a lot of time. Unfortunately he cannot attend a leadership conference to get some new ideas. He has to stay in place and deal with everything that surrounds him, including himself.

The chorus of Act 4 tells us that it is 3 o'clock in the morning, the night before the biggest decision of his entire life. Henry V walks out and meets every single one of his 8,000 exhausted troops. Nowadays, we call this MBWA, management by walking about: being seen and, crucially, being seen not to be afraid. This requires another bit of performance ethic because as a human being surrounded by 40,000, you have got to be bit worried. But as a leader if you show your worry to your people, you create panic.

A lot of modern leaders choose to solve this problem by not visiting their people. We argue that that this is a fatally flawed strategy because in the absence of leadership, people's projections and fears grow worse. How do you show up with visible leadership, exuding confidence in a situation that does not really merit it? This is one of Henry's great gifts that he is able to do so.

At the beginning of Act 4, however, after the chorus tells us about this royal walkabout, Henry operates very differently. He is one-on-one with his brother, the Duke of Gloucester and he says, ''Tis true that we are in great danger.' He is prepared to speak about his emotional reality to a brother, to someone he trusts but he won't spread it among the troops. He then realizes that he does not yet know if he is the right person doing the right thing. He takes a time-out to go and spend some time alone. When he is asked that the nobles want a strategy meeting, he says, 'I and my bosom must debate awhile, and then I would no other company.'

It's a fascinating phrase. Four hundred years before Daniel Goleman came up with the phrase 'emotional intelligence', Shakespeare has his most inspired leader saying his head and his heart have got to have an internal conversation to see if they are still aligned before he has any chance of re-engaging the hearts and minds of his disenchanted troops.

Leaders have to do their own work first. Henry takes the crown off, a symbolic dethroning from the burden of leadership, puts a cloak around his shoulders, rubs a bit of mud on his face so no one would recognize him and goes about alone with his own thoughts, fears, uncertainties into the dark night, facing his inner demons. Eventually, he gets drawn into a conversation with three common soldiers who have never met before, representing the common man who, like many common soldiers of the world over, face incredible loads and do not think they have got a hope.

The soldiers are saying, 'We see yonder the beginning of the day, but I think we shall never see the end of it.' Like many common soldiers facing impossible loads, what are they thinking? If this battle does not go well, it will be a bad matter for the king who led us to it. The nobles have said they won't be ransomed, but when their throats are cut, they can still be ransomed and the soldiers will be none the wiser.

Henry realizes in that moment, despite everything he has done so far right, that when he most needs their trust, he has lost it. Everyone in the crisis is thinking about personal survival. How am I going to get out of this? So, he tries to negotiate with them. He tries to see what responsibility leaders have for their people and what they do not have. He says: 'Every subject's duty is the king's; but every subject's soul is his own.' He as a leader cannot be responsible for the soul or spirit of his subjects.

This is going over the heads of the common soldiers. They just want to know if they are going to get back to England, have a beer and meet their families. At this point all Henry can do is unload his burden. He talks about the burden of leadership. It is tough at the top. He says 'Upon the king! Let us our lives, our souls, our debts, our careful wives, our children and our sins lay on the king! We must bear all.' That is an emotional truth about leadership. That burden is real. Our challenge and our questions for leaders is: what is going to make that burden worthwhile? Even in the midst of deep crisis, can you dig down enough into your core values, into what inspires you as an individual to bring up the inspired energy to share with your people who need some at this time?

Henry is able to do this and he goes back to his troops and speaks the Saint Crispin's Day Speech. This is a call to brotherhood. He says to them that if they don't want to be there, they can go. But those who remain will forever remember 'with advantages what feats he did that day'. He finds a way to ignite the common spirit: 'We few, we happy few, we band of brothers; for he today that sheds his blood with me shall be my brother.' He invites everyone to share that sense of commonality with him, raises their spirits and sends them off for the big battle, which they win.

Shakespeare spends three minutes on the battle, 43 minutes on the dark night. We know which is more important to him as a dramatist. Part good luck, part good judgement, part bad weather, the strategy is okay but what Henry has done has raised the spirit of his people so that whatever strategy is in place, it has the maximum chance of success.

Those are the bits in the story that are connected to motivation and inspiration, our subject today. But just for the sake of completion, I will finish the story for you because next in Act 5 we're off the battlefield and we are in a garden and room where the king of France and king of England have been brought together under the auspices of the Duke of Burgundy who is acting a little like Ban Ki-moon when he brings two sides together. Burgundy was not aligned to France or England at that time.

The first thing he does to them is give them a really hard time. He essentially says to them, both of you have told me that you want France because you believe France is the best garden of the world. Let me tell you what you are doing to France right now. You are taking olive gardeners and vintners and the people who cropped the hedgerows and turning them into soldiers. You are pitching them against each other in big bloody battles in which most of them have been killed and some of the surrounding farmland has been burnt. I don't think that's particularly sustainable, do you? Is this going to help you achieve what you want?

He does this wonderful bit that I think all peace-makers and a lot of consultants sometimes do: speaking truth to power. How do you tell something to someone who has a lot of power in a way that they will listen when you say that they are on the verge of going the wrong way? All of us in leadership have that ability to really speak the truth.

Secondly, there is a proposal on the table. At the end of his life, Henry V of England marries princess Katharine of France, thereby turning an aggressive takeover into a peaceful merger of mutual interest.

The last challenge that Henry has, though, is to try and make Katharine fall in love with him. This complete section of the story would have us believe that Henry wants a real relationship, not a politically arranged marriage. It is arranged for the two of them to meet but Henry being pretty much a warrior will, like many warriors, give his seduction technique a good five seconds. Katharine is not really having it either. He asks her if she likes him and she replies that she really cannot tell. In the middle of the scene, he asks her if she loves him. She replies, that how can she love the enemy of France? And at the end of the scene, he asks her if she will marry him. Katherine replies that she will marry him only if it pleases her father, the King.

That is not exactly an overwhelming emotion of reciprocation. But Henry is wise enough and self-aware enough to know his problem. He says, 'Beshrew my father's ambition! He was thinking of civil wars when he got me: therefore was I created with a stubborn outside, with an aspect of iron, that, when I come to woo ladies, I fright them.' That's an interesting metaphor for leadership. All of you who lead know that there are times you have to put the armour and the sword on. The question becomes: do we know how to take it off? Do we know how to sustain our organizational cultures as well as ourselves and our relationships; the environment with our victories and our great battles?

Burgundy comes in and tells Henry that it's going to take a bit of a time. He is going to have to learn a new way of being. Spend a few months in the garden and he's sure something will blossom between the two of them. On that basis Henry takes a three month engagement as his next strategic option for peace. The play ends with the queen of France blessing the upcoming marriage and wishing for everlasting peace between the French and the English which was a bid that didn't work

That is the story, now if you could come up with questions about that story of inspirational leadership.

Q: We have been seeing in the last decade that charismatic leadership can lead an organization, into disaster. Today's leadership is embedded in humility. What is your view?

Richard Olivier: This question about egoism and humility and charisma is really important. I don't think charisma can be developed. I think charisma is a birth-right. Some people are born to be great musicians, great artists, and great engineers. So also, some people are born with charisma. Charisma in theatre is what we call having a magnetic personality. That means that when someone walks in a room, you are just drawn to them. You don't really know why because they are not at that point famous or powerful. They are just like a magnet that draws our attention.

I have met President Clinton and President Reagan in the past. Reagan was charming but Clinton was charismatic and has that kind of inner magnetism. This doesn't mean that as a leader you are going to do the right thing. All the great tyrants of the twentieth century were charismatic leaders: Hitler, Stalin, Mao Tse Tung, Saddam Hussein were all charismatic leaders. Being charismatic does not mean you are going to do the right thing even though there is a possibility.

I separate charisma from inspiration because I believe everyone on the planet has the potential to be inspired and to know what inspires them and, therefore, if they choose, become an inspired leader. The difference is they are not doing it because they want a big position or they want a big building named after them. They are doing it because they genuinely want to lead the world to a better place for a larger group of people. So, inspiration comes from within. In fact, a lot of inspired leaders are walking around who you will never see convincingly addressing a stadium full of people. But you sit next to them in a management meeting and you go out of that meeting feeling you are in the right job, doing the right thing and are proud to be working for that person. To be inspiring doesn't need to have that kind of stadium-like charisma. But when you meet it, you know it.

Martin Luther King was a charismatic leader. So was Gandhi and so was Mandela. The charismatic leader can also be inspired. When you get someone who has both of these qualities, they will usually change the world. They will shift a lot of systems in some unbelievably important way. But it is very, very rare. Some people have charisma. Some people have inspiration. Very few lucky souls have both. If you just get charisma without inspiration or without much inspiration, you can then tend towards the egoistical style of leadership because charismatic people grow up with everyone paying attention to them; they are used to it. As they move into adulthood, they tend to assume that they automatically deserve the top positions around; the places where people are going to pay lots of attention to them.

There is a technical term for this: Narcissistic Personality Disorder. That is, I simply need people to look at me in order to feel good about myself. It is usually because there is a bit of me inside that is missing. That's the bit that contains feeling of self worth. A lot of charismatic leaders who go to burnout or stay in power too long –Robert Mugabe is a very obvious current example –actually require as many people in the world as possible to tell them that they are okay or they are great because inside they don't believe it. They need everyone else to fill the hole.

It's like the difference between a shining sun and a black hole in space. Inspired leaders are giving energy and the black hole leaders are sucking energy from people. It can be quite attractive to be around egoistical leaders. They will usually treat everyone like their children. They will often become a father figure or a mother figure for a large number of people. When Adolf Hitler is the Fuhrer, everyone gets protected. That's the deal. So you give your loyalty to the leader. You don't question him and he will protect you. It's an adult-child relationship that most of these uninspired but charismatic tyrants have with their people. They don't have equal relationships.

Coming back to the inspired leaders, they are in service of something greater than themselves. They are not doing it for themselves or for their legacy. They tend to have people around them who are willing to meet them on an equal level and to give them straight feedback. When someone is becoming a tyrant, all those who disagree start leaving the Cabinet. The people who left are those who agree with the old policy and are on the same wavelength – exactly like Mugabe and his generals. Mugabe was actually talking about going. I have friends in South Africa who were involved in the peace negotiations. It was his generals who told him that he couldn't go, because naturally they were worried about what would happen to them if they lost his protection.

The inspired piece relates to what happens or what can happen when you are inspired. You find yourself having the energy that you need when you need it, no matter what the difficulty you are facing. It happens because you have got a sense from the inside of what is your gift to the world. There is a fine line between saying, 'I have a gift and everyone needs to hear it,' which can then go into an egoistical place, and knowing that as an individual human being on this planet you are a unique soul with your own bit to offer to the whole puzzle. If I hold back on that bit, which a lot of people do, if I never find out what is the purpose for being on this planet at this time, I will not be able to contribute or offer it.

The other thing that inspires people is whether they have a self-reflective capacity that will enable them to think about their sense of purpose, what enables them as human beings to get up in the morning with a smile on their face knowing that they are going into this organization or to do this kind of work?

George Bernard Shaw, another great playwright, in a play called *Man and Superman* written about 100 years ago said this: 'This is the true joy in life, the being used for a purpose recognized by yourself as a mighty one; the being thoroughly worn out before you are thrown on the scrap heap; the being a force of Nature instead of a feverish selfish little clod of ailments and grievances complaining that the world will not devote itself to making you happy.'

That is a strong statement. Two bits of it that are most important for me is that the true joy in life is being used for a purpose recognized by yourself – not your peers, not your parents, not your boss, not your coaches, no one else in your culture has the right to tell you what your purpose is. Inspired leaders find it often in the midst of difficulty, often as an accident. You know, who knows exactly what Gandhi's life would have been if he hadn't been thrown off a train in South Africa and just got a sense of, hey this isn't right?

Those little moments are the one that begin to awaken someone's genius in themselves. The bit where humility comes in, which is really tough, is how do you keep yourself humble when everyone else is telling you are so great? That is really hard. I think it is by being grounded, by keeping your feet literally on the ground. One of the things that Henry V was known to do when he re-entered London after his great victory and all his nobles wanted to carry him through the city in a golden chariot was to say, no. Instead, he took his shoes off. He put his war helmet under his arm and he walked all the way into London, 20 miles. Keeping your feet on the ground, remaining humble is very important.

The second thing that I think does this is the acknowledgement that when you are inspired, you are an instrument for some other energy that is coming through you. This happens with what I call peak performers in every field who maintain humility. They know it is not theirs. They know that this talent is not mine, it is given to me and it is my job to use it for others. So that sense of being instrumental, for knowing that something plays through me and is not mine is something you will find clearly in Gandhi in Mandela and in many other people.

The third thing is the willingness to have their worldview changed. They have a self transformative capacity that they don't get blinkered by the time they are 21 or 35. No matter what we might think of him, perhaps in later or earlier years, Mikhail Gorbachev had a moment when he really redefined the global history in our lifetime. That moment was when he was on the plane on Air Force One with George W's dad flying from the White House to Camp David. He was looking out of the window, seeing this beautiful land in Washington and he noticed that he was looking over the case of his military accompaniment. He realized that in that briefcase were all the codes that could destroy the entire country down there. Then, he looked at the other window and saw George Bush Sr. next to him with his military attaché and the briefcase with all the codes to destroy his entire country and everyone living in it. He said that was the moment he realized that something had to change. That moment popped him into a bigger picture.

These are times, these are opportunities – the global economic crisis is one of them – for us to subtly rethink not just what we do but how we are doing it and why we do it. As a global population of leaders, business leaders now have more power than kings and queens in medieval Europe.

I will just finish with Henry's speech to his troops at the end which was when he dug really deep and got to see himself in a slightly different way, really thinking of himself as an instrument trying to serve what he saw as the greater good. He comes back into his tent after walking around and he sees that all his people are depressed and are asking for 10,000 more troops or else they haven't got the chance. And he comes in and says:

> What's he that wishes so?
> My cousin Westmoreland? No, my fair cousin:
> If we are mark'd to die, we are enough
> To do our country loss; and if to live,
> The fewer men, the greater share of honour.
> By Jove, I am not covetous for gold,
> Nor care I who doth feed upon my cost;
> It yearns me not if men my garments wear;

Such outward things dwell not in my desires:
But if it be a sin to covet honour,
I am the most offending soul alive.
No, faith, my cousin, wish not a man from England:
God's peace! I would not lose so great an honour
As one man more, methinks, would share from me
For the best hope I have. O, do not wish one more!
Rather proclaim it, Westmoreland, through my host,
That he which hath no stomach to this fight,
Let him depart; his passport shall be made
And crowns for convoy put into his purse:
We would not die in that man's company
Who fears his fellowship to die with us.
This day is called the feast of Crispian:
He that outlives this day, and comes safe home,
Will stand a tip-toe when the day is named,
And rouse him at the name of Crispian.
He that shall live this day, and sees old age,
Will yearly on the vigil feast his neighbours,
And say 'To-morrow is Saint Crispian:'
Then will he strip his sleeve and show his scars.
And say 'These wounds I had on Crispin's day.'
Old men forget: yet all shall be forgot,
But he'll remember with advantages
Harry the king, Bedford and Exeter,
Warwick and Talbot, Salisbury and Gloucester,
Be in their flowing cups freshly remember'd.
This story shall the good man teach his son;
And Crispin Crispian shall ne'er go by,
From this day to the very ending of the world,
But we in it shall be remember'd;
We few, we happy few, we band of brothers;
For he to-day that sheds his blood with me
Shall be my brother; be he ne'er so vile,
This day shall gentle his condition:
And gentlemen in England now a-bed
Shall think themselves accursed that they were not here,
And hold their manhoods cheap whiles any speaks
That fought with us upon Saint Crispin's day.

After the Crash

Lessons for Business

▪

Rajiv Bajaj

▪

Malvinder Singh

▪

Preetha Reddy

▪

Atul Kumar Rai

▪

Moderator

Murali Sivaraman

CEO, Philips Electronics India Limited

Rajiv Bajaj

Managing Director, Bajaj Auto Ltd.

As President and Joint Managing Director of India's iconic automobile manufacturer, Bajaj Auto Ltd, Rajiv Bajaj has reoriented marketing, sales and service interfaces and given a big thrust to export initiatives. With effect from April 2005, he has been Managing Director of the company.

Born in 1966, Rajiv holds a B.E. (Mechanical) with a first class distinction. He graduated from the University of Poona in April 1988 at the top of his class. He also holds a master's in Manufacturing Systems Engineering, which he cleared with distinction from the University of Warwick, UK, in 1991.

Rajiv began his career with the company as an officer of special duty. He led a team of young engineers in 'Streamlined Manufacturing Systems (SMS)' initiative, defining lean manufacturing practices. In 1995 he was promoted to General Manager (products) and Vice President (products), where he redefined the product development processes by nurturing in-house talent, by appropriate technology infusion, and by forging technical tie-ups for critical system suppliers in the supply chain.

Rajiv conceived from scratch all aspects of a new state-of-the-art manufacturing plant in Chakan, Maharashtra, that showcased new benchmarks in quality and productivity standards.

Among his numerous honours, Rajiv was awarded Chief Executive of the Year by the Indian Institute of Materials Management. He was nominated as a 'Young Global Leader' by the World Economic forum. The Marco Ricci Metro Society conferred on him the Young Achievers Award and he has also received the Auto Professional Man of the Year Award.

Rajiv's name figured twice on *Economic Times* India's 20 Top Powerful CEOs and India's 100 Most Powerful CEOs list. NDTV Profit conferred on him the Man of the Year and Business Leadership Award while the Times Group has awarded him for Oneness of Mahavir & Mahatma.

BEFORE I BEGIN, I WOULD JUST LIKE TO SAY THAT I MEAN NO OFFENCE THAT I AM HERE IN A T-SHIRT AND NOT IN A SUIT. THIS IS MY COMPANY UNIFORM AND GIVEN that we were going to be in Delhi, I thought I would use it to my advantage to project an image of austerity.

The brief I received contained four questions in relation to the crash and its aftermath. I will put those questions and what I feel about them before you.

The first question: is the worst indeed over? There is an African proverb that says, 'Don't look where you sell, look where you slipped.' An event and its cause never occur simultaneously. In the context of the auto industry, I believe that while the current symptoms may be passing, the causes that led to these events are alive and thriving. In that sense I don't think the worst is over. It may be over just for now.

The second question: in a crash such as this are there any safe businesses? Does the auto industry fair worse than others? It is a matter of fact, not opinion, that most auto companies the world over have been very poor value builders over the last fifty years. Let me tell you an auto industry secret. We wake up every morning, whether we are in the auto industry in the US, Europe or India, and we thank God every morning for our sexier cousin in the transportation industry, the airline industry because their misdeeds make us look smart and keep us off the bottom of the barrel. Otherwise it is true that the auto industry has generally not been a very smart value builder.

In our industry there is a very popular saying that product is king. Recently Carlos Ghosn, the CEO of Renault and Nissan said: 'There is no problem in the auto industry that a good product cannot sort out.' I differ slightly. I believe that in this industry while product might be king, it is strategy which is ace. If I have to put strategy in one word, I would use the word specialization. In the car industry, the specialist Porsche is the envy of everyone else for its consistent profitable performance. As we move down the ladder of specialization to BMW, Mercedes, Toyota, Volkswagen, etc, profitability diminishes.

In the same way, in the two-wheeler industry, Harley Davidson is the Porsche of our industry. The standing joke in the industry for a long time has been how with just 200,000 motorcycles sold every year, the market cap of Harley Davidson was always several times that of General Motors which sells nine million cars a year. So, specialization is the strategy for the auto industry, irrespective of good times or bad times

The next question, the third one: what are the do's and don'ts that we must remember as we move on? As I just said, the biggest do that we must remember is specialization. Whatever the industry, whatever the profession, specialization alone is rewarding, which means the biggest don't must be that of generalization, or commoditization, because that can never be a rewarding strategy.

Let me explain with an Indian analogy, using the analogy of

If we have the right posture, the right positioning for should be effortless. If there is stress in business, then manner in which we are seeking to expand.

yoga. In yoga, we are taught to first find our centre in the *asana* or posture. It's like finding the centre of the business; the unique position of the brand. Then in yoga we are asked to bend and stretch from this position. In other words, how can we grow our brand from its centre? If we do our yoga right, our mind remains calm. It is not agitated. Our breath is even, not short. Our face is relaxed, not clenched. Our stomach stays soft, not knotted.

It should be the same in business. If we have the right posture, the right positioning for our brand, and if our expansion actions are right, business should be effortless. If there is stress in business, then there is something wrong with the posture or in the manner in which we are seeking to expand.

Finally, the fourth question: why are these lessons forgotten in the good times? Here I will rely not on allopathy, because Preetha will talk about this, but about homeopathy. Dr Samuel

Hahnemann, the founder of homeopathy, said: 'It is the life force that cures, for a dead man needs no more medicine.' So, disease is supposed to be nothing but a disorder of our life force, more commonly known as our immune system. Health, therefore, must first be an inside out process of restoring order to that life force, to that immune system.

In a somewhat philosophical sense, the job of the CEO is to make sure that at all times the life force, that is the brand force of the organization, is correctly aligned. Unfortunately, these lessons are forgotten because we are always looking for the next quick fix and we are always trying to get past the current situation into the next quarter. Anshu Jain referred to the fact that eighteen months ago we were all a lot sicker than we are now and how the antibiotics of easy money was required to cure us of that disease.

our brand, and if our expansion actions are right, business there is something wrong with the posture or in the

Allopathy doesn't cure. Antibiotics don't cure us. They only suppress the symptoms. They drive the disease deeper and deeper into the organism, into the organization. The disease surely comes back, maybe in a somewhat different form, maybe more intensely in the future and this vicious cycle continues.

I have been at Bajaj for nineteen years, starting in 1990. At that time India had a recession. There was then the Asian crisis, then there was the dotcom disaster, then there was the globalization fiasco, now we had a meltdown of some sort. I don't think these are different diseases. These are all symptoms of the same disease and since that disease is only being suppressed, not being sorted out, it keeps coming back every few years.

I would like to finish by quoting Sir Alec Issigonis, a great car man who said that fashion dates but logic is timeless. The problem with business, at least the auto business the world over, is that there is just too much fashion and not enough logic. There is too much art but not enough science. A man much wiser than me said: 'Before we embark on the process of possibilities, we must first start from the purity of principles, from logic and from science.' So, I think whether it's about cars, Kareena Kapoor or Kashmir, the process of possibilities must first start from good principles, only then can we sort out this problem and not get into another crash

Malvinder Singh

Group Chairman, Religare Enterprises and Fortis Healthcare

Malvinder Mohan Singh is the Group Chairman of Religare Enterprises and Fortis Healthcare Ltd. As an entrepreneur, he has diversified business interests in financial services, healthcare, information technology, aviation and travel services.

Malvinder was the Chairman, Managing Director and CEO of Ranbaxy Laboratories Ltd. He unlocked value in Ranbaxy's business model and focused the company on future growth drivers by monetizing large on-going patent challenges, investing resources in high-growth emerging markets and forging strategic research alliances with big global pharma. Malvinder spearheaded the coming together of Ranbaxy and Daiichi Sankyo, a leading Japanese innovator, to create a pharmaceutical powerhouse.

Malvinder is a member of Young Global Forum, an initiative of the World Economic Forum. He is also a member of the board of Fuqua School of Business, Duke University, a member of the Board of Governors of the Management Development Institute and Indian Council for Research on International Economic Relations (ICRIER).

WHEN ONE TALKS ABOUT THE CRASH AND SINCE RAJIV STARTED WITH TALKING ABOUT THE AUTO INDUSTRY, LET ME GIVE YOU AN EXAMPLE of how I see life during the crash from his eyes and from the auto industry.

Imagine yourself on a cold, windy, foggy morning in January, sitting in your car and deciding to drive from Delhi to Chandigarh. As you get on to the highway, you find yourself in a race competition with the best drivers globally. Vehicles range from the best and the most expensive to two-wheelers and bullock carts, all trying to drive faster than one another to get to their destination. Traffic rules exist but adherence to rules is optional. The obstacles include bumpy roads, uneven roads, undulating roads, pot holes, poor visibility (because of the fog), extreme congestion on the road, multiple accidents, and the unanticipated actions of the participants. You try and apply your brakes when you are driving at 100 kilometres an hour and suddenly somebody tries to dash across the highway or, worse, as you are driving you suddenly find a bus that is supposed to be driving on the other side coming directly towards you for a head-on collision. In circumstances such as this, the one who makes it safely to the end point is the person who has invested in a good car, maintained it well, has trained dedicated drivers, and can understand and anticipate traffic behaviour well enough to allow for calculated risks, of course with luck on the side.

During the last twelve to fifteen months, I have had people who have come to me and said you know, you have had the best SUV, you have had the best driver, and you have had a clear road to drive on. But the reality is that my SUV is parked in the garage waiting for the transformation opportunity when I can use it.

Today I will give you stories and examples about how you can drive in a Maruti car, which half of India drives, and still make a success of your business. At the end of the day, navigating through the chaos of business pretty much remains the same. Coming to the first point, which is probably the most fundamental and the most basic, is that in business one needs to ensure that you are able to sustain, manage and grow your operating cash flows.

One always needs to look at the products and services to see how effectively you are engaging and delivering these to your customer. What you can do, how you can better them, how do you increase productivity, how do you minimize costs, look at purchasing efficiencies, look at cost rationalization and align your business model to make sure no matter what you are doing, no matter what business cycle you are going through, you have adequate generation of cash to sustain your business, to grow your business and to invest in the future.

When one tends to go through a crisis and downturn, one tries to go to an extreme of either completely cutting down growth or trying to expand and grow as aggressively as you can beyond your resources. But the key is to find that balance and see how you drive business in the most optimal manner.

Similarly in terms of debt, many people were very, very optimistic. In the good times, they have taken a lot of leverage. When it came to tough times, they are put in a position where because of a liquidity and debt trap and because of lack of cash in the system, they find themselves being driven by circumstances versus driving their business in the way they would like to. Whichever way you look at it, ensuring you have a healthy and operational, effective cash flow, is extremely critical to business.

In times of crisis, there will be transformational opportunities. It is important that one continues to strive towards a vision for the company, continues to leverage and explore these opportunities of how you can transform and leapfrog your business to the next level. Many a time these opportunities won't be there and if they are, they probably will not come at the value that they come at in terms of times of crisis.

I will give you a few examples of what we have done in the last twelve months. As of September and October last year, the financial crisis was really looming large in the Western world. One could feel the liquidity pressure and a whole host of pressures in the financial markets in India. We had a tremendous opportunity that came our way by the acquisition that we did of Lotus Asset Management. It was an asset management company and, for a number of reasons, became available towards the end of October, early November last year. Our teams were fast, quick and decisive. We engaged with the acquiring company and closed the transaction in a matter of three days. Before our competitors realized what was happening, we had done the deal and announced it. Within a month we had taken control of the team of the company. We put a team in place and twelve months from there the Religare Asset Management company has grown five times the business that we had taken over.

Similarly, there was a tremendous opportunity that came our way in the acquisition of Wockhardt Hospitals. In the healthcare business, it has enabled us to have a national presence much sooner than we would have. Today we are in an extremely strong

In time of crisis, there will be transformational towards a vision for the company, continues to leverage and leapfrog your business to the next level.

position to build from this and grow and aim for a leadership position in the market of healthcare. We have a national presence. We are there across most of the cities in India. We are a leader in many of the states in India. We have access to a very strong medical talent pool and an extremely capable management and, most importantly, it has put us in a position to be close to our patients, to be able to understand them more effectively, and to be able to service them closer to their homes. This further emboldens us to dream bigger, to aspire to greater heights and to be able to service the huge demand-supply gap that is there within the healthcare system in India. All of us agree that India can certainly do with a lot more healthcare facilities, capable doctors, and being able to reach out to people in semi-urban and rural areas.

Another exciting opportunity that came our way was when Religare, our finance company went out and made a bold attempt at acquiring the asset management business of AIG. In good times, probably this acquisition opportunity wouldn't have been there. AIG really symbolizes the financial system in the American market. It has assets of over $80 billion. It has a presence in thirty-five countries. This to us was an opportunity that fitted strategically with our vision to be a global leader in financial services. We were in the final two shortlists. We did not get it but that doesn't stop us from aspiring and attempting to make another large acquisition in the financial services space as we move on.

For us it is very clear that at the end of the day when you are looking at acquisition opportunities, you also need to know when to walk away. In good times, we have seen how people have over leveraged themselves and found themselves in a spot. In terms of when the downturn comes, it's always good to look at

opportunities. It is important that one continues to strive and explore these opportunities of how you can transform

opportunities. But one must know how to ensure that discipline of being objective, of ensuring you are able to pick up an asset, to leverage an opportunity but only where you can truly create value and add value for your shareholders. You don't want to be in a situation where you have gone and acquired something which is an asset because you were either over passionate or because you got emotionally drawn and were too close to the situation or it was somebody's ego that said, 'I must get it at any cost.'

At the end of the day, it's business. In business you need to be dispassionate. You need to ensure that you are creating value for your company and for your shareholders. As one continues to grow businesses around the world, we realize and recognize that people are the biggest assets of any organization. But when it comes to a downturn, when it comes to uncertainty, when it comes to where the environment is extremely challenging and there are clouds all over you, where you are not able to see the rays of sunlight, it is important for leaders to ensure that they are able to engage and communicate with people more than they have done in the past. They must be able to reinforce the vision for the company; the direction in which they want the organization to grow. There must be ability to align and galvanize people around the vision. There must be ability for you to go out there and make sure it's not your dream or your vision but a dream and a vision that is shared by people across the organization. When you have people who are dreaming and living that day in and day out, your life will become that much easier because those people will run the company as their own.

It is extremely important to go out and get a team that is completely aligned and to ensure that they stick on the cores. They must walk together on the same road collectively as a team. Within our group we have always believed that you can get ordinary people to do extraordinary things if they are aligned and committed to the same objective. When you get that, servicing a customer – particularly for those of us in financial services and in healthcare – becomes that much easier.

When you walk into a Fortis Hospital, you will see that not only do we provide the best healthcare but that we do it with compassion and care. It is for this reason that a recent all-India survey done by the Government of India, found Escorts Hospital, a leading cardiac hospital, in the number one position: not only as the best hospital but as the best hospital providing customer care.

With these examples, I want to assure you that it is not money in the bank that has driven us but basic, simple management principles. It is the ability to aspire and dream to be a market leader, to drive the agenda for your industry. It is to have a vision, to have an empowered team that is aligned to grow your business to what you want, the ability to think out of the box, ability for speed and decisiveness, and, at the end of the day, to have collective accountability to take that agenda forward.

Preetha Reddy

Managing Director, Apollo Hospitals

Preetha Reddy holds the responsibility of steering the operations of the Apollo Hospitals Group and managing the network of highly skilled professionals that comprise it. Under her able management, the group has grown rapidly and presently has the unique distinction of having seven JCI accredited hospitals – JCI is a subsidiary of the Joint Council on Accreditation of Healthcare Organizations – in the group, the largest number in a group outside the US. She works closely with clinicians to help introduce contemporary protocols and constantly enhance clinical outcomes.

Preetha has worked closely with industry bodies and the government to advance policy decisions on important healthcare issues. She is an adviser and consultant in conjunction with the Tamil Nadu state government for the reorganization of the disaster management programme in the city of Chennai. Preetha is the first woman adviser on healthcare to the Government of India, and also a member of the National Quality Council, which provides guidelines on minimum quality standards in Indian hospitals.

With a keen intent to innovate constantly, Preetha is working closely on the 'Apollo Way' – a new patient-centric healthcare programme designed to enhance patient satisfaction at every level. This ground-breaking initiative is a quest to offer a distinctive patient experience while ensuring optimum utilization of resources and staff convenience.

Under Preetha's leadership, Apollo Hospitals has done truly inspiring work even for the less fortunate. An inspiring example being SACH (Save a Child's Heart) – an initiative to treat under-privileged children with congenital cardiac diseases – and numerous screening camps for cancer and cardiac diseases.

Preetha graduated in Chemistry from the University of Madras, and has a post-graduate degree in Public Administration.

IT IS STRANGE THAT YOU HAVE TWO HEALTHCARE PROVIDERS HERE THIS EVENING. IT GOES TO SAY, OF COURSE, THAT INDIA IS REALLY COMMITTED TO providing high-quality healthcare.

Talking about the slowdown and lessons learnt, probably the only thing that the crisis of the previous year didn't slow down were the theories surrounding it. There have been reams and reams written on the causes and on the way forward but today is a point in time to stop thinking about the past and stop pinning the blame on what went wrong. It is really time to just take notes on the lessons learnt and leverage cumulative learning that will help us stay sharper, more watchful and able to think beyond our industry and sphere of activity and look at the real world around us. It is time now for us to paint our own canvas.

The pundits say that the worst is over and there is a glimmer of hope on the horizon. There is excitement. You see the stock market going up and you think that things are better at least in this part of the world.

I am not so sure. Sometimes we wonder: are we really at the crossroads and are there lessons to be learnt? Do we just sweep the mess of the past few years under the carpet and continue like nothing has happened? Or do we take up the challenge and say let's really clean up the mess, let's think differently, let's look at the destructive innovations and see if we can run our businesses better? To be able to journey ahead is to be absolutely sure that we don't forget what we have learnt in the past year.

Of some of the lessons that we have learnt is first of all the stark truth: the inter-dependence of nations. The concept of a flat, new globalized world has been repeated and repeated again. But the recession really dragged that concept from its academic layer and placed it right in the middle of the corporate world. If falling property rates in one corner of the globe can set in motion a deadly game of dominos the world over, then the writing on the wall is very clear. In future, businesses should not be looking at the nearest competitor in the industry but at the world around us. That is lesson number one: monitoring on a global scale is vital.

Over the past one year, I have often been asked how it feels to be in a recession-proof industry. The honest answer is that I feel relieved but, deep inside I also feel very responsible because a healthcare provider forms the basis of where industries go to when they need you. What is it that we can do? If we didn't change, if we didn't look at better ways of doing things, we would actually be a very irresponsible business. So, we ask ourselves, can our processes be made better? Can they be more efficient? Can we make care more accessible and more affordable?

To find the answers the relentless pursuit to raise the bar continues, and continues consistently. Being steeped in healthcare, my worldview is tinted with the dynamics of the industry. But I am fairly confident that the emerging sense in healthcare is emblematic of many other industries.

Globally, as the statistics show, the demand for healthcare will only increase. This demand has no negative correlation with economic disasters. Healthcare has often been said to be more or less neutral to economic cycles and historically speaking this has actually been correct. But strangely enough, this time around there has been a bit of a twist to the tale.

The US has actually seen a huge slowdown in its own healthcare. There has been such a tremendous slowdown that there are hospitals which are practically empty. Healthcare costs which are spiralling out of control have become a huge debate.

In India we are a lot better off. Cost-effective practices have already been invoked and they have paid off. What has really added value and credibility to us is medical value travel. People from overseas have been coming to our country seeking high-end procedures; not cosmetic surgeries, but deep-seated, high-end procedures that have shown a 15 per cent increase. If we compare this with other Asian countries, then they have shown much more in terms of increase. But I think it's steadily increasing in India too.

Credibility has gone up, trust has gone up in our hospitals. In a way it has been the icing on the cake to see that in an economic downturn, people from other countries are looking at better high-end clinical options in our country. But strange as it may seem, the recession has been a blessing in disguise and that is a big lesson to us. It has helped us shed unhealthy flab. It has made certain healthcare players more agile, responsive, and certainly more patient-centric.

Last year was actually a good year for Apollo. We showed a tremendous increase in terms of volume and in terms of a bottom line but more than anything else, last year was a time when we initiated a number of new projects. They have been extremely exciting for us. Last year was a time for introspection also. The game changed and we had to change along with it. We took a long hard look at ourselves and decided to bite the bullet. Projects were prioritized; some which did not make sense were shelved.

The recession has been a blessing in disguise and that It has made certain healthcare players more agile,

Processes were streamlined and the doctor-patient relations taken to the highest levels of the game. Over 190 standard operating procedures were changed and this had a tremendous impact on our operational efficiencies.

The last year also saw an exciting foundation for what we call the 'Apollo Way'. The 'Apollo Way' is a revolutionary approach envisaged to help caregivers, the doctors and nurses, spend more time with patients by lowering the time they would need to spend on mundane activities, thereby making the entire experience more patient-centric.

Another critical lesson emerged and you could even say would be the way we need to go about business in the future. That's what lesson number three is all about. It is about leveraging collaboration rather than worrying about competition. A seamless boundary-less global healthcare delivery system is imperative to meet the growing demand and to accommodate supply fluctuations in a particular region.

We studied some of the strategies which a country like Australia has used. They have used a core location strategy where one provider puts in high-end equipment and everybody else, regardless of competition, uses it. It cuts down waste. It makes it more cost effective for the patient. There are many examples like that which healthcare providers really need to work on and collaborate together.

The case for collaboration extends to other vital areas – sharing of research, innovations and best practices that are required for us to reach the next frontier. Our mission and our vision is to touch a billion lives. That has probably been the most exciting thing which happened to Apollo Hospitals as a group. When we completed twenty-five years, we analyzed the amount of work we had done and as managers we were very excited that we had treated 18

is a big lesson to us. It has helped us shed unhealthy flab. responsive, and certainly more patient-centric.

million patients. The chairman [Dr Prathap C. Reddy] looked at us and said: 'So what? The country has a billion people.' All of us understand that one hospital provider cannot look after or touch a billion lives. But we can come up with ideas and innovations, disruptive innovations if need be, and impact a billion lives in this country and in this part of the world.

That is what being a responsible healthcare provider is about. How can we leverage collaborations? How can we make a difference? How can we work with governments so that we can at least change laws, change systems and try to impact people's lives? There has been some excitement in the South over the past couple of years. There have been some fantastic insurance programmes in the state of Andhra Pradesh, Tamil Nadu and, to some extent, Karnataka. People are getting access to high-end healthcare. This is because of stringent processes, meticulous planning and a lot of innovation.

So in the future it's all about a collaborative effort and a systematic focus to touch people's lives.

The next lesson we learnt is that India's dichotomy works to our advantage. India doesn't exist in the cities. There is a huge India, a huge Bharat, which is out there in the rural areas, which many of us are not exposed to. It was during the recession that Apollo Hospitals unfolded its most powerful growth strategy, the Apollo Reach Hospitals. I am personally most excited by the Apollo Reach Hospitals and the huge potential that it represents. Under this model, we will take affordable and high-quality healthcare to India's smaller towns and rural India.

Healthcare, as I said earlier, needs a culture of disruptive innovation. The entire business paradigm would immensely benefit from the natural process of disruption. Once business models adopt new technology and markets replace incumbent institutions and mindsets, there will inevitably be higher quality and more value for everyone. Over the past year, I have learnt that to be high tech is not necessarily high cost. The solutions are out there. Those at the helm play a role in safeguarding the organization's future. I believe we should encourage reinventing the wheel because with every reinvention the wheel just gets better. Our thrust with innovative thinking has seen tangible results.

Today Apollo is Asia's largest healthcare group and has earned the trust of 18 million patients. In the wake of recession or even otherwise, there should be no stone left unturned in leveraging the power of science and technology to foster innovation. This is true for healthcare players and organizations in today's world. Technology can actually help in every facet of our company from keeping costs down to developing predictive models to becoming more customer-focused. It can help transform the way we work and we should never cut down our research and development budgets in times of recession because that is really what makes a difference for us. At this time, we actually harness technology to provide telemedicine and use telemedicine to become one of the largest players in the world.

But the magic mantra for us is the customers' trust. We need to surpass boundaries to keep that trust with us and deliver whatever we need to at this time. To me business as usual is no longer good enough and is never going to be good enough. For the sake of future generations, we need to focus more on being innovative, being more nimble and providing cost-effective healthcare in this part of the world so that the rest of the world looks at us as an example.

Atul Kumar Rai

CEO and Managing Director, IFCI

Atul Kumar Rai is the Chief Executive Office and Managing Director of IFCI (Industrial Financial Corporation of India Ltd) since July 2007. Before joining IFCI, Atul had worked for over 20 years in various positions in the Government of India. His assignments have involved a diverse range of activities from hands-on management to regulation and, finally to the most abstract level of formulating policy.

An Honours graduate in Economics from University of Delhi, he also holds a post-graduate qualification in Economics from Jawaharlal Nehru University. He started his career in Forward Markets Commission in 1987 where he worked for four years in the development of forward and futures trading and setting up of new commodity exchanges. Between 1991 and 1993, Atul worked on policy making in the Planning Commission. His presence in the Ministry of Industry from 1993 to 1996 coincided with the dismantling of industrial licensing regime and sweeping tax reforms, both of which happened to fall in his domain. Between 1997 and 2002, the Delhi Development Authority had him handling management in a field organization. In 2002, he joined the banking division as a director, managing ownership matters of government-sponsored financial institutions. During this period, he set up two institutions, the India Infrastructure Finance Company Ltd (IIFCL) launched in January 2006, and SASF (Stressed Assets Stabilisation Fund) in 2004, a special purpose vehicle (SPV) which manages the bad debts of IDBI Ltd.

Atul continued as a director at IIFCL in an executive capacity until he joined IFCI. In the interim, he was Chairman of Dena Bank's Board. He was a Director for three years on the Board of Vijaya Bank, IIBI and IIFCL.

BEFORE WE PROCEED WITH THE POST-CRASH LESSON FOR BUSINESS, THERE IS A QUESTION OF THE CAPACITY OF BUSINESS TO LEARN LESSONS. IF WE ARE HOLDING a class, we ought to make sure that there are some students in it and that they are not all off gallivanting in their private jets or partying in yachts.

The history of Western capitalism, replete with its booms and busts, is not really reassuring on the capacity of business to learn lessons. At the formative core of every business lies a process of innovation, a kind of unlearning or de-learning or even anti-learning. Business does not do business as a class. Booms and busts are intrinsic to the process of creative destruction in a capitalist economy. Each bust prepares the ground for innovations leading to the next boom.

To put it differently, there is a creative part of business which challenges established learning. Let me hope that the creative part of business survives not only the events of 2008 and 2009, but also that of this session. Secondly, let us remind ourselves that the crash refers not to a single event as crashes often do, but comprises a multitude of subprime crisis, financial meltdown, credit fees, regulatory omissions, and so on.

We have been more used to the word 'economic crisis' to describe the situation. If the word 'crash' catches on, it may well auger an important lesson in how the taxonomic shift from crisis to crash came about. One may ask, for instance, if the word 'crisis' has served its purpose with the financial bailouts last year to the entities in the US and Europe. I recall a series of business conferences in 2007, which warned of the impending crisis. Stalwarts of the financial world argued in favour of rescue packages for the beleaguered entities. The rescue did happen which saved some businesses. But for the business as a whole, it might prove a lesson worth learning: even against its better instinct if one cries wolf, one may stand in good prospect of being saved by the tiger.

On the other hand, the G20 summit noted in its statement at Pittsburgh that it agrees to do everything necessary to ensure recovery, and it worked. So, it's all over now. To call the episode a crisis is an unnecessary lengthening of the pain and reminder of the shock that we have put behind us.

No, it was no crisis. It was just a blur, a momentary lapse. Of course, I should never have let big brother finance be at the wheel. But I was quick enough to take over as soon as he yelled for me. So, we are all safe and it's going to be fine; just a scratch but there have been scratches before. It never was so beautiful a vehicle anyway. It was just the one which never got fossilized.

The point is that these events are not forgotten ten, twenty or many more years later or even described as a crash, crisis, collapse of something else altogether different. The third thing that the events in question highlight is our collective failure to predict the consequences of our own actions. The crash or crisis is not an act of God. Some might even go further and argue that there are limits to the ingenuity of God in wreaking havoc. A collective failure to

Increased fiscal spending can only be a short-term remedy. of growth.

predict the consequences of our actions is not just a characteristic of this crisis; it is constitutive of this crisis.

Perhaps one goes too far looking for villains either in the corporate board rooms or bedrooms where the search is now headed. If there was excessive leverage, part of the problem lay with the savings glut and easy money. Part of the problem also can be said to have been with the privileges accorded to a class of financial institutions called banks. Some businesses had no option but to be excessively leveraged in order to stay in business.

Next, the issue about economic management. There has been some sanguinity about implications of fiscal deficits especially in times of lack of aggregate demand to absorb the output. Simply put, the logic is that it is possible that private consumption and investment demand are insufficient to absorb the aggregate output. In these times, to avoid the economies from slipping into a downward spiral, the only option is to increase government spending.

That's the ancient argument. It is not certain if it really applies the stark lesson of 1970. 1970 is evidence that it does not. But even if it does, the point is that increased fiscal spending can only be a short-term remedy. It cannot restore the economy to a long-term trend rate of growth such as it might be. I do hope that the fiscal packages put together by the governments all across the world amounting to more than 10 per cent of the world GDP over the last one year help restore stability. But the question of their having impact on growth is definitely a more subtle one. It's not certain at all. Long-term growth depends on demographies, on productivity.

The only point I want to make is that as President Bush noted earlier at this summit, the centre of the world is shifting east. That has an opportunity for the economies of the east perhaps to look at

It cannot restore the economy to a long-term trend rate

a contest with the American dollar as the international currency of exchange. That means perhaps also working on institutional credibility of these societies and governments which for some time may not be a bad thing to happen in this part of the world because when you want your credibility to be accepted by the world it needs more than economic size or military might.

I don't know what wonder Rajiv Bajaj does. He operates in the premium model. He believes in quality. In a recession time conventional wisdom says that premium and needs don't work. But here he comes with his Quarter 2 results and a mind-blowing margin of 22 per cent – that's over 14 per cent or 13.5 per cent that he had registered a year back. So, one needs to hear from him on where is the recession.

Malvinder Singh is in a truly enviable position. He rode the crisis with Rs 10,000 crore, an ideal time to hunt fish, catch assets available on sale and do an amazing job in consolidating his healthcare leadership by acquiring Wockhardt. He has many other things hidden up his sleeve in terms of financial services and investments in real estate.

Moderator | **Murali Sivaraman**
CEO, Philips Electronics India Limited

Q: My question is directed to Malvinder Singh. Was the selling of Ranbaxy your best business decision in recent times?

Malvinder Singh: The sale of Ranbaxy had nothing to do with the crash at the markets. We were a global business. My reading and sense was very clear that it was time for the innovation segment of the global pharmaceutical industry and the generic piece of that pie to come together. I saw the landscape changing, and changing very rapidly, and I was convinced that this was the right model for the pharma industry to evolve and grow in a sustainable manner. Therefore, I took the decision that I did for innovation and generics to come together. It so happened that the way they came together was through a sale of a stake. But that's not the key point here. The key point is about having conviction that this was the right business model for us to go to the next level.

Q: My question is for both Preetha and Malvinder. In these difficult times, what are the disruptive innovations and partnership approaches that you expect from your suppliers? This question concerns both short-term and long-term partnerships.

Preetha Reddy: It's superb to have fabulous, high-end technology that is really making a difference in people's lives but only in cities. Bharat is away from the cities. We need technologies which will be mobile. We need technologies which will be cost-effective. We need scanning devices which we can take to the remotest locations. I was sitting next to Rajiv Bajaj and it struck me, why can't we make an auto, fitted out by Philips and take it to rural areas, transmit via satellite on the hub and spoke model and get the diagnostics up?

There are so many things we can do. As managers we need to empower people to run the business so that senior management takes time out to look at innovations, look at better ways of doing things. I believe there are some phenomenal things which can happen out of India.

The second thing is that India is very lucky to have IITs across the country. The IITs today want to get into the healthcare space; to help handle healthcare better. Large companies like Philips and GE need to get into these campuses and use young minds to find out how we can come up with some fabulous technology which will impact the rest of the world.

Malvinder Singh: The current business model we have is very centric to the metros and the bigger cities. This is not a business model that will transform delivery of high-quality healthcare to India. India cannot wait much longer for this to happen and, therefore, disruptive innovation is required from various stakeholders. Take, for example, health insurance. Look at the amount of money the government is actually spending in the healthcare sector, whether on infrastructure building, primary healthcare or trying to provide access to healthcare to the people. Now you could put together all that money and give a health insurance policy with an option to the people to choose their healthcare provider. Let the decision and choice be left to the consumer.

At the end of the day, when it comes to technology, equipment, telecommunications and being able to provide access in terms of delivery of care, doing the tests and doing the diagnosis much closer to the customer, we need to create it not from a viewpoint of, 'Look, healthcare is a right and, therefore, it must be free.' If it needs to be sustainable, it has to be a viable economic model. That viability is going to be a function between the healthcare delivery providers, the suppliers, the technology people, the telecommunication companies and the government.

Q: This question is also to both Preetha and Malvinder. What are you doing to make medical facilities more accessible to the poor?

Malvinder Singh: Firstly, we do provide service. In terms of the hub and spoke model that we have, we have a reach of 40 hospitals across the nation with the Wockhardt acquisition having come through. We are able to leverage the capability of our doctors.

We are able to go out into towns and villages and provide medical treatment to people who really can't afford it.

Most of our hospitals are not in a mandatory position where they need to provide a certain level of free healthcare because we have not taken land at a concessional rate. But having said that, we do provide healthcare to people who are needy and cannot afford it. We have ways and means to ensure that they get treatment. Beyond that, it's really going into the interiors, educating people, engaging with them and having doctors and nurses go to villages and provide treatment. Over a period of time at places where we have been repeatedly visiting, we have been able to impact both treatment and preventive healthcare.

Preetha Reddy: I think healthcare for the poor is a responsibility which corporations like us have to look at. We have two or three specific initiatives which we have taken up over the past few years. One that is really close to my heart is what we call SACH, or Save a Child's Heart. Under this initiative, we provide completely free cardiac surgeries for children. We have done almost 3,000 completely free cardiac surgeries for children and this is something that the entire team at the hospitals is delighted about.

Healthcare for the poor is not charity. You cannot just dole out healthcare. You have to give the people something which they can come back to you for. That is why we have taken some villages where we have actually built two hospitals in a completely rural location. It's for people to be able to access healthcare. We have a healthcare scheme at Rs 1 a day which the people pay and they come to the hospital, use the facilities and their dignity is maintained. They don't come and stand in line and say, "Please give us free healthcare." They have a card, they have paid for it and they come and access healthcare and this model is being replicated by many industries in their own smaller towns.

Also, we have tied up with the microcredit and microfinance people. Those who work with them have access to healthcare by a savings scheme. The main thing which I really want to emphasize today is that there is human dignity. You cannot dole out healthcare like you are doling out charity. You have to allow people to access facilities and give them methodologies and ways to be able to do it.

Q: My question is for Malvinder Singh. From 1994 to now in a relatively short period of fifteen years, you have moved from being a management trainee at Ranbaxy to this iconic position in the pharmaceutical, financial and healthcare sector. How do you plan to grow forward?

Malvinder Singh: Well, if I look back, I never thought I would be where I am today. My father always said to me, "Whatever you do in life, make sure you do it well. You can attain a leadership position not only in India but at a global level if you create centres of excellence and you do them with a very strong set of values."

Ranbaxy was a business that my grandfather started. My father made it global. I had the platform to build upon that and take it to the next level. But over the last seven or eight years, we as a family have invested in two new businesses, which is healthcare and financial services, something completely different from what the inheritance was in the global pharmaceutical space. These offer very exciting opportunities. We have aspirations, dreams and visions to make sure that we can create Fortis Healthcare and also Religare Enterprises into global brand; brands far bigger for India than Ranbaxy was. It is that dream and that vision that takes us and our teams to the next level of growth.

Q: This is for Rajiv Bajaj. If Tata can produce a Rs 1 lakh car, why can't you produce a Rs 10,000 motor bike? And second, what is the status of your own small car project?

Rajiv Bajaj: In this industry, products sell but brands profit. We recorded a 22 per cent EBIDTA (earnings before interest, taxes, depreciation and amortization) last quarter and that is pretty unusual for the auto industry. The centre of Bajaj lies in making sporty motorcycles that are affordable for everyday use. That is our centre. The centre of our other brand, RE lies in making little autorickshaws that do the last mile job, hopefully lending reach to healthcare, taking it into Bharat as Preetha put it. These are our two brands, and the greatest risk is to stray from your centre and position.

A small car that is perhaps priced low but not necessarily low-cost would really not resonate with our strategy to be a high EBIDTA company. I have learnt the hard way trying to compete with my main competitor Hero Honda that just making a cheaper clone of Hero Honda won't get us anywhere. That is why we had a different strategy to be exactly the opposite to make the bigger, faster, more expensive, sexier motorcycle. That's what succeeds. 'Me too' doesn't succeed. It's the one who does the opposite who succeeds.

In the same way, I am very sceptical about building a car business by making a cheaper clone of a Maruti. That is why we have consciously chosen to stay away from that. On our own car project, I am not sure it's of interest to a wider audience.

Q: There is global pressure today on India to reduce emissions and I would address myself to Mr Bajaj who manufactures small vehicles. Would you agree to a proposition where the government puts restrictions on the use of individual vehicles on the roads in order to check pollution and reduce consumption of energy?

My second question is on the pharma side. The government has a programme which has never been taken up called the Jan Aushadhi Programme. It is related to the distribution of generic medicine and was intended to have been done through the public sector units and outlets run by NGOs and the Red Cross at the district hospital level. Wouldn't such a programme encounter resistance from the private sector because it would to some extent impact its business?

Rajiv Bajaj: What you are suggesting is actually already a reality. China is the world's largest two-wheeler market with about twelve million vehicles and 200 manufacturers. Apparently nobody makes money. India is about half that size with two manufacturers, Hero Honda and ourselves, and we make sizeable profits. So, clearly China may be bigger but India is more rewarding and I think the government has had a lot to do with it although this may not be explicitly something that we are aware of.

Just picking on the two points that you mentioned, from time to time there has been a strengthening of the emission norms in India. Today, for example, cars in Europe are contemplating to get to, let's say, 100 grams per km of CO2 at some point of time. India is nowhere close to that. Indian motorcycles are actually the most emission-friendly motorcycles in the world because our emission regulations are the tightest in the world and we meet them by a factor of safety of more than 50 per cent. A typical motorcycle sold in India emits about 30 or 40 grams per km of CO2 which is absolutely outstanding. For a long time it will be as practically close to low emission or zero emission as we will get.

The second aspect of mileage, well, a motorcycle that burns fuel more cleanly not only emits lower emissions but obviously also delivers the highest mileage. Indian motorcycles are actually the most fuel-efficient motorcycles in the world. I recently met Harley-Davidson COO Matt Levatich and I joked with him saying: 'Your bikes don't comply with our emission regulations. That's why you have to allow our mangoes into the US so that your bikes can come in here.' That is the standard that Indian motorcycles have set: the highest quality, the highest mileage and the lowest emissions. This is very important for us because in our business, capital itself is not an entry barrier. We have to compete on knowledge and by setting high standards of emission and mileage. The government has actually ensured that cheap low quality motorcycles from outside India don't come in and infest our roads. The regulations are in place and we already meet them.

Malvinder Singh: In terms of generic products being accessible in a deeper manner within the country, the market mechanism today provides for that in terms of ensuring access goes down as deep as possible into the villages. But having said that, in terms of pricing, pharmaceutical products in India are the cheapest that you will find anywhere in the world. From a pricing viewpoint, there is ample choice for the customer and the doctor to prescribe medicines that are as cost effective as you can get. There is no other market in the world where you will get pharmaceutical products cheaper than what you get in India.

Murali Sivaraman: Atul, a final word from you. As you are redefining your business model and seeking a strategic partner, do you want to go down the commercial banking line like your fellow ICICI and IDBI have done?

Atul Kumar Rai: I did mention that part of the problem in the financial sector is the privileged status of banks because banks alone are entitled to accept deposits. Thanks to regulations, we have a very high entry barrier where you need Rs 200 crore of capital plus we have a situation where no new bank has been licensed. Probably we do need more competition in banking.

There are two committees of the government which have gone into this question and have stated that the banking space needs to be opened up to players at all levels: at regional levels, at local levels as well as the national level. Between 70 and 75 per cent of banking is with the public sector. So, is it the threat of competition or is it a kind of a situation where the concern is the stability of the financial system? This is unlikely to be opened up in the near future. For any entity like ours, this is not a question that we can decide on our own.

Let me just very briefly mention what are the issues. One of the issues which have come up is that larger institutions pose a greater degree of risk, so you should have smaller institutions. Therefore, perhaps, the size of the institution or bank should be smaller rather than larger. That might be an indicator that more banks may be allowed to function. But until then we really wait on the sidelines. On the other hand, we have been able to build a good business in terms of capitalizing our core competency. In fact, in some ways, in a 9 per cent growth economy you have ample opportunities for everybody. That is the best part of operating in the Indian environment today.

ADITYA BIRLA GROUP

Presenting Partner

A US $28 billion corporation, the Aditya Birla Group is in the League of Fortune 500. It is anchored by an extraordinary force of 100,000 employees, belonging to 25 different nationalities. In India, the Group has been adjudged "The Best Employer in India and among the top 20 in Asia" by the Hewitt-Economic Times and Wall Street Journal Study 2007. Over 60 per cent of its revenues flow from its overseas operations.

The Group operates in 25 countries - India, UK, Germany, Hungary, Brazil, Italy, France, Luxembourg, Switzerland, Australia, USA, Canada, Egypt, China, Thailand, Laos, Indonesia, Philippines, Dubai, Singapore, Myanmar, Bangladesh, Vietnam, Malaysia and Korea.

GLOBALLY THE ADITYA BIRLA GROUP IS:

A metals powerhouse, among the world's most cost-efficient aluminium and copper producers. Hindalco-Novelis is the largest aluminium rolling company. It is one of the three biggest Producers of primary aluminium in Asia, with the largest single location copper smelter.

- No. 1 in viscose staple fibre
- 4th largest producer of insulators
- 4th largest producer of carbon black
- 11th largest cement producer globally, 7th largest in Asia and 2nd largest in India
- Among the world's top 15 BPO companies and among India's top 4
- Among the best energy efficient fertiliser plants

IN INDIA:

- A premier branded garments player
- The 2nd largest player in viscose filament yarn
- The 2nd largest in the chlor-alkali sector
- Among the top 5 mobile telephony companies
- A leading player in Life Insurance and Asset Management
- Among the top 3 super-market chains in the Retail business

Rock solid in fundamentals, the Aditya Birla Group nurtures a culture where success does not come in the way of the need to keep learning afresh, to keep experimenting.

BEYOND BUSINESS – THE ADITYA BIRLA GROUP IS:

- Working in 3700 villages
- Reaching out to 7 million people annually through the Aditya Birla Centre for Community Initiatives and Rural Development, spearheaded by Mrs. Rajashree Birla
- Focusing on healthcare, education, sustainable livelihood, infrastructure and espousing social causes
- Running 41 schools and 18 hospitals

Transcending the conventional barriers of business to send out a message that "We Care".

AERENS GOLD SOUK GROUP

Associate Sponsor

Aerens Gold Souk Group (AGS) is a four decade old, diversified conglomerate having interests in real estate, retail, entertainment & hospitality sector. Within the real estate sector, the Group is exposed to retail, residential, commercial, township and SEZ projects. The company is ISO 9001:2000 and ISO 14000:2004 certified and complies with International standards in management and construction.

Having established several Gold Souks (specialty malls for jewellery) & Gold Souk Grande (large format multi specialty malls), Aerens Gold Souk Group is creating the first of its kind Gem and Jewellery Park in three states of India. With projects spread across 24 different cities in 9 states of India, Aerens Gold Souk Group plans to create 100 million square feet of premium space thereby fulfilling its motto of 'Lifestyling India'.

Aerens Gold Souk Group aims to establish landmarks that redefine the way we live, work and play. This pioneering spirit of doing the extraordinary has been the hallmark of all the Group's ventures whether it is the creation of India's first specialty jewellery mall Gold Souk (in Gurgaon, Delhi & Jaipur), or the first large format multi specialty mall Gold Souk Grande (in Ludhiana, Kochi, Chennai, Indore, Hissar), or even the creation of the first Gem and Jewellery Park in Gurgaon & Kochi.

OIL AND NATURAL GAS COMMISSION

Associate Sponsor

Oil and Gas division was formed in 1955 out of GSI and was subsequently converted into Oil and Natural Gas Directorate and finally into Oil and Natural Gas Commission on 14th August 1956. In 1994, it became a Corporation, and in 1997 was given status of 'Navratna' by Government of India. ONGC was recognized as a "Flagship" Oil PSU in the year 2000.

ONGC is one of the largest E&P companies in the world in terms of reserves and production, with hydrocarbon reserves exceeding 1 billion tonnes of Oil and Gas and produces more than 1 million Barrels of Oil Equivalent (MMBOE) per day contributing around 80% of domestic production. It also contributes over 3.5 million tonnes per annum of Value-Added-Products including LPG, C2-C3, Naphtha, HSD, SKO and ATF.

ONGC has established 6.4 Billion Tonnes of in-place hydrocarbon reserves with 339 discoveries of oil and gas. Out of these in-place hydrocarbons on domestic acreages, ultimate reserves are 2.3 Billion Tonnes of oil plus oil equivalent gas (O+OEG). It has cumulatively produced 753 million metric tonnes (MMT) of Crude, 442 Billion Cubic Meters (BCM) of Natural Gas and 54.2 Million tonnes of Value Added Products (VAP) from 136 domestic onshore production fields and 7 domestic offshore fields.

ONGC, the 369th ranking Fortune Global 500 Company (2007) has also been ranked as Numero Uno E&P Company in Asia and the third largest E&P Company in the world in Platts Energy Business Technology Survey 2007- based on Assets, Revenues, Profits, EPS and Return on invested capital. ONGC is 21st among the top 50 publicly traded global Oil & Gas companies (PFC Energy ranking, January' 2007).

INDUSTRIAL FINANCE CORPORATION OF INDIA

Associate Sponsor

IFCI Ltd, (formerly known as Industrial Finance Corporation of India), the first Development Finance Institution of the country, was set up in 1948 to provide impetus to industrial development through medium and long-term finance. In 60 years of its existence, IFCI has evaluated more than 4800 projects, with a well-diversified sector portfolio and extended cumulative financial assistance of over INR 400 billion. The direct employment generated as a result of its financial assistance is estimated at almost 1 million persons. In 1993, IFCI transformed from a statutory corporation to a company under the Indian Companies Act, 1956. With pan-India presence, IFCI has been undertaking techno-economic and financial viability studies for a variety of projects and extending financial assistance. IFCI today provides a host of Advisory Services in the areas of Project Appraisal, Risk Analysis, Credit Syndication, Placement of Debt and Equity, Corporate Restructuring, Infrastructure and Legal Advisory.

Through specialized subsidiaries and associate organizations, IFCI has emerged as a major player providing comprehensive financial solutions ranging from Merchant Banking, Insurance Broking, Venture Capital, Depository Services, Factoring Services to Education, Real Estate, Asset Reconstruction and Securitization. IFCI has come to be rated amongst the world's top 500 global financial brands.

AQUA MANAGEMENT CONSULTING GROUP

Associate Sponsor

Aqua Management Consulting Group (Aqua MCG) is a premier advisory and execution group committed to delivering superior supply chains and maximizing business value for our clients.

OUR CORE OFFERINGS ARE:

- Operations and Supply Chain Consulting & Implementation
- Information Technology Consulting & Implementation
- Operations & Supply Chain Outsourcing

Aqua MCG differentiates itself from other consulting firms with its resolute domain focus, a philosophy of symbiotically working with clients from blueprinting through to execution & implementation, the humility & willingness to learn & constantly improve capabilities & offerings, with an unwavering focus on maximizing client value.

Our team comprises professionals with strong consulting experience, good domain knowledge and execution leadership. We use structured methodologies, analytical rigor and defined metrics to deliver value for every project we undertake. Our expertise includes certifications/ trainings in CSCP, CPIM, Six Sigma, TOGAF, SOA, Project Management, ERP / SCM (SAP (R/3,CRM,BIW,APO), JD Edwards, i2, BPCS), BPM, CoBit, ITIL, CMM, Lean, TOC etc. -

By virtue of collaborating with our clients, gaining in-depth industry knowledge and investing heavily in research & development, we have built our Knowledge Centre that regularly publishes articles & reports and organizes leadership workshops.

BHARAT SANCHAR NIGAM LIMITED

Summit Partner

Bharat Sanchar Nigam Ltd. (BSNL), the leading Telecommunications Company in the country reaches out to 76 million customers and provides comprehensive range of telecom services that includes: Wireline, CDMA Mobile, GSM Mobile, Internet, Broadband, Carrier service, MPLS-VPN, VSAT, VoIP services, IN Services etc. Creating a paradigm shift in the digital communications, BSNL has recently launched its revolutionary 3G services in 11 cities which will soon be expandable to 700 cities across the country.

In the emerging digital communications landscape, BSNL is optimizing its Quality Telecom Network for Converging technologies to provide faster and easier access to information and multiple services. The company is presently expanding its 2G network with additional 34 million lines, out of which, more than 11 million lines are already. BSNL is the only service provider, making focused efforts and planned initiatives to bridge the Rural-Urban Digital Divide ICT sector. In fact there is no telecom operator in the country to beat its reach with its wide network giving services in every nook & corner of country and operates across India except Delhi & Mumbai. BSNL is numero uno operator of India in all services in its license area. The company offers vide ranging & most transparent tariff schemes designed to suite every customer. BSNL's technological prowess, its nationwide coverage, reach, comprehensive range of telecom services and the desire to excel has made it the No. 1 Telecom Company of India.

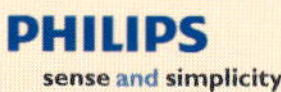

PHILIPS ELECTRONICS

Summit Partner

Philips Electronics India Limited, a subsidiary of the Netherlands-based Royal Philips Electronics, is the leading Health and Wellbeing company. Philips has an unmatched range of internationally acclaimed products backed by superior design and technology and an excellent distribution and after-sales service network. Philips has been operating in India for over 75 years and employs over 4,500 employees around the country.

As one of the nation's most well-known and well-loved brands, Philips is a part of practically every Indian's life. Philips products find use in virtually every aspect of daily life - at home, at work and on the move. Operating in the sectors of Consumer Lifestyle, Lighting and Healthcare, today Philips stands as a source of easy to use, trendy and innovative products that enhance the quality of consumers' professional and personal lives.

MINISTRY OF TOURISM

Incredible !ndia

Summit Partner

The Ministry of Tourism functions as the nodal agency for the development of tourism in the country focusing both development of domestic and international tourism recognizing socio-economic benefits of tourism. The Ministry of Tourism plays a crucial role in coordinating and supplementing the efforts of the State/Union Territory Governments, catalyzing private investment, strengthening promotional and marketing efforts and in providing trained manpower resources. The functions of the Ministry in this regard mainly consist of the following:

All Policy Matters, including: Development Policies, Incentives, External Assistance, Manpower Development, Promotion & Marketing, Investment Facilitation, Planning, Co-ordination with other Ministries, Departments, State/UT Governments, Regulation: (a) Standards (b) Guidelines, Infrastructure & Product Development: (a) Central Assistance, Human Resource Development: (a) Institutions (b) Setting Standards and Guidelines, Publicity & Marketing: (a) Policy (b) Strategies (c) Co-ordination (d) Supervision, Research, Analysis, Monitoring and Evaluation, International Co-operation and External Assistance: (a) International Bodies (b) Bilateral Agreements (c) External Assistance (d) Foreign Technical Collaboration, Legislation and Parliamentary Work, Establishment matters, Vigilance matters, Implementation of official language policy, Budget co-ordination and related matters, Plan-coordination and monitoring.

KINGFISHER AIRLINES

FLY KINGFISHER

Summit Partner

Kingfisher Airlines is India's only Five Star Airline rated by Skytrax, and the only one to offer premium first class service on domestic routes. It offers over 385 flights daily connecting 72 key Indian and international destinations and has won an impressive line-up of prestigious international awards including 'Best Airline in Central Asia' recently at World Airline Awards 2009.

Kingfisher Airlines offers world-class, in-flight entertainment with personalized video screens with 10 channels of chartbusting Kingfisher Radio, 5 channels of the FUN TV and 16 channels of Live TV onboard its flights. The Kingfisher Class experience also includes extra-wide seats, spacious leg room and large overhead storage space, international-class cabin crew and designer interiors.

STEEL AUTHORITY OF INDIA

Summit Partner

Steel Authority of India Limited (SAIL), the leading steel-making company in India, is a fully integrated iron and steel maker, producing both basic and special steels (bars, rods, coils, scheets, structurals etc.) for domestic construction, engineering, power, railway, automotive and defence industries and for sale in export markets.

SAIL produces iron and steel at five integrated plants and three special steel plants, located principally in the eastern and central regions of India. SAIL's has its own Central Marketing Organisation (CMO) with a widespread marketing network. SAIL's International Trade Division (ITD), in New Delhi undertakes exports of steel products. Other units of SAIL include SAIL's Consultancy Division (SAILCON), Research and Development Centre for Iron and Steel, Centre for Engineering and Technology, Management Training Institute, Safety Organisation, Raw Materials Division, Environment Management Division and Growth Division.

FIAT INDIA AUTOMOBILES LIMITED

Summit Partner

Fiat India Automobiles Limited (FIAL) is a 50-50 Industrial Joint Venture between Fiat Group Automobiles S. p. A., (Fiat) and Tata Motors Limited (Tata). The state-of-the-art facility at Ranjangaon pune, Maharashtra. which is owned by FIAL, is capable of producing 200,000 cars and 300,000 engines, besides 300,000 parts & accessories. This plant currently manufacturers Palio Stile, Linea and Grande Punto. The facility also manufactures Fiat's successful 1.3 litre Multijet diesel engines and 1.2 & 1.4 litre Fire gasoline engine. Apart from Fiat cars, the facility will also produce Tata passenger and next generation cars with investment exceeding € 650 Million. The plant provides direct and indirect employment to more than 4,000 people.

PARKER-THE LUXOR GROUP

Summit Partner

Coveted as a masterpiece for more than a century, PARKER offers an exclusive range of luxurious writing instruments, legends in their own right, and lifestyle statements relevant to every generation. Recognized as an iconic writing instrument, the Parker range features a unique blend of optimum performance, unfailing reliability and aesthetic design. Parker was launched in India in 1996 by the Luxor Group which is the largest manufacturer of writing instruments in India, producing over 1,000,000 pens per day in all shapes, sizes, designs and colors. The Luxor Group was founded in 1963 by Mr. D K Jain, and today it is one of the largest manufacturers and exporters of writing instruments in India.

HP

Summit Partner

For over 70 years, HP has helped people, businesses, and communities around the world apply technology in meaningful ways and harnessing new thinking and ideas to deliver reliable products and services. Established in 1988, India is one of the largest and most diverse sites for HP outside of the US and its USD 4bn annual R&D investment fuels the invention of products, solutions and new technologies.

HP's personal computing division the Personal Systems Group focuses on providing simple, reliable and affordable personal computing solutions and devices for home and business use, including desktop and notebook PCs, workstations, smart handhelds, personal storage and access devices. Its diverse portfolio of products and mobility solutions help people manage business more efficiently and stay in touch in an increasingly interconnected world. HP has been ranked as the leader across all categories in the Indian PC market according to IDC's Asia/Pacific Quarterly PC Tracker, quarter on quarter, across commercial and consumer products.

More information about HP (NYSE: HPQ) is available at http://www.hp.com/ .

RELIGARE ENTERPRISES

Summit Partner

One of the largest and fastest growing integrated financial services group with a pan-India presence and presence in multiple international locations, Religare Enterprises Limited (REL) offers a comprehensive suite of customer-focused financial products and services targeted at retail investors, high net worth individuals and corporate and institutional clients.

Apart from financial services, Religare as a brand is extended to diagnostics through Super Religare Laboratories which is South and South-east Asia 's largest diagnostics network; in wellness retail through Religare Wellness; as well as air charter and travel solutions via Religare Voyages.

REL has a presence in over 500 cities and towns controlling 1,837 business locations all over India . For more information, log on to www.religare.in

AIRCEL

Summit Partner

Aircel, a part of Maxis Communications Berhad, Malaysia, is India's fifth largest GSM mobile service provider with a subscriber base of over 25 million and is the fastest growing mobile operator in the country. It is the market leader in Tamil Nadu, Assam, North-East and Chennai. . Aircel is now present in 18 Telecom Circles (Mumbai, Pune, Uttar Pradesh East, Uttar Pradesh West, Delhi, Andhra Pradesh, Karnataka, Kerala, Kolkata, Assam, Bihar, Chennai, Himachal Pradesh, Jammu and Kashmir, North-East, Orissa, Tamil Nadu and West Bengal) and with spectrum secured for all the remaining circles (a total of 23 circles in India), the company is on track to become a leading Pan-India Operator. For more information, please log on to www.aircel.com

CHIVAS

CHIVAS

Summit Partner

Savouring the smoothest scotch in the world is like raising a toast to good luck. Good luck lives in the very name "Chivas" that comes from the Gaelic seamhas meaning lucky or blessed with fortune. Born in Strathila, Speyside, Scotland in 1801, this honey fruity whisky with a rich taste and creamy smoothness was aged for a minimum of 12 years, Chivas Regal was the favourite of Queen Victoria, who awarded it the Royal Warrant in 1843.

One of the smoothest whiskies in the world, with a rich heritage, Chivas Regal was also the favoured drink of the "rat pack" 'Ole Blue Eyes' Frank Sinatra, Dean Martin and Sammy Davis Jr. Enjoying a close association with America's boom years, Chivas rose in popularity to become the singular choice of scotch aficionados in the United States

Today Chivas is one of the best selling premium whiskies in the world. A symbol of the good life, a robust youthfulness is at the heart of all Chivas Regal blended whiskies that have blended with times while retaining their original soul. This perhaps is what led Colin Scott, the master blender to create a new blend of aged whiskies in 1997: the Chivas Regal 18 Year Old.

Living life to the fullest is very much the Chivas Regal philosophy on life. Something that is reflected in 'This is the Chivas Life', that is a celebration of the arts, music and extraordinary travel experiences. Around the globe, scotch lovers in over 200 countries live the Chivas Life by raising a toast to the world's most famous Scotch brand.

NATIONAL THERMAL POWER CORPORATION

Summit Partner

The Leading Power Company in the country and among the largest in the world, NTPC has been playing a major role in meeting the power needs and also contributing to the economic and social development of the country.

NTPC is India's largest power utility with an installed capacity of 30644 MW through 15 coal based, 7 gas based and 4 Joint Venture power stations. With nearly 19 percent of the installed capacity, NTPC generated 206.93 Billion Units (BUs) electricity in 2008-09, about 30 percent of electricity in the country.

NTPC aims to become a 50,000 MW company by 2012 and a 75,000 MW plus company by 2017.

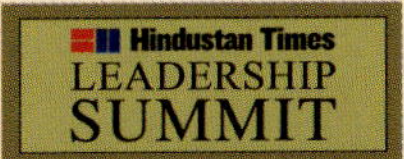

POWER FINANCE CORPORATION

Summit Partner

The Power Finance Corporation Limited (PFC) is a leading Power Sector Public Financial Institution and a NBFC, providing fund and non-fund based support for the development of the Indian Power Sector. Occupying a key position in the Government of India's plans for the power sector, PFC performs a major role in channelizing investment into the power sector and functions as a dedicated agency for its development.

PFC is a Schedule-A, Navratna CPSE, under the administrative control of the Ministry of Power. The main objectives of PFC are to finance Power Projects, in particular, Thermal and Hydro Projects, Power Transmission & Distribution works, Renovation & Modernization of power plants, System Improvement and Energy Conservation schemes, etc. The main beneficiaries of PFC's financial assistance are; State Power Utilities and Municipal Utilities, joint, central and private sector power utilities. As of 31st March, 2009, cumulative sanctions of PFC stood at Rs.2,32,551 crore and a cumulative disbursement of Rs.1,13,119 crore. The Corporation earned a net profit of Rs.1970 crore during the year 2008-09.

POWER GRID

Summit Partner

POWERGRID, the Central Transmission Utility (CTU) of the country, owns & operates a power transmission network of 72,800 ckt. kms. of transmission lines and 124 Sub-stations with transformation capacity of 82,000 MVA. Availability of this gigantic transmission network which wheels about 45% of total power for the country is consistently maintained over 99%. POWERGRID has also installed more than 20,000 Km Telecom Network connecting major cities of India.

During FY 2008-09, POWERGRID achieved a turnover of Rs. 7,029 Crore and Net Profit of Rs. 1,691 Crore. POWERGRID has already established National Power Grid with an inter-regional power transmission capacity of about 20,800 MW, which is envisaged to be enhanced to over 37,000 MW by 2012. POWERGRID has also been offering consultancy services to various power utilities in India and aboard.

CARZONRENT

Summit Partner

A pioneer in shaping the personal ground transportation industry in India, Carzonrent (India) Pvt. Ltd. (CIPL) is India's # 1 personal ground transportation service provider today offering a complete bouquet of end-to-end long and short term car rental solutions through its fleet of 5000 cars across the country.

A brainchild of Mr. Rajiv K. Vij, CEO, Carzonrent (India) Pvt. Ltd., was launched in the year 2000. "Cor" the branding of Carzonrent signifies the fact that Personal Ground Transportation is the "Core" business of Carzonrent.

Carzonrent has taken potent steps towards organizing the industry and regularizing its operations. Carzonrent became the first company to offer a one-stop-solution for all car rental, taxi & car lease services. The company introduced technology in the car rental domain, employing GPS and navigation devices in their cars. The setting up of 24x7 customer support center ensured that there was a continuous flow of services and that the customers got fully integrated and coordinated services.

AIRPORTS AUTHORITY OF INDIA

Summit Partner

Airports Authority of India [AAI] was constituted on 1st April, 1995 to take up the challenges in the competitive environment. Over the years, civil aviation, world over, has gone a sea change and the AAI has fully equipped itself to meet the challenges both at national and international levels. AAI manages 134 airports including civil enclaves spread across the country. AAI provides CNS/ATM [Communication, Navigation, Surveillance / Air Traffic Management] services at all the civil airports in the country, which covers Indian airspace measuring over 2.8 mn sq. nautical miles. CNS/ATM services are also provided by AAI at 9 other airports, not managed by AAI.

The main functions of AAI inter-alia include construction, modification and management of passenger terminals, development and management of cargo terminals, development and maintenance of apron infrastructure including runways, parallel taxiways, apron etc., provision of CNS services which include provision of DVOR, DME, ILS, ATC radars, visual aids etc., provision of air traffic services, provision of passenger facilities and related amenities at its terminals thereby ensuring safe and secure operations of aircraft, passenger and cargo. AAI is partner in joint venture companies for the development of Delhi and Mumbai airports where its stake is 26% AAI's stake in each of the two greenfield airports recently developed at Bangalore and Hyderabad is 13%. AAI provides CNS/ATM services at these airports, as well.

PEVONIA SPA CARE

Summit Partner

Pevonia Spa Care meets with the demands of the evolving Spa, Salon & Wellness Industry. We consider ourselves as a 360' facilitator in the Wellness Industry and offer solutions from conceptualization, designing, sourcing, operating and marketing. Our dedication to clients remain highly personal. Every project in which we participate receives the individualized attention that it deserves. We are committed to providing our Clients with the finest service possible.

The Founder, F.J. Singh, who, Combined with Years of Experience not only as a creator but also as an Operator, with a Design & Architectural Background & having the passion for the Industry, is the leading force to his team of Experts. Brand Creation & Marketing is his forte, which simplifies & ensures our motto "concept to completion"...is not just carried out, but carried out with excellence.

HINDUSTAN

हिन्दुस्तान

Media Partner

HT Media group's Hindi newspaper Hindustan ranks as the 3rd most-read newspaper in the country and the fastest growing among the top 10 dailies in India. Known for its fair, unbiased and secular news reporting and analyses, the width and depth of Hindustan's editorial, including the newspaper's acclaimed supplements, is quite unparalleled.

Hindustan is expanding rapidly in the state of Uttar Pradesh, dominates Bihar with a three-fourth readership share in the state. In Jharkhand also, Hindustan has been the market leader since the formation of the state. Hindustan is all set to become the leading Hindi newspaper in the country. Hindustan is also available on-line in epaper format.

HINDUSTANTIMES.COM

hindustantimes.com

Media Partner

HindustanTimes.com, with over 2 mn unique visitors and 100 mn page views per month, is one of the largest news portals in the country. It has consistently been ranked amongst the top 10 news sites in the world by Forbes and offers in-depth coverage and analyses to its users.

In keeping with athe objective of continuous improvements to enrich the user experience, HindustanTimes.com has a host of innovative features such as homepage customisation, newsletters, news alerts, blogs and rich multimedia.

MINT

Media Partner

Mint, the business daily from Hindustan Times in exclusive content partnership with The Wall Street Journal was launched in February 2007. Mint has endeavoured to deliver 'Clarity in Business News' - a need clearly articulated by discerning business news readers. Available 6 days a week in Delhi, Mumbai, Bangalore, Chandigarh & Pune, Mint gives you clear, relevant and well-analysed Indian as well as international business news.

Mint is a differentiated product offering, not just in terms of editorial content but also in design & format. The association with WSJ enables it to tap into the best global news resources to bring international news relevant to Indian consumers and business. The readership profile of Mint is ahead of that of the competition and accurately reflects Mit's emphasis on clarity and credibility of content aided by unmatched international business news content from The Wall Street Journal.

CNN-IBN

Media Partner

CNN-IBN is India's Best English News Channel, and is one of the most respected and dynamic media brands in the country today. CNN-IBN has in a short time, redefined the limits and has set new standards for journalism in Indian news television through its differentiated programming, philosophy of inclusive journalism, and the spirit of 'Whatever It Takes'. CNN-IBN continues to be India's window to the world and world's window into India.

CNN-IBN has won a host of prestigious awards including News Television Awards '07 and '08, Indian Telly Awards '07 and Indian Television Academy Awards '07 for Best English News Channel; Ramnath Goenka Excellence in Journalism Award '07 in different categories and the Popular News Channel of the Year Award in Asia Brand Congress '08.

IBN7

Media Partner

India's Channel of Impact - IBN7 is a Hindi News Channel with a single motive and promise to present the news in a "no nonsense manner" and deliver truth in context to the discerning viewer. Guided by the same principles which made CNN-IBN a cult brand, IBN7 with its committed journalistic force that embodies and believes in the spirit of 'Khabar, Har Keemat Par' has the highest share of impact across all TV channels. IBN7 is emerging as the thought leader in the cluttered Hindi news space.a

CNBC-TV18

Media Partner

The undisputed leader in business news and information in India, CNBC-TV18, is trusted by business leaders for its insight, analysis and real-time market coverage. With one of the largest and most comprehensive television content libraries in India, CNBC-TV18 has been the platform for thought leaders across India, giving India's decision makers unparalleled news, analysis and perspective.

Not only has the channel revolutionized business programming in India, helping viewers to understand and profit from the markets and from their businesses, it has also built loyal communities, by interacting with people of all ages through non-markets programming, special on-ground events and a series of awards that have set the standards for industry benchmarks.